To my wonderful son Dale, who inherited my love an hunting and fishing, just know that these skills enabled me to a yps lead my paratroopers into battle in 1966 during which our battalion commander, LT. Col. Mertel announced that my "C" Company, 1/8th CAV, BN. (Airborne) was the very finest companies. We killed the most NVA and VC enemy and lost only four of my brave troopers." During this year of 1966 I refused two Silver Stars as our coward battalion executive officer, a West Pointer told me to beg for them! Love to dear Dale Dad, Minneapolis, minnesota, Thanksgiving, 2009

WAR STORIES OF THE INFANTRY

WAR STORIES OF THE INFANTRY

AMERICANS IN COMBAT, 1918 TO TODAY

MICHAEL GREEN & JAMES D. BROWN

ZENITH PRESS

To all the U.S. Army and Marine Corps infantrymen who have served and fought for their country since World War I and upheld the proud traditions of their service.

First published in 2009 by Zenith Press, an imprint of MBI Publishing Company, 400 First Avenue North, Suite 300, Minneapolis, MN 55401 USA.

Zenith Press titles are also available at discounts in bulk quantity for industrial or sales-promotional use. For details write to Special Sales Manager at MBI Publishing Company, 400 First Avenue North, Suite 300, Minneapolis, MN 55401 USA.

To find out more about our books, join us online at www.zenithpress.com.

Designer: Helena Shimizu
Maps: Patti Isaacs

Front cover image: Soldiers from Company A, 1st Battalion, 36th Infantry Regiment, 1st Armored Division, search for weapons caches along the banks of the Euphrates River near Hit, Iraq. *photo by Cpl. Brian M. Henner/ courtesy of U.S. Army*

Library of Congress Cataloging-in-Publication Data

Green, Michael.
 War stories of the infantry : Americans in combat, 1918 to today / Michael Green and James D. Brown.
   p. cm.
  ISBN 978-0-7603-3569-7 (hb w/ jkt)
 1. United States. Army. Infantry—Biography. 2. Soldiers—United States—Biography—Anecdotes. 3. United States—History, Military—21st century—Anecdotes. 4. United States—History, Military—20th century—Anecdotes. I. Brown, James D. II. Title.
 UD23.G74 2009
 356'.1140973—dc22

                            2008041430

Printed in the United States of America

CONTENTS

ACKNOWLEDGMENTS 1

INTRODUCTION 3

CHAPTER 1   World War I (1914–1918) 7

CHAPTER 2   World War II (1939–1945) 35

CHAPTER 3   Korean War (1950–1953) 121

CHAPTER 4   Vietnam War (1965–1975) 141

CHAPTER 5   Grenada and Panama (1983–1989) 177

CHAPTER 6   Operation Desert Storm (1991) 203

CHAPTER 7   Somalia (1993) 223

CHAPTER 8   Operation Iraqi Freedom (2003–2004) ... 267

INDEX 305

ACKNOWLEDGMENTS

Besides those individuals' stories that appear in this book, the authors would like to thank the following persons for their help in providing the contact points for many of the interviews found within this work. These include Jonathan P. Roth, Jennifer K. Yancey, Elsie Jackson, Ericka I. Loze-Hudson, Jason Toepher, William Castle, Michael E. Hanlon, Kenneth W. Estes, Fred Allison, Virgil Roberts, and Martin W. Anderson.

Thanks also go to Charles Merrill for the transcribing and giving permission to use the World War I war story of Sgt. Charles Leo Boucher. The same appreciation goes out to Kim Kovaril for the editing of the World War II war story of Pvt. Ed Poppendick and for Sharon Hutto Marks for transcribing her father's, Staff Sgt. James C. "Buck" Hutto, World War II war story and for allowing the authors permission for use of it in this work.

A special note of thanks goes to the Korean War Educator, a non-profit educational group dedicated to preserving the history of the Korean War online. Mrs. Dale M. (Lynnita) Brown who maintains a website at www.koreanwar-educator.org heads the organization.

Organizations that provided help in collecting stories for this book include the U.S. Army National Infantry Museum, the Media Relation branch of the Fort Benning Public Affairs Office, *Infantry* magazine, the Donovan Research Library, and the U.S. Army Office of the Chief of Public Affairs (New York Branch). Other organizations that provided support for the authors include the Marine Corps University (History Division), the U.S. Army Heritage and Education Center, and the Great War Society.

INTRODUCTION

Every Marine is, first and foremost, a rifleman. All other conditions are secondary.

—Gen. Alfred M. Gray,
29th Marine Corps Commandant (1987–1991)

Our literature is replete with military histories; stories of conquests made and empires expanded or lost, of political, economic, social, or religious goals achieved or failed. Such accounts are told not only in text, but in the pictorial language of maps recolored and redrawn, and of boldly swooping arrows tracing the progress of campaigns across countries and continents. Their military forces are depicted as so many game pieces deployed across irregular and multicolored chessboards. This isn't one of those books.

These accounts weren't set down by men who write history; they are the words of men who made history. The infantrymen, whose stories these are, were at the cutting edge of the arrows you have already seen drawn across the maps. Theirs are not the tales of countries conquered, but of farmer's fields crossed under fire dragging a wounded buddy. Their victories were not of cities captured or fortresses reduced, but of machine-gun bunkers silenced and hedgerows crossed.

War is a terrible undertaking, and infantrymen bear the worst of it. Artillerymen, aviators, cavalrymen, and tankers see our share of the terrors of combat, but anybody who's ever been in a fight will tell you that the infantry always has it the toughest.

An infantryman knows more than one treatment for malaria, and can state his personal preference. He knows why you crawl through the jungle alongside a trail instead of walking along it. An infantryman knows why that rock out in the clearing looked like it was crawling closer to his foxhole last night. And he knows that no foxhole is ever deep enough to protect him from that one-in-a-million mortar round that has his name on it.

A common thread running through these stories is that almost none of these guys started out trying to be a hero, and even fewer ended up trying to be one. They were sons of Iowa farmers and New Jersey grocers, and Texas ranchers, who were just trying to do their duty and keep alive in the process.

Some of the stories start with accounts of how these boys joined the U.S. Army or Marine Corps with visions of sharp uniforms, travel and adventure, steady pay, and barracks room camaraderie, but none of that lasts even as far as their second paragraphs. An infantryman's life is hard enough in training, but once the fighting starts, it's all downhill from there. What you do see is that all these boys fought not so much for the high ideals of soldiery as for each other. Although family and friends back home are treasured memories, every soldier's world soon shrinks to encompass his fellows in the platoon, the company, the battalion. Unlike the red-shirted, and hence nameless and expendable, members of a *Star Trek* "away team," every soldier in a unit in combat is a brother to every other. Losses are keenly felt, and men now dead for decades past are still remembered in these men's thoughts and prayers.

What is even more remarkable in these stories is that they are even remembered at all. Most of us will be fortunate enough to not see even one violent death in our entire lifetimes. These men have seen comrades fall as a daily occurrence. No one could fault them if they just blotted these events out of their memory, as a kind of psychological self-defense. Most of them, however, remember their experiences as if they happened yesterday. Not everything . . . just the important stuff. They may not remember what month it was, but they can remember the last conversation they had just before a buddy died in a first-aid station in a World War I battle. They can't always remember exactly which hill they were defending, but they remember exactly how many Browning automatic rifle (BAR) magazines were in the bandolier they carried up to the last remaining dugout in Korea. They might not even know whether they were in Germany or Belgium, but they remember the name of that sergeant from Texas who got shot by a sniper in the tree line across the road. They remember the important stuff, like never letting your buddies down when they need you.

The editors have resisted the temptation to pretty up the language of these stories. The sentence structure and grammar may not always be right, but we think it's more important for you, the reader, to hear their stories in their words. We have changed the narratives only where absolutely necessary for clarity, and then made the least editorial intrusion we could. It is our hope that you will receive these imperfections as proof of their authenticity. The stories themselves come from a wide variety of different sources, including interviews, after-actions reports, unit histories, *Infantry* magazine, and written memoirs.

Each story reflects the perspective of the individual and his position in the military and his rank at the time the story or stories took place. Obviously, officers often have a much different view of combat than those of the enlisted personnel as is apparent in the stories found within this book. Many of the stories are horrific and reflect the nature of war. Most provide examples of infantrymen overcoming various obstacles, be it the enemy, the terrain, the weather, and doing their duty as American fighting men.

The Queen of Battle

We are members of one of the oldest professions in the history of the world. However, from time immemorial critics, historians and conquerors have looked askance at the lowly foot soldier. Ingenious minds have long endeavored to conceive something to replace us. From the forgotten soul who invented the chariot, to the development of the modern panzer division of tanks, one idea has ruled the trend of war—crush the infantry. But we have replied: Arbela, Crecy, Guadalajara, and Stalingrad are ours. We have a heritage that is equaled by none. We do not have the glamour that the public has spread over the Air Corps or the Navy; nor are we a specialized task force as are the Marines. We are, the Doughboy, the Dogface, the Poilu, and the Tommy; the men who dig, fight, and die; the jack-of-all-trades; the men who must and will win all conflicts. We are the riflemen who proudly wear the crossed rifles, we will surmount all obstacles and all barriers, alone and unaided if need be. For we are, THE INFANTRY.

—The Infantry School, Fort Benning, Georgia, 1943

1 | WORLD WAR I
(1914–1918)

Sgt. Charles Leo Boucher, U.S. Army

The April 1918 battle of Seicheprey was an early test of the relatively unblooded soldiers of the American Expeditionary Force. Veteran German storm troopers initially overran the American positions, but at the end of the day, Sergeant Boucher and his national guard comrades of the 26th "Yankee" Division held their line.

WE RELIEVED SOLDIERS FROM THE 1ST DIVISION, and although this sector was supposed to be a quiet one, it wasn't long till it was turned into a "hell on wheels" for us. Replacements were now coming in, which had a tendency to boost our morale for the time being at least. Just before our taking over in the Toul sector, and on the last day of our hike from the Aisne front, we had quite an experience as we climbed the slope of a good-sized hill. We saw nothing out of the ordinary until a large opening on the side of this hill came into view. This proved to be one of the openings or entrances to the famed Chalk Mines of Soissons. As we marched down a slope, which led us into the mines, thousands of lights came into view, and routes leading in every direction. Allied troops were coming and going: British, French, and Italian. Guides from the French Army took over and led us into a section assigned to us until we moved on the next day. Four pieces of two by four [boards] were used, two long and two short, and after they were nailed together, heavy screening was attached. Then the forms were placed on sturdy legs, forming our bunks for the night. I began to explore our new surroundings. Well, it didn't take long for me to get myself completely lost. I had located a French canteen, and as soon as I had made my purchase, I turned to go back to our location. Oh, brother! There were plenty of routes, but I wasn't sure which was the right one. In the meantime, a French sergeant saw me and realized that I was lost, so with a little French I had picked up plus a bit of English he understood, he took me to his outfit first, where a good-sized party was underway. One of the noncommissioned officers had just been promoted, and a celebration was in order, and I was invited as their guest. Plenty of food and wine was consumed, and then I was guided back to my outfit. I was told that there were over twenty thousand troops billeted in this particular section of the mine, and without guides, one could travel all night without getting to his destination, so once again, I was just "Lucky Charlie."

The entrance to the Mines of Soissons was well camouflaged so that enemy planes might not spot it from above. Come morning, we hiked out onto a country road, which was camouflaged for quite a distance. Like in previous occasions, when moving up into the front lines, we were greeted with heavy cannonading, and the horizon was a sheet of flames. When you're dog tired, lousy, and hungry, the rat-tat-tat of machine guns and the booming of artillery just have a tendency to put you to sleep. Soldiers constantly under fire must snatch rest what and where they can as the circumstances may permit. Mother Nature takes over, and that is all there is to it.

The last move up took us to the base of Mount See, in the Toul sector, which was at the time occupied by the enemy. They were so well situated that we were exposed to their view day and night.

Technically speaking, they could look right down into our trenches from the mountains. We had to do something about it as soon as humanly possible, so on the morning of April 19, 1918, our captain sent a runner to my dugout with orders to report to him immediately. As I entered the post commander's dugout, I was seated at a long table that had been hastily improvised by placing long planks on trestles running the length of the dugout. Maps had been laid out on the table, and candles were sputtering at either end, and the rest of the dugout was in darkness. Some of our company officers and noncommissioned officers had been sent to Chaumont, General Pershing's headquarters, for training periods. Lieutenant Johnson and Lieutenant Carruth were already seated, and the noncommissioned officers from the rest of the platoons also were seated. Then Captain Griswold stood at the head of the table, and he began to explain the plans arrived at for the takeover. He addressed me, personally, as I was senior noncommissioned officer of the 1st Platoon of C Company. He told us all that the French intelligence division had tapped the enemy's wires and found out that an attack of "German shock troops" was in the making. They did not, however, find out when the attack was to take place, but they had decided it would take place tonight. He then pointed out on the map a position at the base of Mount See that I was to occupy with my platoon.

Our platoon, plus a platoon from Company B and one from Company D, was to relieve the 3rd Battalion of the 102nd U.S. Infantry. Then, the "skipper" explained that we were not to advance beyond a given point, and my men were to be deployed to the best possible advantage as a strongpoint, which, later, proved to be a suicide post. I was then ordered to keep the information of an impending attack away from my men and, furthermore, [told that] if the attack materialized, we were to hold our post until the very last man. Then my captain asked me if I had anything to say before the meeting broke up. I asked for additional men, as we suffered recent casualties, and I was left [with] between fifty-five and sixty men, including a couple of machine gunners. The group began looking at each other, but no one volunteered to give me any additional men. Finally, however, Lieutenant Carruth said he would give me a squad from his platoon and said I could pick out the squad I wanted, so I chose Corporal Gritzback and his men. In the fighting that took place during the night and the following day, I lost every one of them, killed in action.

As the day wore on and darkness began creeping towards us, I formed the men in single file alongside the Church at Mandres. The usual orders were passed along the line: no smoking, no lights, and no talking. I also ordered them to remove and sheath bayonets so as to avoid any accidents. We moved along a well-camouflaged and torn up road till we came to a garden gate that was still standing, and we dropped into a communication trench. We had to keep closed up so as not to lose contact with the man ahead. On our way in, we were considerably helped by the light of the moon, although it was tough in spots where we had to expose ourselves on account of rock formations.

When the enemy sent up Very lights or flares, we simply froze in our position, resembling trees or posts until the lights died out. We made record time in relieving the 3rd Battalion. Recognizing the point that had been designated on the map where we were ordered to make our stand, I placed one machine gunner at either end of our platoon. I also put a bayonet man on either side to challenge anyone coming near our position. The rest of the men were allowed to rest up as best they could in the bottom of the trench.

Another noncommissioned officer and I crawled out on our bellies about midnight to inspect the barbed wire emplacements in front of our position. The wire had been cut in zigzag style, so when looking at it from the front, it seemed solid. We found out, however, that it had been cut to prepare for an attack. No sooner had we regained our position than the moon was clouded over, and it was so dark you couldn't see your hand ahead of you, so I decided I should let my men know what we were in for. It hadn't been easy keeping the news to myself, so now I ordered bayonets fixed and hit the parapet. No sooner was that accomplished than hell let loose as Austrian 77s and German 88s blasted away at us. It had been altogether too quiet while taking over our new position, with only intermittent shellfire plus an occasional rat-tat-tat from machine guns, but now we got the business. The barrage lasted until dawn began to show, and our first casualty was discovered. He was almost completely covered with earth, and the blood was pumping from his mouth, ears, and eyes. Nothing could be done for him, so he just choked up and passed on. We all knew what we could expect after such a heavy barrage, and since we were short of ammunition, I ordered our men to hold their fire until the Prussian shock troops hit the barbed wire. We hadn't long to wait, and just as they arrived at the barbed wire, we opened up on them.

They advanced in close formation, and soon the wire and the ground in front of us was covered with their dead and wounded. They then crawled over each other only to be mowed down by our deadly fire. The shouting and screaming of the wounded and dying wasn't easy to listen to and very hard to forget. A friendly platoon had been captured in the Bois de Remieres on our right and another on our left, so now we were surrounded on all sides, and our casualties began to pile up on us. I had been wounded early in the morning by a hunk of shrapnel, so I used a shoelace and a piece of wood I cut from a duckboard in the trench to make a tourniquet and stop the bleeding and hobbled about the rest of the day, as best I could.

Corporal Gritzback was in charge of a machine-gun squad, and his gunner, Private Lilley, was hit on the head and killed, so Dodi Gritzback lifted his body off the gun and took over. He mowed them down as they kept on coming in on us and, finally, he was hit just below the brim of his helmet. The helmet was scooped off his head, and [it] hit one of his men on the face, opening up his cheek. Then Corporal Coe got a bullet in the guts, and we laid him on the parados [a bank behind a trench or other type of fortification, giving protection from the rear]. He kept hollering, "Charlie! Oh, Charlie, for God's sake, do something for me." I gave him some water from my canteen. Then, I ripped open his shirt, and there was a hole in his belly. Then a piece of shell hit him in the neck and decapitated him completely, so his misery was over. The enemy had overestimated our strength, because those of us who could stand up used the rifles and ammunition of our dead comrades to ward them off. About the middle of the afternoon, the hand-to-hand fighting died down, and "Fokker" planes flew low over our position. We lay still alongside our dead buddies, for at the least sign of movement, their Fokkers opened up with machine-gun fire.

I must have lost a lot of blood, for "Gwatsy" Mendillo, who was doing a fine job as a rifle grenadier, tried to cheer me up by saying, "Gee! Charlie! We got them good this time, and they're running for the woods." He didn't have a scratch on him, so far, so I said, "For God's sake, keep your head down, Gwatsy," but it was already too late, for a hunk of shrapnel dug through our parapet, hit him in the chest, and opened it up, and he died almost immediately. How he succeeded in speaking, I still do not know, but his last words, to me, were, "Charlie! They got me."

George Cooper, from Roxbury, Massachusetts, was one of our machine gunners [that] I had posted on the right end of our position. He was hit on the right shoulder early in the morning, and the enemy rushed him. I was on the point of throwing a grenade, only if I did, then he also would have been killed, so they captured him, and, as it turned out, he was the only one of our platoon to be taken prisoner, for we had decided we would fight to the end rather than be captured.

Just before darkness set in, I heard a noise in a gully that ran into our trench, so I figured it must be the enemy mop-up patrol. I only had a couple of bullets left in the chamber of my .45 [pistol]. The noise stopped, and a head popped into sight. When I was about to fire, I gave another look, and a white and distorted face proved to be that of George Cooper, so I grabbed his shoulders and pulled him down into our trench beside me. He must have had about twenty bullet holes in him, but not one of them was well placed enough to kill him. He made an effort to speak, so I told him to keep quiet and conserve his energy. I had a few malted milk tablets left, and I forced them into his mouth. I also poured the last of the water I had left in my canteen into his mouth. Then he asked me if I had any bullets left in my revolver and begged me, with tears rolling out of his eyes, to please, for God's sake, kill him. He screamed, "Charlie! I just cannot stand the pains any longer." It is an awful decision to make, but I just could not up and kill my buddy like that. "No, George," I told him. "When night falls, we will crawl under the barbed wire, find the road, and crawl back to our lines." Just then, a German Fokker flew overhead. As I turned to look, he grabbed my .45, as the holster was open, but before he could use it on himself, I got it away from him, and then night overtook us.

Now we began to crawl towards the road, and on our way out, he gained strength enough to talk. He explained how he was taken to an enemy first-aid station where his wounds were dressed, and then the doctor motioned to have him taken to the rear of their lines. But the sergeant major pushed him towards our side and No Man's Land and pulled out his Luger automatic [pistol] and shot him down. Then, he began to crawl towards our lines little by little, being shot at consistently by the enemy snipers, until finally he arrived in our position.

Before darkness had set in, Art Hubbard had skirted the Bois de Remieres and gotten back to our outfit. I had asked him, on leaving, to have reinforcements sent up to us, but in the mean-time, a box barrage had been dropped around us, and as a result, no one could get through to us. Our regiment had given us up, since we were known to have been completely surrounded, and they assumed we were all killed or captured. When we hit the road, it was pitch dark, and when flares lit the sky, we searched for the steeple of the church at Mandres, but it had been destroyed by shellfire, so now we had to decide if we should turn to the left or to the right, as there remained nothing to guide us. To make things worse, a heavy gas attack was sent over with chlorine shells. Our gas masks had been torn by shrapnel, and what was left of our uniforms was torn into shreds and was muddy and bloody. Out of our original platoon of over sixty men, there were only eight of us still alive, and all were badly wounded.

Our orders to hold our suicide post had been carried out. But, Oh God, at what a price! We finally decided to follow the shoulder of the road to our right. We kept crawling along on our bellies, as we had no food and we were weak from loss of blood. Soon, the road was being splattered by rifle fire, but the sound was that of our good old 30-06 Springfields [rifles], for we had been taken for an enemy patrol. With what strength we had left, we hollered, "For God's sake, let up." So they came towards us and scooped us up in their arms and carried us into a first-aid station. We were given hot drinks and also were given shots in the arm to deaden our pains, and then we were placed on stretchers to wait for the ambulances to take us to the 101st Sanitation Train.

George Cooper's stretcher was placed next to mine, and then we talked. He cracked a joke about when he borrowed my rifle when we were on guard duty along the Mexican border. We both had a good laugh, and then George straightened out and died.

In order to get to the field hospital, it was necessary to go through "Dead Man's Curve," which was full of deep shell holes and was under constant bombardment. Another gas attack had been launched, and the Klaxon horns were shrieking and blasting all along the lines. I was alone on the floor of the ambulance, and the driver stopped and asked me if I had a gas mask. I said, "No, but for God's sake put yours on, and I will cover my head with my blanket." Dead Man's Curve was one hell of a place, but our good old Ford ambulances plowed through the shell holes and bombardments and didn't let up till we arrived at the field station, where I was given more shots, a cup of hot cocoa, and cigarettes.

I was placed in a squad tent to await further transportation to the evacuation hospital at Toul. I was constantly drugged to kill the pains, and as soon as the effects of the drugs began to wear off, I opened my eyes, and all that I could see were lights all around me, and I was on the operating table. I could barely see the doctor, and then, off in the distance, as my left inner ear drum was fractured, I dimly heard the doctor asking the orderly when I was brought in from the field hospital. The last words I could hear were "I'm afraid we may be compelled to amputate his leg." Then I was gone again, this time with ether.

When I came to, I was sitting up in a bed in a large ward of the Toul Hospital. Although I was half-cocked from the effects of ether, I was cussing to beat hell. For I thought I was back up in the front lines, and I was hollering at my men, "Give 'em hell, the SOBs!" until I felt the hand of an orderly on my shoulder, and he was saying, "Take it easy, soldier, there are women around." He was referring to our army nurses. I then lay back and calmed down a bit. Then I remember a well-built elderly nurse with gray hair bending over me, and she said, "Try and be as quiet as you can, as you have just had a severe hemorrhage of your wounded leg, and since you've lost so much blood already in the trenches, you need every drop of blood you have left." And then she bent over me and scooped me up in her arms from the blood soaked sheets and put me in another bed, nearby. She gave me a shot and left me to rest.

Cpl. Frank L. Faulkner, U.S. Army

Overshadowed by the better-known exploits of the 2nd Infantry Division's 4th Marine Brigade, Corporal Faulkner and his fellow soldiers of the division's 3rd Infantry Brigade served just as valiantly alongside the marines in blunting and then counterattacking against the seemingly overwhelming Third German Offensive.

ON THE 12TH OF MARCH, 1918, traveling in our usual manner, we embarked for the front. We traveled to Dugny, a place about five kilometers from Verdun. From here we hiked about eight kilometers to a place called Genicourt, just back of the trenches. It was here that I saw my first view of shell-torn towns and also my first air battles. At that time, it was quite a novel sight, but it soon grew familiar, as they were a daily occurrence.

On March 17th we went in the trenches; of course, we had to travel in the dark. We had full packs, and much of the travel was over the hills and through the woods, so when we reached there, we were pretty well tired out.

We relieved the French, so we did not know much about what sort of a place we were in, but we were told the direction to look for the Germans. It was in a wood; most of the trees had been broken off by shellfire, and only the stumps were left. They looked much like the forms of men, so we spent the rest of the first night shooting up the stumps. That night sort of put us on our feet, and shell-fire lost some of its terrors to us. In fact, we soon became able to enjoy a siesta in spite of heavy artillery fire. To say that it does not give you a queer feeling any time when the shells are landing close about you is stretching it a trifle. I went through some mighty heavy barrages afterwards, but I never felt so apprehensive as on that second night.

We were relieved in about twelve days. We came out to a little village just back of the front called Montharon. Here we drilled some days, but since there was considerable shelling there, it was necessary to be careful. From there we went back to Genicourt and stayed a few days, and then [we] went back in the lines near Rupt-em-Woerve. This time the trenches were in bad shape, and it had rained. The water was sometimes quite deep, and one's feet were wet at all times. The dugouts were in very bad shape: damp; dirty; full of cooties, rats, and other vermin. We were all mighty glad to get out of there.

It was in this sector that the first Distinguished Service Cross was awarded to a member of the regiment. It was given to a fellow by the name of Frank Alekno, who ran two hundred yards for help after receiving a fatal wound. [The story] was published in the papers. It went something like this: there was a patrol of seven Germans, including one officer, a sergeant, and a corporal. Alekno, with the assistance of the help he summoned, attacked them and killed the officer and fatally wounded the corporal. From the papers on the body of the officer and the statements of the wounded corporal, some very valuable information was obtained. The rest of the Germans escaped, but I think one was wounded. Both the corporal and the sergeant who went to Alekno's assistance were wounded more or less seriously. I was about 250 yards from where the action occurred. I heard the shots but did not know what had happened afterwards. I knew Alekno well, as he was in our company. It was [in] this sector that we had our first shell gas attack. Several of the fellows were gassed, but fortunately I escaped.

When we came out from this sector, we went to Woimbly and stayed there several days—three I think. It was there that I spent my first and only time in the brig; we had just come out of the trenches the night before, and our clothes were all wet and muddy, especially the leggings. Since the town was a shell-torn place and contained only a few French soldiers guarding some wine stores, I did not think it amiss if I allowed my leggings to dry while I went across the street to the kitchen for some grease for my shoes. On the way over, I met the officer of the day, and he requested the pleasure of my company. Not being accustomed to be so highly honored, and thinking perhaps I might be of service to him, I went along cheerfully. When we had progressed down the street a ways, he turned me over to the guard and told me I was a prisoner. I asked him what the idea was, and he told me that next time that I appeared on the street, perhaps I would have my leggings on. I just laughed and went in, because I could not feel very guilty.

From Woimbly we went into reserve again at a place opposite Fort Tryon toward the front. Here we did not do much during the days, but at night we dug trenches and put up barbed wire entanglements. The dugouts on this sector were quite different from those we had been in; they were bombproof (that is, if a bomb did not hit them). Inside they were quite dry and lighted with electric lights, but many of the fellows here were taken sick with trench fever and were a long time away from the company. One of our forms of diversion here was to go swimming in the Meuse Canal. The water was awfully cold, but it was wonderfully good to be able to keep clean again.

We left this place on the 9th of May, being relieved by the French. We hiked down along the canal to Montharon and stayed there that night and the next day; then we went on down to a place where we could take the train. (It was in Montharon that I received notice that I was made corporal. I was a little dubious about liking the job then and became more so.) The train took us as far as Robert Espaigne, where we disembarked. I was chosen as the goat to go as an assistant to the billeting officer. It was a job that I was not hankering for, and it fully came up to my expectations. The billets were miserable affairs, and the platoons seemed to think that I had picked them out. In assigning billets, I took them as they came, but each platoon took exception and seemed to think that I had a personal grudge against them, especially since they landed in the rain and there was considerable waiting to get them all inside. Here we drilled and maneuvered to get the new men initiated into the mysteries of extended-order drill. It was here also that we received our two-months' delayed pay and the last one that I received until I received casual pay after I came out of the hospital.

Our exit from here was by a rather long hike to Ravigny, where we entrained for Chaumont-en-Vexin, north of Paris and back of the Somme front. We did not go direct to Chaumont by train but detrained at Meru at about 10 a.m. and hiked twenty-four kilometers through the boiling-hot sun at a forced-march time. The hike killed five mules but only three men. However, many were overcome by the heat, and we were all pretty well used up. Here we drilled and maneuvered some more. We were allowed to go to the village at night, and it was by far the nicest town that we were ever allowed in.

From here we received a hurry call to go to the front. The Germans were just making their drive from Paris through Chateau Thierry and the Paris-Metz road. We took motor lorries and arrived at the front on June 1st. We had to hike a long distance after we left the motor lorries, but on the 29th of June we arrived in a wood just [in] back of the front, and the next day we went up to the Coloumb front and stayed there three days.

Our kitchen did not reach us for some time, since they had to hike the 125 kilometers to get there. There were several days that . . . [were] pretty slim for food, but there was some farm stock that had been abandoned there, so we helped ourselves and had fresh veal, fresh pork, honey, and chicken. After we left that front, we came back to the previously mentioned woods and the following night went in the lines at Triangle Farm just at the right of Belleau Wood. This was the 4th of June. The next day was the attack of which so much is read, but only the marines are mentioned. Nevertheless, the 9th and 23rd were there, and they did just as deserving work, for they were sacrificed that the marines might win their objective.

I was on a point of a hill where I could see both the marines and the "doughboys," and if there was any difference, the marines had the better protection, and they had an artillery barrage. We had neither; the 9th and 23rd advanced about three hundred yards across an absolutely open field and without a barrage, except the hot one that the Germans put over against them. They drove the Germans out of the woods before them, only to find that it was not the purpose of the command to hold the position so costly gained; it was merely so that the marines could gain theirs. The marines had boulders and stone fences to protect them, and their loss could not be any greater than the 9th and 23rd. In K Company of the 23rd, there were twenty-six men left for duty, and [there were] twenty-eight men in M Company. B and C Companies lost heavily also.

I did not see a single man hesitate in either brigade. They walked right up in the face of the heavy machine gun and artillery fire. And although you could see them falling fast, those that were left passed steadily on. When they found that they were not to hold the ground that they had taken at such cost, they felt pretty sore.

On this front, the artillery fire was intense until we were relieved on about July 12. We stayed three days on that farm. Since we had taken up an advanced position during the attack that was in the open, we could only obtain food at night, and then we did not have much to obtain. We withdrew to be a support position and stayed there about three days, digging trenches. Then we went back up in the front line and stayed several days. When we came out . . . we went in reserve down in a wood where our kitchen was located. On the 19th of June, we returned to the position that we had held in support and continued there until we were relieved.

We spent our . . . nights digging trenches in front of the front line and going on patrol. I took the automatic rifle [BAR] on these patrols and also acted as covering party for the working parties. While here we used to go out in the woods and make coffee with a dry wood fire, for the dry wood did not smoke, and we could make it in the daytime. This coffee was a lifesaver. Days we used to also dig dugouts for the officers at battalion headquarters. In this position, we had numerous gas attacks, some of which were quite severe. On one occasion there . . . [were] only eight men left out of one platoon fit for duty. I was gassed somewhat myself, but not enough to go to the hospital. I got the gas while working all day in a patch of woods that had been gassed the night before.

From this position, we withdrew to a place opposite Monreal and stayed until the 16th, when we left for the Soissons front. By hiking and motor lorries, we reached the front the night of the 17th. I never saw so many men, guns, ambulances, and various kind[s] of equipment as there . . . [were] back of this front. We knew that something was coming off, but we did not know the importance of it until some time after. That night it rained, and it was pitch dark, and we hiked up to the front. The roads were congested with equipment and tanks, and only a flash of lightning would show us the way. The next morning, at 4:30 a.m, the barrage opened, and we went over the top. It was the most wonderful barrage I had ever heard. And I have heard none like it since. It sure made us feel good.

By noon we had taken about five kilometers. That afternoon we started on our second attack and took the town of Vierzy. It was when I was going up the other side of this cut that [I arrived in the town where] I received my wound. A first-aid man was right there, and he dressed it, and a couple German prisoners that were taken just beyond helped me . . . [for] about three miles to the first-aid station. Here my wound was redressed, and I had to wait about a day and a half before the ambulance could get through to take me to the evacuation hospital at La Fontaine. From there I was sent to Pierrefont, and from there to Senlis, thence to the French hospital at Chantilly, where I was operated on by a French woman surgeon. Then I was shipped to the American base hospital at Angers, where I remained until I recovered.

After recovery, which was one day less than a month, I was sent to the classification camp at Saint Agninan. This was a miserable place. It was a dirty, dusty, hot sand heap, and the noncoms that were in charge were a frontline duty–dodging, hard-boiled lot. From here, we were sent back to the replacement camp for the IV Army Corps, to which the 2nd Division then belonged. Here we were picked out on experience and time over there, and as to whether we had been wounded or not, and also on our education. We were then sent to Toul as observers with the IV Army Corps. After a brief preparation, we took part in the Saint Mihiel drive. In that capacity it was new but awfully interesting work. The accurateness with which we could view the action made our work both interesting and valuable; reports were sent in from our post four hours ahead of any other source.

Pvt. Clarence L. Richmond, U.S. Marine Corps

Since 1915 the Germans had occupied Blanc Mont, massively fortifying this commanding prominence. By the end of September 1918, the time had come to retake Blanc Mont. Included in the fifty-four thousand Americans assigned to the task were Private Clarence and the other marines of the 4th Marine Brigade. It would prove to be one of their toughest battles.

AT DARK ON THE 29TH [OF SEPTEMBER 1918], we boarded camions [trucks] and headed towards the sound of guns. We left the camions, just out of Suippes, passed through the town, . . . hiked to a place not far beyond, and pitched pup tents just at dawn. It was raining a light drizzle. After getting some sleep, I looked around to see what could be seen. A battery of seventy-fives had sent over a barrage from this place, as was indicated by several huge piles of empty shells near us. The battery had evidently been moved closer to the front. A huge 12-inch howitzer was still sitting just a few yards from us. It was too muddy to move it. The shells were about two and a half feet long. The howitzer was for close range only. It was not fired any while we were there, but a large-caliber gun was fired pretty near during the night. I did not try to find where it was.

It remained cloudy and rainy all during the day. The next day cleared up, and the sun came out. Going to the edge of the woods, I could see in the distance, probably about three or four miles, the battle as it was being waged—could see the flashes from a battery of seventy-fives, and after borrowing a pair of field glasses, saw some cavalry taking part in the fight. I watched the battle for some time. Finally, [I] had to take the glasses back to Sergeant Inman of our platoon.

Just at dark on October 1st, we prepared to move. I was still acting as a stretcher bearer, having turned in my rifle and ammunition a few days previously. A few minutes before we began to move, I went over to the main highway, about a half a mile away, to get two more stretchers. Before I got back, my company had already started. It was dark, and I had some difficulty in locating my pack. Shouldering it, I next had some more trouble in finding my place with the company. After we got out in the open field, several shells fell pretty close, one falling close enough that a large lump of mud hit me on the helmet. I had just put my helmet on as the first shell hit; [I] had been wearing [my] overseas cap.

No more shells fell near us until we had nearly reached our positions. Traveling the highway, we passed through the remains of a little village once known as Suain. Now there were only crumbled walls, under which were dugouts. There were but little remains. Passing on, we began to cross the original French frontline trenches, No Man's Land, and then the German trenches. The road ended, there being now nothing but deep trenches, enormous shell holes, and mine craters. Being able to see only by starlight, it was not possible to get a good view of the sector. This sector had been the scene of four years' bombardment, no material advance being made by either side, the French taking a few yards, and then the Germans retaking it. One mine crater looked to be about fifty feet across and fifteen feet deep. The French had been attacking at this place for several days.

As we drew nearer the lines, flares were shot up every few minutes, like the Germans were uneasy, and I guess they were. A few shells fell close by, wounding a few, as I heard cries. After some delay, we were assigned to a position alongside a road. [I] saw several dead lying around just before we fell out. It was now beginning to get light, and we worked fast digging in. When it got good daylight, I found that we were just outside the little town of Somme-Py. Nearly all the buildings were a wreck, and shells continued to fall in the town all day.

There were a good many planes in the air during the day. A good many trenches ran all around in our vicinity, so I spent most of the day looking around, and [I] explored two dugouts. [I] probably should have been back in my "hole." [I] found some French bread lying on the ground, and even though it was molded, ate some of it. The day passed without anything happening. Most of us made our holes better during the day. We had a sloping hill in front of us, which gave us good protection from fire.

At dusk, [I] went over into Somme-Py with Captain Dunbeck, our CO [commanding officer], in order to locate our dressing station, though I never came back to it during the days that followed. Just as we reached where we were going, a good many shells fell dangerously close, fragments flying all around. A few wounded were brought to the dressing station while we were there. When I got back to our positions, I learned that a shell had hit in the road beside our positions, wounding two fellows. The shell had hit about ten or fifteen yards from my hole. I turned in early to try to get some sleep.

During the night some of the 9th Infantry passed by. One fellow jumped right up on top of my roof, knocking dirt down on me, and then swiped a French canteen full of water I had. I wouldn't have minded the damage he . . . [did] to my hole so much, if he had only let my water supply alone. After they passed by, nothing more bothered [me] during the night.

In the morning, the 3rd, I awoke to find the company all assembled, ready to go. No one had called me. They had had some chow, which had been brought up during the early morning. [I] did some quick work getting ready and proceeded to see what could be found in the way of eats. [I] was lucky to find a piece of bread and a syrup bucket with about two or three spoonfuls in the bottom. That was all I could find. Overcoats had been issued to everybody but me, and there seemed to be none left. The morning was pretty cold, there being a heavy frost. The lack of an overcoat did not worry me, as I knew that I could have a dozen by night, if I needed that many.

Passing through Somme-Py, we took a position in support, just as it got good daylight. The barrage had started just a short while before. Several batteries of seventy-fives were located rather close to the lines. They were all firing away as fast as they could. We passed over the front lines as they had been that morning. There were several dead Frenchmen lying around. We crossed an open field, which was being swept by machine-gun fire. There was nothing to give us protection. A fellow about two feet in front of me fell, a machine-gun bullet glazing the side of his head. It was not serious, and he walked back to the dressing station. Coming to a ravine, we stopped for a while. The boys in front took cover just below the crest of the hill in front of us, while we took cover in a deep trench running the length of the ravine. A good many shells fell a few yards behind us; evidently some battery had our exact range. By following the sound of the shell with my eyes, I could see the ones that hit close to us. We often had arguments as to whether a shell could be seen in the air. This was the first time I had verified the fact that they could be seen, but only when they hit close.

The shelling eased up a little, and we cleared the crest of the hill in front of us. Quite a few shrapnel shells burst just in front of us, the shrapnel raking the ground all around us. No one had yet been wounded near me, so [I] had no one to carry back. We still held a support position and started to dig in soon after noon. The ground was not very favorable for digging, and before we had finished, [we] received orders to change our position.

A gap existed on our left, and our battalion was ordered to fill it. Our objective was the crest of a portion of Blanc Mont ridge. As soon as the Germans saw what we were attempting to do, they met us with heavy machine-gun fire and trench mortars. I think they had every conceivable kind of trench mortar. Some of the shells sounded like they were lopsided as they hit all around us, many of them exploding in the air before hitting the ground. Machine-gun fire became murderously heavy as we ascended the slope of the hill.

Private Hamilton of our platoon fell with a machine-gun bullet through his chest. Hamilton carried a French automatic rifle. Just before coming to the front, he had been given a summary [court martial] for something he had done. Getting him on a stretcher, we headed for the rear to find a first-aid station. We had not gone more than a hundred yards when a trench mortar hit about twenty feet from us and wounded one of the fellows. Stopping a few minutes, I bound up his wound, and we proceeded. Hamilton died before we reached the dressing station. Not wishing to leave him on the field, we buried him in a shell hole, putting up a little improvised cross and fastening one of his identification tags to the cross.

It was dark when we got back to the company. The battalion had taken the crest of the ridge but was still under heavy fire. If it had not been for the trenches that run along the crest of the ridge, [I] do not believe we could have held our gains. Machine-gun fire was extremely fierce right on top of the ridge. I had some difficulty in getting to where the 43rd was. Company CP was located in an excavation previously made for a large gun, though the gun had never been put in place. It was unsafe to stand upright, as quite often some machine gunner turned the muzzle of his machine and raked the top of our "big hole." However, as long as they did not come over the top down on us, we were reasonably safe. Anything to eat, other than emergency rations, was out of the question. However, I was not to go hungry, as I had brought two cans of milk with me from Courtesols. A can of milk and some hard tack was a dish the others envied. Having lost out on the breakfast that morning, and [having had] nothing at noon, milk and hard tack was something not to be rejected with contempt. It helped fill a vacant place.

The fire became less and less as the night passed. About three o'clock in the morning we moved from our position out into the open. Firing had almost ceased by this time. A deserter came over to our company and was immediately taken in charge. We laid out in the open for about an hour and a half, [until] finally, just before daylight, [we] took up a position along a road right on the crest of the ridge. Here we formed attacking waves and waited for good daylight. The Germans located us and began to drop shells along the road, killing and wounding several.

With absolutely no artillery support, we were off when it got light enough to see. We could see where the Germans had hastily dug in during the night. They had dug only very shallow holes. Several field pieces were captured at the very beginning. We crossed a narrow-gauge railroad track and saw several dugouts. We met strong resistance, mostly machine-gun fire. We still had no artillery support.

Enemy planes hovered close overhead and kept their guns turned down on us nearly all morning. Our own planes were not so numerous during the early morning, though they showed up in great numbers later on. We soon detected that [we] were being fired on from almost the rear on our left, indication that no advance had been made by whoever was on our left flank. There became about as much danger of being shot from the rear as from the front. We were pursuing a course almost parallel with a main highway, and as a consequence were under direct observation. As we cleared the crest of a rise, the machine-gun and artillery fire became so fierce we were unable to continue our advance. The October sun was warm, and as we would rest a few minutes now and then, I would lie flat on the ground and almost fall asleep due to being sleepy and from the effect of the sun's rays, even though machine-gun bullets clipped the ground here and there all around me. Finding we could not safely advance beyond the crest of the hill, we fell back a ways and dug in. Artillery fire was point-blank.

Then my work began. All morning I had not seen a single one of the other stretcher bearers. I had been carrying a stretcher alone and had not yet used it.

While the others were digging in, I got some other fellows to help me and commenced to carry wounded back along the highway. Ambulances came up within a half mile of where the battalion dug in. The road, being under direct observation, was subject to heavy shelling. There were so many wounded that we were not able to evacuate near all of them. There were calls everywhere for stretcher bearers. Some were only slightly wounded, while others were pretty badly shot up. Some bore their pain in grim silence, while others, even though only slightly wounded, acted as though they were nearly killed. One fellow, who seemed to be pretty badly wounded, said, "Never mind the pain, boys, go right on." This was in contrast to those who begged to be carried easier, when we were carrying them as easy as was possible under the circumstances. We continued to carry wounded till darkness called a halt to our work. When night came, I, for one, was pretty tired. One of the ambulances received a direct hit, during the afternoon, and was burned up. [I] never learned if the driver was killed or not.

An ammunition dump blew up close to one of our sergeants during the afternoon. He became very near shell-shocked.

During the night, we were not shelled very much, though a few large shells fell near us on our left. We could hear them coming several seconds before they landed, and when they did hit, the earth fairly trembled. A counterattack was reported on our exposed left flank just at dark, but it was repulsed by battalion headquarters and medical men.

The next day, October 5, the French connected up with our left, and we were not bothered any more from that direction. I continued to carry wounded the second day we were in this position. One fellow who had an artery severed in his leg by a piece of shrapnel, I bandaged with a tourniquet just above the wound and rushed him back to the dressing station. [I] saw that he had immediate attention, as the tourniquet had to be loosened quite often. Another fellow had his whole heel shot off. Another had his head severed from his body as clean as if [it] had been done with a knife. During the afternoon of the 5th, the 6th Regiment leapfrogged us and took up the attack. Also our artillery began to give us support early on the 5th. From then on we had plenty of artillery support. Our dressing station was moved up closer but received a direct hit, killing and wounding again several in the station at the time. The enemy kept up a lively fire just over our heads. Machine-gun bullets and "whiz bangs" just cleared our parapets. It was a "close shave" sometimes.

Rations came up to us during the night of the 6th. I helped carry them to the company and was surprised to note that we got some canned pork and beans. This item was up to this time a "scarce article" with us. I celebrated by keeping two cans for myself and a "buddy." Coffee was sent up in a water cart, and we were told to carry our canteens back and fill them. Gathering up about eight canteens, I went back to where the water carts were, one for each company, and filled them with cold coffee, for it was cold by the time it reached us. Just as I started back, a battery of our heavy guns began dropping shells within our lines. The first round fell about a hundred yards in rear of me. I could hear the guns when they were fired and could also hear the shells before they hit. Doing some double-time, I could tell by the sound of the second round that the shells were coming closer. A few seconds before they hit, I fell flat on the ground, and, as soon as the air was clear of flying shell fragments, [I] did some more double-time, only this time faster. In spite of my speed, the shells kept hitting closer each time. By this time signal rockets were being sent up, indicating to the battery that the range was short. Just as I thought the next ones would get me, the battery ceased firing. If they had not ceased firing when they did, there would have been one less marine that night. The next day I saw where shells had hit and torn up the earth. After a while, the battery started firing again, but the range was still short. They soon got it adjusted, and the shells fell on the Germans instead of us. I didn't go after any more coffee that night.

During the morning and afternoon of October 6th, I lay in our positions and watched everything going on, as if there was no war. It was interesting to watch our planes in the air, for they were numerous by this time. Squadron after squadron of bombing planes came over and, after dropping their "load" on the Germans, flew back. Several fighting planes would accompany each squadron. Sometimes the German planes would drop out of the clouds above, and there would be a battle royal in the air. One time a German plane flew pretty low right over us. Again, a large French plane came up to the front alone, just before dark. Several German planes dropped from above and attacked it. The big plane spiraled towards the earth and, when near the ground, leveled out back towards the rear, but before it was lost to view, I saw that it was on fire. [I] do not know if it was able to land before burning up or not.

Just after dark on the night of the 6th, we moved back to the rear, to a place where we "jumped off" on the morning of the 4th. Here we had a good trench for protection. The 51st Company had lost all their officers, and Lieutenant Thayer, of our company, took charge of it. The other companies had also lost nearly all of their officers. We were shelled some in this place, and several were wounded, and one [was] killed. I helped carry all the wounded back to the rear. One wounded fellow on a stretcher was deserted by those carrying his when some shells fell near them. I saw that he got back to the rear at once.

Our shelling was probably due to some artillery fellows firing a captured seventy-seven right beside our positions. Our platoon commander, Lieutenant Stokes, who had only recently been made from a Top, offered a sergeant a hundred francs for his hole, but the sergeant said he would rather have the hole than the money.

The 36th Division relieved us and undertook to carry on the attack. As they filtered through us, I talked with several of them. They were from Texas and Oklahoma and had a good many Indians among them. They said that they had not yet been under shellfire, and this was evident from their actions when shells came . . . [anywhere] near. They attacked on two successive mornings while we were there. The report was that they did not make much headway at first. [I] remember one Indian . . . [man] going to the rear who did not seem to be wounded anywhere. I asked him what was the matter, and was much surprised to hear him say that he was gassed, as he had a cigarette in his mouth at the time. When a person is gassed, smoking is out of the question. Several of our original stretcher bearers turned up about this time. No one seemed to know where most of them had been.

2 | WORLD WAR II
(1939–1945)

Pvt. Ed Poppendick, U.S. Marine Corps

Less than a year after Pearl Harbor, the discovery of a Japanese airfield under construction on Guadalcanal required America to go on the offensive, with the 1st Marine Division chosen to assault this now-strategic outpost. Due to a shortage of transport vessels, it was an invasion on a shoestring, with Private Poppendick and the rest of the division's 7th Marine Regiment not even arriving until six weeks following the August 7, 1942, landing.

OUR BATTALION GOT ITS FIRST VIEW of Guadalcanal on September 18, 1942. The island looked beautiful. It didn't look like there was anything wrong with it. When we finally got to "the Canal," we went in and they took us back and forth on the landing craft off the McCawley because the Japanese were in and out, bombarding the shoreline. When we landed, a couple of times we heard, "'Bout time you got here!" or "Well, you finally got here today, why'd you guys get here so late?"

I remember that first day on Guadalcanal, when we were getting off the ships, we shot down one of our planes. It was just one of the navy planes that came flying by, and what happened was a couple of guys got itchy trigger fingers, and then the next thing, boom, there was hell to pay.

When I first saw some of the marines already on Guadalcanal, they were pretty beat up. The marines were barely holding their positions along the rivers, the Matanikau and Lunga, and they still held only the perimeter around the airfield. All they had, all the marines had, was a string of barbed wire just around the airfield; in front of that was No Man's Land. The marines were in back of the wire; anything coming through at you, you had to stay there and fight or you'd lose the airfield. It was hard for the marines on Guadalcanal because the odds were stacked against us in a lot of ways, like not having enough men or supplies and other things. While I was on the Canal, it sure wasn't the Ritz. A lot of the food we had was Japanese stuff because we didn't get to unload all of our supplies. We had rice, different things, canned goods, and rations, whatever you could get from the Japs; a lot of their food was still around the airstrip because when the first group of marines came in, the Japs and the laborers took to the hills, and they left everything behind.

There were a lot of casualties the night we originally landed because there was a cruiser, I believe it was, that had one of those float planes dropping flares on our position so the Japanese could see where they were shooting. They dropped the flares, and the cruiser would hone its shells in on where the flares fell. They shot a lot of shells into that lit-up area, and we lost a few guys there. We were in a coconut grove, and a guy not too far from me chewed through his poncho. He had suffered an injury, and he didn't want to give away our position. I think his name was Hattrie, and he was from New York. Just so he wouldn't scream out, he just kept chewing through and through. Hattrie survived, but he had shrapnel through his legs.

The next day we were a little leery, a little scared. People don't realize that when you get shelled, you have no place to go. You're trying to dig a hole, and you can't, and pieces of shell, they are sharp, and you can hear them going by, swish! If you got hit with one of those, you'd know it. I found out that this kid, not too far from me, had been hit by shrapnel, and another guy that was near me, his helmet had a big hole where a piece of shrapnel had gone through it. That shrapnel, it's razor sharp. When it hits you, you're going to feel it. We had quite a few guys who were killed and injured that time. First night out, and we got shelled; I thought to myself, "This is really it."

The thing is, the 5th and 1st Regiments, they saw a lot of atrocities when they first came in, like in the battle of the Tenaru. The Japanese sneaked in on the marines, and some were pretty well beat up—butchered, when they tried to help the Japs. The Japanese soldiers had a tendency to wield a sword and didn't think too much of slitting your throat or cutting your head off or whatever they wanted to do. At least the Germans didn't do anything like that. I also heard some marines mention something about a couple of priests that were murdered on Guadalcanal along with some nuns; seeing this kind of thing made some of the marines stop acting according to the rules of war, if there were such things.

During the day, we kept pretty close to our foxholes unless we were manning one of the machine guns. If it rained, any shelter would be made by a poncho or something like that to try to keep water off you. At night, when you got into your foxhole to sleep, you were warned not to get out because it wasn't safe. When you dug a foxhole, you made it deep enough so you would hear someone getting close to you before they saw you first. If anyone went by, you were told to use your knife, then find out who it was crawling along, because the Japs would sneak into our lines and try to kill anyone they found. If you got out of that foxhole, boy, I'll tell you, one of your buddies might shoot you.

At nighttime, you could really hear the land crabs. You'd sometimes mistake them for Japs once in a while until you realized what they were. You were always listening for someone creeping up on you. When you first heard one of those crabs, you figured someone was coming, just from the noise that they made. It was nothing to shoot off your rifle when you heard the damn things. Pretty soon all the guys would be shooting at one little crab.

One time I got so sick in my foxhole, and I couldn't leave because I could have gotten shot. I was so sick I couldn't move. I had diarrhea and everything else. And the next night I thought, "I got to get the hell out of this hole!" but I couldn't because someone would shoot me. Then somebody yelled at me, "Shoot that son of a bitch!" I was in a hole by myself, and there were two or three other foxholes around, and I smelled bad enough that they wanted to shoot me.

We were on duty, on the line most of the time. But when we did get off the line, we didn't have a lot to do to relax. We could go down to the river to bathe, swim, or wash our clothes. That was one thing: they didn't want you to look too dirty! When you came out from washing up, you'd take over the position of the other guys, and they'd go down to the river for their turn to get cleaned up. That was about it for relaxation. Probably the only thing we did otherwise was fixing up the belts on the machine guns. Each belt held about 450 rounds of ammunition, and you had to fill the belts with bullets.

Boy, I remember when I got malaria. It must have been just a couple of weeks after I landed on Guadalcanal, maybe around the end of September. I think when you get that stuff it . . . [takes] a little time, and then it just . . . [seems] to get worse and worse. You got a little headache and fever, and a lot of times you . . . [didn't] know what [was] going on with you. When the fever got too high, then you thought, "Geez, I gotta do something about this." I got so sick they sent me back to the beach to give me some quinine or Atabrine, whatever the doc had on hand. I thought the Atabrine didn't suppress malaria too well, and the guys didn't like it because it turned you yellow. But, when you had malaria, there . . . [wasn't] too much you . . . [could] do; it just had to work its way out. When I got down to the beach, the doc put me to bed because my temperature was over 104 degrees, and he said, "Oh, you've got it now." Well, the Japs suddenly started shelling the beach, and as sick as I was, I thought to myself, "I'll just take my chances on the line."

Everyone was getting malaria and getting sick from other things too: You had malaria [and] dengue fever; You'd get bit[ten] by something, and your leg would start rotting; Or [you'd get] diarrhea and everything else from what you had gotten to eat. It was lousy, really. When you got sick, you really got sick. It didn't take too much. You didn't feel like doing anything, but you still had to fight. I think just about everyone I knew on Guadalcanal . . . had something of one sort or another wrong with them.

Chesty Puller, the commander of the 1st Battalion, 7th Marines, got us going first thing, right on patrols and everything. Then Puller went to [Alexander A.] Vandegrift and started to beg him for action. So . . . one time, all of Company D went out, and Chesty was with us, leading the party toward the Matanikau. We went from one hill to the next. Anyway, it was getting [to be] dusk, and Chesty decided, "Okay, guys, we're gonna go up one more hill, and then we'll bivouac." That was all right because it was getting too damn dark; who wanted to go down into the next valley in the dark? We started to head up the hill, and the next thing, we heard a couple of shots. Puller yelled, "I got a couple of the bastards!" Well, I don't know what the hell happened. Geez, everything started to go.

This kid Randolph that had just gotten in our outfit . . . didn't last too long. That happened a lot with new recruits who were coming in with no battle experience. Having been in the island for a little bit, [I] had already learned a lot about different things, and [I] tried to pass on some knowledge to the new guys. But no one can take a standard ten or twenty minutes, or even two hours, to explain . . . what's going to happen in a battle. Even if you had all the time in the world to explain it, there's always a new situation that you've never been in before. You just told the new guys to keep their heads low and stay away from going up any paths. Once you were in actual battle conditions, you had to learn a lot of things real fast, and your previous training was never enough. Anyway, this kid Randolph—a nice kid from Louisiana—I had just gotten to know him. You don't get to meet too many of the guys enough to know them because once you get used to them, it's like everything else; you get to know them, and they're gone. Randolph got hit when they called for the small mortars. He had the mortar base plates, and he made the mistake of going up the path. As he went, geez, they just riddled him right down the side with a machine gun. He really got it.

The battalion tried to make it to the top of the hill, but it was raining so hard we kept slipping back; for every two feet up, you went back five. The men were told to hold on to the person in front of them so the Japs couldn't infiltrate our line. We did this because . . . [we] had to watch out for who was in front of . . . [us]; the Japanese had this tendency to mix in with our own guys and kill them. We then went back to our main camp with whatever wounded we had.

I can say that our wounded sure had it better than the Japs when it came to care. The Japanese weren't getting much of anything in the way of aid. Their medical treatment wasn't all that good—just commit hari-kari, I guess! Our guys had the corpsmen, . . . [who] took very good care of us. I can't say anything bad about the corpsmen. They were always there. They were limited in what they could do on the spot, but they always had their little bag of goodies to give you something, like plasma, compresses, sulfa, morphine, what have you.

Once the medics treated the guys, you tried hard to get them back as soon as you could to give them the best chance of surviving. I remember one sergeant who was hurt, and we got halfway back, but he died. Sometimes, the wounded would die on the way, and other times you'd get all the way back with them, and they would die on you then. If you had to go two or three miles up a hill and then down a hill with someone that was injured badly, they weren't going to last too long.

After the battle was over, I had to identify Randolph's body. When you saw a dead marine, it was really a tough situation. But you were glad it wasn't you. Afterwards a group of us buried Randolph. [We buried] anybody that was killed . . . right on the spot. Someone would make up a map of the graves so they could go back and dig our guys up. We always went back for the fallen when we had the chance. A lot of times . . . [they would] bury the marine in his poncho and take his canteen and put all the information in the canteen and bury him with it. In a lot of actions, you didn't know what was going on, who was missing or not missing. If you got buried in a hole from a shell, no one would know anything about what happened to you except you were gone. As for the Japs, it didn't bother me that much to see a dead one. Sometimes, for two or three days these bodies were lying around, and they smelled and every other thing.

Another major battle our company fought in was near the Matanikau River, marching inland from the coast. They put us in some landing craft, and we disembarked on the beach at Point Cruz, this bit of land that juts out a little into the ocean. The Higgins boats—the ones with ramps—dropped us off. I didn't do so great on the landing. I stepped off the boat and sank like a stone. The other guys were stepping over me, and then someone pulled me up by my pack straps. I almost drowned.

We were all supposed to meet up with the 1st Raider Battalion, Edson's Raiders. Lieutenant Richards was my platoon leader. The corporal, Chiles, was in charge; and then there was the number one man, the gunner; and then [there was] the number two man; and I was the number three man; and then [there was] the number four man. We were a machine-gun squad, the .30-caliber water-cooled ones. They're heavy! I think the one part was thirty pounds and the other part about forty-five pounds or something like that, so . . . [one] guy carried one part, and one carried another.

We started in from the beach, and it was pretty easy going through the coconut trees on the plantation there. After we had gotten in about twenty-five or thirty yards, this kid next to me looked at our platoon sergeant, Bucky Stowers, and said, "I think the Raiders are in back of us." Then the Japs came in; we had no idea they were coming in behind us to attack. All of a sudden, my squad was fighting down at the bottom of the hill while the rest of the guys had made it to the top to dig in. I heard gunfire, and the platoon sergeant, Stowers, . . . [had his gun] shot right out of his hand. He was right there, a couple of feet away from me, when it happened. I don't know where in the hell he went after that. The next thing I knew, this kid next to me, the number four kid, was shot in the head. His name was Dick; he was a Jewish kid from New York. I could have touched him; he was that close to me when he got shot. It's amazing when you think of the way things go; it could have just as easily been me that got hit. The number one and two men were both shot: one was Anderson and the other Amichi, I think they were called. The corporal in charge, Chiles, . . . had his head blown off. Somebody said he got hit with an exploding shell, like a dum-dum bullet or something. And then the other kid was shot; he was from Ohio, Steubenville. He got shot maybe two or three times. I don't know if he was killed or not. Corpsmen would pick up the wounded and evacuate them out, so often you never knew what happened to the guys who were hit. The guys in my squad all got shot so quickly; we didn't even have the guns set up or anything. Seven guys in the squad, and I was the only one left.

[I knew] the Japs were still going around since I heard them talking; I didn't know what the hell they were saying. I laid there not knowing what to do. I just hugged the ground, figuring my turn was next, so I decided to play dead and stayed that way. Then I heard my lieutenant, Richards, say something. He didn't know if I was dead, too. He was behind a log about ten or fifteen feet away from me, and when he realized I was still alive, he started hollering, "Do you think you can make it back here?"

I yelled back, "I'll try it." I just took the ammunition this way, the spare parts that way, grabbed my rifle, and throom, I must have looked like Jesse Owens running. I hit that log and went over, and all I could hear was a machine gun going, the leaves coming down, and Lieutenant Richards shouting, "Oh boy, this is it!" After I recovered for a while, Lieutenant Richards told me, "Okay, from now on, you're my runner." I didn't think that being a runner was any worse than being a gunner. The thing is that you were scared all the time anyway.

I don't know why, but Puller didn't go with us that day, and when he heard we were in trouble, he was really down and out because he couldn't get to us. The guys back in camp later told me that Puller went down and commandeered a destroyer or something to shell the area where we were trapped. This one guy, Sgt. [Robert D.] Raysbrook, . . . used the flags to tell the destroyer what to do, and every once in a while, he dropped down because he was being shot at. [Sergeant Raysbrook was awarded the Navy Cross for his actions.] He got the message over, and the men on the ship relayed back for our group to try to get to the beach, so they could pick us up.

The guys on the destroyer told our commanding officer that they were going to lay down a barrage so we could make it to the beach. That's what they did. The shells came in a pattern that created a corridor we could use to get to the beach; the shells kept the Japs away from us. When the shelling was over, our officers told us, "Okay, get going down the hill." When we got to the beach, we were laying low in the water because we thought the Japs would come back and kill us. Eventually, the Japs started firing with a large gun. What a noise it made; it scared the hell out of you. We were waiting for the landing craft to get us, but they wouldn't come in because they thought we were the Japanese. One guy in the Coast Guard, [Albert] Munro, . . . was using his craft to shield the men from Japanese fire. He got a medal for it, I think.

When the boats finally did come in, most of our guys stayed with the injured, carrying them out as far as they could without drowning. We were up to our necks with the wounded, trying to hold them up and get them into the boats. When we were ordered, "You go," they'd take every third or fourth guy into the landing craft. When it was your turn, you went; until then, you laid in the water facing the jungle. Finally, my time came, and I waded out to get into the boat. One of the sailors in it remarked to me, "I never saw so many beat up guys as you." The thing was, the ones the navy could get to, they picked up. Those navy guys were taking a chance picking up the wounded, since their boats could . . . [have gotten] knocked off if one of the Japanese destroyers were around; those Japs wouldn't let anything go in for the wounded.

As for the first major combat experiences, we weren't too prepared for what to expect. Even though the 7th was supposed to be in pretty good shape from training and everything else in the jungle, when we got to the Canal, things were a lot different; nobody had really helped me with what to expect, not all the training I had or the marines on the island. The only thing I knew was that you had to dig a hole deep enough to try to keep your body from being shelled or hit with a bullet.

When you are actually in a battle, no amount of training can prepare you for the feeling that you don't know where you're going or what you're going to do. All that you [knew was] that you . . . [were] going in; other than that, they didn't give us too much information. You just had to be leery and know there was a possibility that anything could happen, like what happened on the Matanikau: the Japs came around the back, and we hadn't expected to get hit that quickly.

We got down to the beach and unloaded the ships, and by then it was too dark to get back safely to our encampment. Lieutenant Richards told us, "Okay, there's a tent, and we're all gonna stay here." That night, all of a sudden, this floatplane came over our bivouac dropping flares—Washing Machine Charlie. He used to get to me, coming off a cruiser and dropping flares so that the ship could hone in on where we bivouacked. Along with the flares coming down lighting everything up, you could see the muzzle blasts from the ships from the shells [they were firing]. Anyway, we [were] in the tent, and the Japanese started shelling us. When the shells started falling, everybody scattered. I asked Lieutenant Richards what he wanted to do. I didn't get any answer, so I thought, "He must be gone." I dove into a foxhole, and there were two guys already there. Then a third one came in on top of me, and somebody else came in, and there were about five of us in there. We stayed in that foxhole until five o'clock in the morning or something like that, whenever it started getting light. Finally, the cruiser took off, and all of us got out. I was shaking like hell. I didn't know what was going on, and one of the guys, this one was a commander or something, said to me, "Take it easy, take it easy, son; you're all right." But I kept shaking like hell, and I didn't know what to do, so I started to look for my officer, Lieutenant Richards, because I didn't know where he was. I found out he ended up not too far away where he had gone into another hole. One of the Jap's shells hit the hole, and all five of them in there were killed. In a foxhole, you could bury somebody quick if it took a direct hit. Just lucky I didn't go with Lieutenant Richards, I guess.

Puller was one of those officers that came up through the ranks; it took him a long time before he was made a corporal and so on. He was in Nicaragua, a lot of other places, before he got promoted to [be] an officer. But Chesty, he always kept in mind that he had been a private for a long time and always remembered what it was like to be one. Not all of the officers had been privates, and those that were didn't always recall being one. Chesty was strictly for the Corps and was someone that believed in it.

I saw Chesty walking around quite often, but I didn't see Vandegrift or [Roy S.] Geiger. They never came on the front line that I noticed, and I didn't usually have a reason to go over to the CP [command post]. Chesty was always around, though.

At Henderson Field they always had the American flag flying, . . . and I don't even think it was that big of [a] flag. It kind of kept us going. When the Japanese bombers came in to hit the field, our fighter planes, Grummans, would go up to meet them. I never met or talked to any of the fighter pilots, because I was on the line all the time. When you're on the line, you don't go anywhere else. You would hear guys talking about the fighter pilots and the dog-fights, so we did know what was going on. I did know the Cactus Air Force didn't have much in the way of planes, parts, or pilots.

I don't know if it was October or November, but they figured we must have shot up two or three thousand Japs in that battle for Henderson Field. We had the lines that we had secured, and the area, on a map, looks so big, but it's just the size of New Haven. We had set up machine guns along a ridgeline above the airstrip. When the Japanese hit us, we were on the line singled up, which meant that there was only one battalion holding an area that should have been held by two. D Company was spread out between different companies, and our platoon was assigned to B Co[mpany]. We all got hit pretty good that night. [We were] not too far from the airport, with the Japs attacking through the jungle. . . . It couldn't have been too easy for the Japanese, because some of them were pretty sick. They weren't too quiet, [because so] many men [were] moving around. You'd hear somebody saying, "Hey Joe, where are you?" and you'd wonder who it was talking like that, because some of them could speak English and sounded like the guy next door. [During] any battle with the Japanese, you were leery because you didn't know what to expect. When the Japs came in, geez, they were crazy. They sure made a battle of out of it. The mortars, eighty-ones, took care of a lot of the Japanese, and the army had some tanks down on the beach near the bank of the Tenaru River that took care of some more. This was also the battle where Johnnie [John Basilone] got his Medal of Honor. His machine gun was set up just a little ways from where our platoon was. I guess our outfit was decorated quite a bit; [we] had quite a few medals after the battle.

When we first landed on the Canal, the only things we had were the packs we would carry. Anything you carried in your pack, . . . you used. You had your poncho, and if you didn't have a poncho, you were out of luck; you had to sit in the rain. If you had room for extra socks, you were all right, but if not, they just put them in storage someplace for you. All the rest of your gear, clothes, whatever you had, you packed . . . a certain way in this duffel bag, your sea-bag. We were supposed to get our sea-bags on Guadalcanal, but I never got mine.

When we left Guadalcanal, we were dirty, hungry, and we looked like a bunch of ragamuffins. We didn't have a hell of a lot going for us when we left. Most of the guys were ill with a little bit of everything: malaria, dysentery, you name it. We didn't [have] many of our possessions left, just what we had on as far as clothes were concerned. Basically, I left the island with the clothes on my back and pretty much nothing else. It must have been . . . January 5, 1943, when we sailed on the *President Adams* to Australia.

Shortly after I got to Melbourne, Australia, I had another bout of malaria. They sent me to a hospital in Adelaide for three weeks, and then I went back to the army hospital in Melbourne. I guess somebody figured out that I wasn't going to get any better, and I was issued my orders to go back to the United States. [It was] just about the happiest day of my life. Of course, when I left the Canal, everything was heaven in comparison. I was one of the lucky ones; the rest of my unit was supposed to ship to Cape Gloucester in New Britain and then to Peleliu, but my malaria prevented me from going. On Peleliu, they had some pretty good battles; I lost a lot of friends there. It was just one of those things that I didn't go with them: lucky sometimes and other times, whatever. But every once in a while, you start thinking about those guys, and you have thoughts in your sleep about what happened, and you think about these things.

Lt. John Spaulding, U.S. Army

There were five invasion beaches on Normandy for D-Day. The 116th Infantry Regiment drew what became known as Bloody Omaha with its first two battalions, including Lieutenant Spaulding and the 1st Section of Company E landing in the first wave.

WE LOADED INTO LCVPs [LANDING CRAFT VEHICLES] from larger ships at 0300, June 6, 1944. The companies were divided into sections, and each LCVP had thirty-two men, including a medic, plus two navy men. I was the leader of the 1st Section of Company E, and we were scheduled to go in on the first wave. My assistant section leader was Tech. Sgt. Philip Streczyk. Streczyk, later wounded in the Huertgen Forest action, was the best soldier I have ever seen. He came into the army as a selectee and worked his way up to platoon sergeant. He was in on the landings at Oran and in Sicily. If we had more men like him, the war would soon be over.

We unloaded into LCVPs in a very rough sea. It took us much longer to load than it had during the practice landings because of the rough water. After boarding the LCVPs, we went an undetermined distance to a rendezvous point. Here the navy crew took

49

us around and around, getting us soaked to the skin. Many of the men got seasick immediately, and others got sick as we moved toward shore.

About 0400 our boats lined up in a V-formation and headed in. As we went towards shore, we could see the outlines of other boats around us, and overhead we could hear a few planes. Between 0545 and 0600, we saw the first flashes from the shore. We didn't know whether the flashes were from our planes bombing, as we had been told to expect, or from German artillery. We caught sight of the shore at about 0615.

We also saw a few of our fighter planes. About 0630 the rocket ships began to fire, but most of their rockets hit in the water.

In the meantime, the navy had been firing, and the dust from the debris, combined with the early morning mist, made it difficult to see the coast.

As we came in, there was considerable noise from the shore and the sea. En route, we passed several yellow rubber boats; they had personnel in them, but we didn't know who they were. They turned out to be the crews of amphibious tanks that had foundered.

About eight hundred to one thousand yards out, we began receiving ineffective machine-gun fire from the shore. As we neared the shore, we reached the line of departure; here the odd-numbered boats swung out abreast on one side, while the even-numbered boats went to the other side. We approached the beach [Omaha] in this formation.

Our instructions were to land just to the right of a house identified by location and coordinates, which was to be the left boundary of my position. We were to cross an antitank ditch near the point designated E-1 and scale the seawall. Once we had done this, we were to send patrols into Saint Laurent to link up with

E Company of the 2nd Battalion, 116th Infantry, which was supposed to land on our right flank and then push on to the high ground behind the town. According to plan, the air force was to have destroyed the beach defenses by this time, enabling us to land without any great opposition.

We hit the line of departure at around 0630, someone gave the signal, and we swung into line. When we were about two hundred yards offshore, the LCVP halted, and a navy crewman yelled for us to drop the ramp. Staff Sergeant Fred A. Bisco and I kicked the ramp down. Meanwhile, the other navy crewman on the LCVP had mounted a machine gun on the rear of the craft and had started to return fire. By now we were beginning to receive not only machine-gun fire but mortar and artillery fire as well. Some of the men said they were German 88mm rounds, but during my entire fight in Europe, I have only seen three 88mm bursts.

We had come in at low tide, and the obstacles were visible, sticking out of the water, and we could see teller mines on many of them. No path had been cleared through the obstacles, so we followed a zigzag path in to the beach. It is difficult to know whether the navy could have taken the boats in any farther, since it is possible that they would have become stuck on the sand bars.

Because we were carrying so much equipment, and because I was afraid we were being landed in deep water, I told the men not to jump out until I had tested the water. I jumped out of the boat slightly to the left of the ramp, into water about waist deep. By then it was about 0645. Then the men began to follow me. We headed for shore, and the small-arms fire became noticeable. We saw other boats to our left, but none to our right. We were the right front unit of the 1st Infantry Division. We had seen some tanks coming in, but we didn't know which unit they belonged to.

As we left the LCVP, we spread out in a V-formation about fifty yards across. The water soon became deeper, and we began to swim when it was over our heads. There was a strong undercurrent carrying us to the left. I pulled the valve on my lifebelt; fortunately, it inflated and saved me, although I lost my carbine. We lost none of our men, but only because they helped each other, or because they got rid of their equipment.

About this time Sergeant Streczyk and Pvt. George Bowen, the medic, were also in the water, carrying an eighteen-foot ladder, intended to assist in crossing the antitank ditch or any other obstacle. They were struggling with it just as I was having the worst time trying to stay afloat. As the ladder came by, I grabbed it. Streczyk yelled, "Lieutenant, we don't need any help!" not realizing that I was trying to get help, not give it! I told them to leave the ladder, so we abandoned it in the water. By now, we could touch bottom, and I had swallowed a lot of water. We pulled out Sgt. Edwin Piasecki, who was about to drown. Private Vincent DiGaetano, who was carrying a seventy-two-pound flamethrower, yelled, "I'm drowning; what do you want me to do with this flamethrower?" Streczyk told him to drop it, so he did. In addition to our flamethrower and many personal weapons, we lost our mortar, most of the mortar ammunition, one of our two bazookas, and much of the bazooka ammunition. However, those men who made it to shore with their weapons were able to fire them as soon as they hit the beach, proving that the M1 Garand is an excellent weapon.

As we were coming in, I looked at the terrain and saw a house that looked like the one we were supposed to hit and said, "Damn, the navy had hit it right on the nose!" I later found out that we had actually landed near another house 1,500 yards to the east of our intended landing site. (One reason the navy crew failed to hit the right part of the beach was that the dust created by the naval gunfire, combined with the early morning mist, made it difficult to see the coast.)

We first ran into wire down near the water's edge; Staff Sergeant Curtis Colwell blew a hole in the wire with a bangalore torpedo, and we picked our way through. I personally didn't see the gap he had blown, because I was still dazed from the landing. I didn't see any mines except antitank mines on the beach. Private William C. Roper, a rifleman, became our first casualty when he was hit in the foot by small-arms fire just as he reached the beach. Then, just after we got ashore, one of my two BAR (Browning automatic rifle) men was hit; next wounded was Pvt. Virgil Tilley, struck in the right shoulder by a shell fragment. By this time, I noticed a number of my men on the beach, all standing up and moving across the sand. They were too waterlogged to run, but they went as fast as they could; it looked as if they were walking in the face of a really strong wind. We moved straight inland across the shale beach, toward the house we had spotted.

We first stopped at a demolished building with brush around it. We were forced to halt there by a minefield at the first slope off the beach. My section was spread out; they had deployed the minute they hit the beach, according to instructions. They had been told to get off the beach as quickly as possible and had walked on across because nobody had stopped them.

As we were crossing the beach, my runner, Pvt. Bruce S. Buck, approached me, and I tried to contact E Company using my 536 radio; I extended the antenna and was trying to transmit when I saw that the mouthpiece had been shot away. Instead of discarding the useless radio, I folded the antenna and slung the 536 over my shoulder, proof that the habits you learn in training can often stay with you even when you are scared.

By the time we reached the house, we were receiving heavy small-arms fire; we organized as skirmishers while returning what fire we could. Sergeant Streczyk and Pvt. Richard J. Gallagher advanced to investigate the minefield we had discovered to our front. They decided we couldn't cross the obstacle and set out to find a bypass through the thick brush. Meanwhile, the rest of us were taking cover behind a low wall of the house, while a German machine gun kept us under fire. Private Lewis J. Ramundo was killed here, the only man in my section killed on the beach. One other man was killed later in the day.

On our left, we had bypassed a pillbox, from which machine-gun fire was mowing down F Company people several hundred yards away. There was nothing we could do to help them, since we still could see no one on our right flank, and there was no one to help us on our left. We still didn't know what had become of the rest of E Company. Behind us, boats in the water were in flames, and I saw a tank come ashore around 0745. After a couple of looks behind us, we decided not to look back anymore.

At this point, it was still early morning, and in spite of heavy German rifle and machine-gun fire, we had sustained few casualties. We returned fire, but without apparent effect. We were nearly at the top of the first hill of the beach when Private Gallagher returned and said to follow him up a defilade about four hundred yards to the right of the pillbox that was impeding F Company's advance. I called my men forward, and we cautiously moved along the defile, keeping our eyes open for the little box mines the Germans had planted throughout the area. We made it through without mishap, but a few hours later H Company sustained several casualties while moving through the same area. The Lord was with us on that one.

A machine gun above us took us under fire, and Sergeant Blades attempted to knock it out with a bazooka; he missed and was shot in the left arm almost immediately. Private Curley, a rifleman, was the next man hit. When Private Tilley was wounded shortly after landing, Staff Sergeant Phelps had picked up his BAR and now attempted to engage the machine gun; [he] was soon hit in both legs. By now, nearly all of my section had moved up, and when we rushed the gun, the lone crewman threw up his hands and yelled, "Kamerad!" We could have easily killed him, but since we needed prisoners for interrogation, I ordered the men not to shoot him. He said that he was Polish, that there were sixteen Germans in the area, and that they had been alerted that morning. He added that their orders were to hold the beach. They had taken a vote on whether to fight and had decided against it, but the German noncommissioned officers had forced them to remain in their positions. He also said that there were sixteen Germans in the trench to the rear of his machine gun and that he had not fired on any Americans, although I had seen him hit three.

I left Sergeant Blades, who had been wounded in the assault, in charge of the prisoner, guarding him with a trench knife. We moved our wounded into a defile, and Private Bowen, the medic, gave them first aid. He covered his whole section of the beach that day; no man waited more than five minutes for first aid, and his actions did a lot to help morale. He later received the Distinguished Service Cross for his actions on D-Day.

Meanwhile, Sgt. Clarence Colson, who had picked up a BAR on the beach, moved along the crest of the hill, firing from the hip. He engaged the machine gun on our right, firing so rapidly that his ammunition carrier had difficulty keeping him supplied with ammunition. We were on top of the hill by 0900, advancing cautiously. We were the first platoon of the 16th Infantry to hit the top. By now, my section was down to twenty-one or twenty-two men. We had spent more time in the rubble of the house at the foot of the hill than anywhere else and had also lost time in the capture and interrogation of the prisoner.

At about 0800, Lieutenant Blue of G Company came up and contacted me; he had followed our trail after his company had landed in the second wave behind us. A few minutes later, the commander of G Company, Captain Dawson, came along and asked me if I knew where E company was. Since I still had seen no one on our right, I told him I didn't know. He said that E Company was five hundred yards to my right, but he was thinking in terms of where they were supposed to land; as it turned out, they were actually five hundred to eight hundred yards to our left instead. I later found out that E Company had lost 121 men. Captain Dawson said that he was going into Colleville and told us to go in to the right. He had about two sections of men with him at that time.

I went over and talked to Lieutenant Blue about the information we had gotten from the prisoner and asked him to give us some support where the sixteen Germans were supposed to be. Moving in that direction, we soon ran into a wooded area and discovered a beautifully camouflaged trench that ran along in a zigzag fashion. We were afraid to go into the trench, but instead moved along the top of it, spraying it with small arms fire. We used bullets instead of grenades because we had very few grenades and thought that bullets would be more effective anyway. We did not fix bayonets at any time during the attack. We turned to the right and hit a wooded area; since we drew no fire from there, we yelled to Lieutenant Blue to move out, and he started for Colleville. We moved toward Saint Laurent; G company went on to

Colleville; and H Company arrived and went into Colleville under Lieutenant Shelby.

Our men were spread out over an area one hundred to five hundred yards wide, and Streczyk and Gallagher volunteered to scout the area to our front. They located a machine gunner flanked by two riflemen, and when Streczyk shot the gunner, the riflemen surrendered. Both of the prisoners refused to give any information. We continued to the west with them in tow. Meeting no resistance, we were soon in hedgerows and orchard country. Watching our flanks and front, we scoured the wooded area, sending one sergeant and three or four men to check out suspicious areas. Although we usually set up an automatic weapon to cover such areas, we did not have any machine guns at this time. We crossed two minefields, one of which had a path through it that looked like it had been in use for a long time. We first saw the ACHTUNG—MINEN! sign after we got through this minefield; we still had an angel on our shoulder.

We now found a construction shack near the strongpoint overlooking the E-1 draw. Sergeant Kenneth Peterson fired his bazooka into the shack, but no one came out. We were about to move on when I spied a piece of stovepipe sticking out of the ground about seventy yards away. By now, we were once again receiving small-arms fire, so I formed my section into a semicircular defensive position, and Sergeant Streczyk and I went forward to investigate. We found an underground dugout and an 81mm mortar emplacement, a position for an antitank gun, and construction for a pillbox. All this overlooked the E-1 draw. The 81mm was not manned, but it had beautiful range cards and lots of ammunition. The dugout was constructed of cement and had radios, excellent sleeping facilities, and guard dogs.

We started to drop a grenade into the ventilator pipe, but Streczyk said, "Hold on a minute," and fired three shots into the dugout. He then yelled in Polish and German that he had interrogated the prisoner earlier [and told] . . . the occupants to come out; four unarmed men came out, carrying two or three wounded. I yelled for Colson to bring a squad forward just as we began receiving small-arms fire from our right flank, off to the west. I yelled for Piasecki and Sakowski to move forward to the edge of the draw, and a firefight ensued. By then, it was about 1000 [hours], and the navy began placing time fire into the draw. In the course of the firefight, Piasecki deployed six or seven men, shot several Germans, and chased the rest into the draw, where the naval gunfire caught them.

When Colson came over, I started down the line of communications trenches leading to the cliff over the beach. We were now behind the Germans, so we routed four out of a hole and got thirteen in the trenches. The trenches had teller mines, hundreds of grenades, and numerous machine guns, and they were firing when we came up. We turned the prisoners over to Streczyk. We had had a short fight with the thirteen men; they threw three grenades at us but didn't hit anyone. We found one dead man in the trenches but didn't know if we killed him. If we did, he was the only German we killed. Several of us went on to check the trenches.

At this point, I did a foolish thing. I had picked up a German rifle after losing my carbine in the water but found I didn't know how to use it too well. When I started to check on the trenches, I traded the German rifle for a soldier's carbine but failed to check it. I soon ran into a German and pulled the trigger, but the safety was on. I reached for the safety catch and hit the clip release instead, so my clip hit the ground. I ran about fifty yards in nothing flat. Fortunately, Sergeant Peterson had me covered, and the German put up his hands. That business of not checking guns is certainly not habit forming.

58

We next took out an [antitank] gun near the edge of the draw. There was little resistance. We now had the prisoners back near the dugout. We had split the section into three units. From the draw to the right, we got a little ineffective machine-gun fire at this time. We tried to use the German 81mm mortar, but no one could operate it. For the first time, I saw people across the draw to the right (west). I supposed that they were from the 116th. They seemed to be pinned down.

About this time, two stragglers from the 116th Infantry came up. I didn't ask what company they were from but just took them along. We went back and checked trenches since we were afraid of infiltration by the Germans. In the meantime, I sent the seventeen to nineteen German prisoners back with two men the way we had come. I told the men to turn the prisoners over to anyone who would take them and to ask about our company.

At this point I saw Lieutenant Hutch of Company E (second section, which had been directly to my left in the boats) coming up. I pointed out a minefield to him, and he told me that there was a sniper near me. We had sniper fire every few feet now and were getting pretty jittery. The navy's time fire was getting very close, too, and we sent off our last yellow smoke grenade to let them know we were Americans.

About 1045 Captain Wozenski of Company E came up from the left. He had come along practically the same route we had used. I was very happy to see him. We had orders to contact Major Washington, 2nd Battalion executive officer, just outside Colleville. Our objective was changed; there were to be no patrols into Trevieres that afternoon as we had originally been told there would be. We never crossed the E-1 draw. Instead, we went along the trail toward Colleville. We were to swing into the fields to the right of Colleville. Lieutenant Hutch and I had about thirty men; as a first lieutenant, he was in charge. Lieutenant James McGourty had also come up with Captain Wozenski. Three of our section leaders had been killed on the beach; Hutch, McGourty, and I were here together.

We ran into Major Washington; he was in a ditch outside town. Earlier, Captain Dawson had come up to Colleville, his original objective. G Company was already in and around the town. We got some small-arms fire in this area, but no one was hit. Lieutenant Hutch and I contacted Major Washington about 1300. He told us we were to go to the right of Colleville and guard the right flank of the town. We went out and were surrounded in about forty minutes. Lieutenant Knuckus of G Company, with about fourteen men, came up and said he had the right flank, so we reinforced him. Altogether, Hutch, Knuckus, and I had about forty-five men.

We had set up our defensive position to the west of Colleville. We selected a position where no digging was necessary, often using drainage ditches. We were now in orchards and hedgerows. We moved cautiously, because we didn't know where anybody was. About 1500 [hours] we got German fire. DiGaetano was hit by shrapnel fire, and Sergeant Bisco was killed by rifle fire. Only one round of artillery came in (we thought it was from one of our ships). It exploded about three hundred yards from us with an orange and yellow flash.

As we looked back toward the beach, we saw several squads of Germans coming toward us, and we had no contact with the battalion. Just as a Company G runner started over to us and got to the edge of our defenses, they opened fire on him. After he fell, they fired at least one hundred rounds of machine-gun ammunition into him. It was terrible. But we do the same thing when we want to stop a runner from taking information. Of course, we didn't find out what he was coming to tell us. We fired until we were low on ammunition that afternoon. I had six rounds of carbine ammunition left; some of the soldiers were down to their last clip, and we were still surrounded. We called a meeting of Lieutenants Knuckus and Hutch, Technical Sergeants Ellis and Streczyk, and me. About 1700 we decided to fight out way back to the battalion. We sent word for the men to come to us in the ditch where we were, several hundred yards south and west of Colleville.

About 1900 or 2000 we set up automatic weapons to cover us as we crawled down the ditch back toward Colleville. Lieutenant Hutch went in front. We got back to the battalion and ran into Company C of the 16th Infantry on the way to reinforce us. We didn't know where we were. We found Major Washington in a little gully at the west of town. He said we were to go back to about the same point with Company C in support. We took up a defensive position five hundred to seven hundred yards from our original positions; this was closer to Colleville. We were still in hedgerows and astride enemy avenues of approach. I think part of the company area bordered on the roads into Colleville. We now had machine guns (I believe they were from Company H). By now, it was about 2100, nearly dark. It was quiet except for some aerial activity.

We spent the night of the first day in the positions near Colleville. We had been in almost constant contact with the enemy since we hit the beach.

Of the section, two men were killed on D-Day, Private Ramundo on the beach and Sergeant Bisco later. Eight were wounded. Five men got DSCs [Distinguished Service Crosses], which were later awarded by Gen. Dwight Eisenhower.

Staff Sgt. James C. "Buck" Hutto, U.S. Army

The 82nd Airborne Division's night drop at Normandy led to a month of heavy combat for Staff Sergeant Hutto and his mortar squad. Then came Market Garden with its daring daylight drop into Holland followed by the brutal Battle of the Bulge and the near continuous combat across Germany to the end of the war in Europe.

I WAS NINETEEN WHEN I ENLISTED in the United States Army in December 1942. I wanted to enlist in the Army Air Corps, but the army recruiter talked me into enlisting in the paratroops. I thought the tough training would help me survive, so I became an airborne trooper.

From my home in Gaston, I had to hitchhike to the recruiter in Columbia and then to Lexington to get a release from the draft board. From there, I went right back to the recruiter. He gave me two bus tokens to go to Fort Jackson, where I spent two nights and then shipped out for training.

I went to Camp Blanding, Florida, for basic training and then on to Fort Benning, Georgia, for jump school. I later took part in various training maneuvers conducted in Cheraw, South Carolina, and later in Tennessee. I spent time at Camp Mackall, North Carolina, and Camp Shanks, New York. My commanding officers were Gen. Matthew B. Ridgway, Gen. James M. Gavin, Col. Roy E. Lindquist, and Lt. Col. Louis G. Mendez Jr.

On December 27, 1943, we shipped out to Belfast, Ireland, on the USAT [U.S. Army Transport] *James Parker*. We billeted on the estate of Cromore near Port Stewart in northern Ireland, where we spent about two months training. When it was almost time for the invasion of Europe, they sent us to Wollaton Park near Nottingham, England, to prepare for D-Day. Our job was to jump

into enemy territory and destroy railroads, disrupt communications, and . . . prevent the enemy from completing their mission. I
was a "Red Devil," a paratrooper in the 82nd Airborne Division; I
was the squad leader in a mortar squad.

I remember that I had tried my best during training to beat
this certain other guy, Clayton, on the mortar. You had to run ten
yards with a shell, place it and aim it just so, and then shoot. I gave
it everything I had so I could beat Clayton, and I did. Then they
said, "You did so good that you're the gunner!" I didn't want to be
the gunner on the mortar squad because he had to carry the mortar! As it ended up, half of the time in combat, I didn't even have a
mortar with me.

At Wollaton Park in Nottingham, there was a brick wall about
seven feet high around the park. It was a beautiful place, with
hundreds of deer and a big lake. We 508th troopers were there
in an area also enclosed by barbed wire. I always said this was
to keep the women out! There were lots of girls, mostly nice girls,
some college girls, waiting outside the gate night and day. They
were there waiting for us to go on leave or to get a pass.

We didn't know exactly when the invasion would be. But when
it was four or five days before D-Day, they put all of us at an airfield inside a huge hangar with barbed wire entangled around it.
We could not get out to talk to anyone, and they couldn't get in to
talk with us. The air force brought us chow, and their driver got out
at the gate, and our army driver drove the truck on in.

I jumped my first combat jump into Normandy, France, on
D-Day, June 6, 1944. We jumped at night around 2 a.m. The moonlight was pretty bright, and you could see a good bit below our
C-47. Our pilot dropped us at around five hundred feet; he said
that he wanted us all out safely rather than have the whole plane

shot down. Our chutes barely had time to open, and the Germans were really letting us have it with antiaircraft fire and tracer bullets. Many troopers were killed before they hit the ground or shot while they dangled from parachutes caught in trees or on buildings. We were all scattered out from our DZ, our drop zone.

I landed in a field bordered with hedgerows. As soon as I landed, I spotted a little white horse and a donkey. The donkey was as scared as I was, and he was running like crazy around and around the field. I just lay there, still in my harness. Then the donkey ran between me and my parachute and got tangled in the suspension lines. He started dragging me toward a barn. I had noticed the barn when I landed; the roof had been knocked out of it, and the Germans were in there shooting out of it at our planes. The donkey was dragging me by my parachute straight for that barn!

I got out my trench knife and cut the suspension lines on the chute. I was within fifty feet of that barn when I was finally cut free. I spent the rest of the night in those hedgerows, doubting that I would live much longer.

Once I heard a German patrol a few feet away and then the sound of the bolt on a machine gun being pulled back. I thought that they would shoot out all the hedgerows and that I would get it. But they moved on, and at dawn they evacuated the barn. I left to try to rejoin my regiment.

I recall being pinned down by German machine gunners in a wheat field a few days after the jump. You could hear the machine guns firing across the field and see the bullets cutting down the wheat stalks in long swaths, like they were harvesting it.

My best friend, R. J. Dennett, jumped right behind me in Normandy. He was taken prisoner by the Germans. I didn't see him again until we visited him and his family thirteen years later in his hometown of Drexel, Missouri. He told me that when he said he would see me later, when we jumped, he didn't think it would be thirteen years later.

Most of all, I remember when dawn came on the morning of D-Day. I saw, at dawn, many, many paratroopers dead, drowned in the flooded marshes of Normandy. Some were only a few feet from a dike or solid ground. But they had drowned there in the dark where they landed in the water. They could not see how close the land was, or they couldn't tell which direction to go to reach solid ground. Their packs with all their equipment weighed over ninety pounds, and in the dark they didn't know how close to land they were, or they could have cut them off. Their chutes were flapping over the water when dawn came. Still in their chutes . . . I saw many drowned like this.

In Chef Du Pont right after the drop, I was crawling down the hedgerows mostly looking for ammo. All the dead were lined up, all over and against that hedgerow in both directions. I glanced up and saw an 82nd boy. He was looking ahead, raised up. His hands were pulling a belt tourniquet around his leg. It was shot or blown off. I thought that when I got to him, I would move him to where they had placed the wounded. Then I saw that he was dead, already stiff, shot exactly between the eyes. I guess he had raised his head too high trying to keep the belt tight on his leg so he wouldn't bleed to death and was shot in the head. He looked alive; I thought he was alive. He was looking off into the distance with staring eyes like he was looking ten thousand miles away. That was as spooked a feeling as I ever had during combat, all those dead lined up under that hedgerow and him, dead, staring.

Against the next hedgerow back were the wounded, lined up like the dead ones before. One doctor who had a heel wound himself was trying to help them all, mostly just giving them morphine. They were wounded real bad.

I remember an old couple in Chef Du Pont. I was assigned a roadblock at a gate near their house and not too far from that hedgerow. Every once in a while, I would go and ask them for some bread. It was from a round loaf, and they would cut me a big slice and spread lots of thick butter on top. This was better than ice cream to me after all those C-rations. The people were always good to share their food with us—all over Europe.

I came across a wounded trooper, really young, who kept calling for his mother. When I could get over to him, I knelt down and wrapped my arm around behind him to lift him up so that I could give him my morphine. My hand went into a big cavity in his back and touched his beating heart. I just held him there like that. He died in my arms, calling for his mother.

Rene Croteau, from Louisiana, died on July 4 in Normandy. Our squad was going from house to house, cleaning up. Much of the fighting was hand-to-hand there, but I remember that Croteau died in an open field.

There was a young French boy around fourteen or fifteen years old who had taken up with us, especially with Croteau because he could speak French. We had given this French boy an 82nd uniform and boots. He had little feet, and we had given him our Lieutenant Williams' paratrooper boots because he had little feet, too. Lieutenant Gene Williams had been killed in combat. I remember that the next day a telegram came for him telling him that his wife had given birth to twin sons.

This French boy ran out onto that field when he saw that Croteau was down and tried to drag him off the field. Croteau was already dead. The boy was killed there with him. After that, we all wished that we knew the boy's family so that we could tell them how he had died, that he was brave, and that all the paratroopers mourned him.

Someone in our squad shot a big dairy cow and then cut steaks off of it while the cow was kicking. We built a fire using a kind of plastic explosive and then hung the steaks near the fire. When they were almost ready, we got orders to move out, and we left, the fire, the steaks hanging there, and the cow, still kicking.

In France, we had no sleep and were eating C-rations in the rain or wherever. Once our squad stopped to eat in a pasture where there were dead cows, all stiff and bloated. One trooper took a look around as we ate and said, "Better 'n home, a picnic every day!" Then he jumped back up to sit on a dead cow to eat. When he did, all this rotten mess squirted out of the cow's back end!

I remember taking cover in these deserted or bombed-out big, old French chateaus. They all had wine cellars; some still had bottles in them. We would drink four-star brandy and chase it with the champagne. But it was the calvados that really made a lasting impression on me!

In July, I shot myself in the left hand with a .45 [pistol]. I thought the chamber was empty. They operated on it in a field hospital in France. I was then shipped to a hospital in Oxford, England. I remember a trooper there in the hospital who had a bad leg wound. I would go visit him in his room. He was a boxer from the Midwest. In Golden Gloves, he said. He got gangrene in the wound, and they amputated his leg at the knee. He was bad after that, and they amputated again at the hip. I didn't see him again, but I heard he died soon after that.

Also while I was there at Oxford, one of our nurses kept after me to fix her bicycle. She was a pretty girl; I think her name was

Miller and that she was from Boston. I finally went and looked at her bicycle, and I couldn't find anything wrong with it. The other guys laughed when I told them that and said, "That's not what she wanted you to fix, Buck!"

I recuperated there at Oxford until mid-July. After I recovered, I did training with the 82nd replacements doing night jumps in preparation for Operation Market Garden in Holland. I missed Hill 95 while I was out with my hand. I often think that this may have saved my life, because our regiment saw some bad combat in July in France. Our company was at a low strength, around fifteen men, when we finally returned to base camp at Nottingham. We should have had one hundred or more troopers.

Normandy was worse than Holland. Nobody can explain to you how bad combat can be; no one can tell you how horrible it is until you are in it. I try not to think about the war, but after the 508th reunions I think about it afterward a lot more. I'll think about it in bed sometimes, and I can't sleep.

I was in France until around July 15 and then was shipped back through Southampton to Nottingham, England, to train replacements and to get ready to jump at Nijmegen, Holland. We were to secure the bridge over the Waal River as part of a joint operation with the British 1st Airborne and our 101st Airborne. It was a daytime combat jump on September 17, 1944.

I lost some of my best friends in Holland. My squad leader and assistant squad leader were killed, along with many others. Lieutenant Mitchell, from Greenville, died almost as soon as we hit the ground in Holland. A horrible death, a bullet hit his white phosphorus grenade that hung on his belt and detonated it. The powder never stops burning. He was covered with it. A slow, terrible death.

Some of my worst times in Holland were as a scout for Company I. You couldn't see the Germans as frequently as in Normandy, but you could smell them and know that they were nearby or had just been there. I guess they could smell us, too.

We would scout into Nijmegen at night, and it would be so dark that you couldn't see your hand in front of your face. You had to walk with one foot on the edge of the road just to know where you were. I remember doing this with my buddy Baldwin (from Houston, Texas). We were about twenty-five yards ahead of our company. He would be on one side of the road, and I on the other. I just kept hoping that we wouldn't bump into each other and scare each other. I knew he was pretty scared, and I was afraid he would bump into me and cut me in two with the Thompson that . . . [he] carried.

Some of our worst fighting, combat, for our company was on the other side of the Nijmegen Bridge, the German side. We were able to take the bridge and the brickyard, but we lost so many men. We lost our squad leader and our assistant squad leader here fighting to secure the bridge. My platoon sergeant made me the squad leader, and I had to take over the attack. I remember that for days later, even after we had taken the bridge, there were still German snipers up in the steel structure of the bridge. Someone told me later that this was the first time Allied forces had actually penetrated into Germany. This was also part of the largest airborne assault in history.

In Nijmegen, I remember listening to wounded all night, but there was still shelling going on, and we couldn't get to them. When light came, I crawled out and came to a German officer and a German sergeant, both badly wounded. The officer's groin was all blown out, and the sergeant had a leg wound, I think. The officer was conscious and motioned to me. I came over close and got out my morphine. Paratroopers were issued morphine injections because they knew that we probably wouldn't have a medic available most of the time in combat. So I rolled up his sleeve and gave him my morphine injection. After that, he motioned for me to take his watch. It was a gold watch. I tried to tell him I didn't want it, but he kept on and on motioning. So I finally took it just to calm him down. Later, I asked our medics about him, and someone told me that one of the two had lived, but I don't know if it was him.

I remember in Holland these burned-out brick walls, at least twenty feet high, still standing on the corner end of what had once been a big house. We had taken cover there and kept our sleeping gear there. We were out talking to some soldiers in a jeep about mortar ammo when a few yards behind us that thick brick wall suddenly fell down. WHAM! We would have been killed sure.

I was sent out with another trooper to set up some C-4 plastic explosive to blow up a bridge. We each took a side and went down the embankment near the base of the bridge. I stopped short when I saw a German directly in front of me pointing a rifle at me. I thought, "This is it," and waited for the bullet. I didn't hear one. Then I realized that he was dead, with his head forward as if he were aiming his gun. I heard my buddy yell to get the hell out of there, and we ran. The bridge blew, and it seemed to literally "rain" bricks for a long time as we ran to get away. I think we used too much C-4!

After spending about six weeks in Operation Market Garden in Holland, we were sent in November to Camp Sissonne near Reims, France for some R&R.

It was December, and I was excited about making the regimental football team and about getting my helmet and uniform, which was to be issued the next morning. Then we got notice to be issued combat equipment, clothes, boots, and combat ammo. We stayed up all night doing this and left at dawn in a convoy for Belgium. The Germans had broken through the defensive line, and they were sending us to close it.

We traveled in truck convoys in the freezing cold weather all day and all through the night, stopping only for "piss stops." We arrived at midnight near Bastogne. The truck convoy with the 82nd went towards Liege, and the 101st, located behind us, went on towards Bastogne. Here they met a German Waffen-SS Panzer division and eventually became surrounded in Bastogne.

The 82nd spent the next few weeks trying to rescue the 101st Airborne, rout the Germans, and close the Bulge. It was during this time that Gen. Anthony McAuliffe of the 101st replied, "Nuts!" when the Germans asked him to surrender.

In the Battle of the Bulge, it was terrible hard because you had to fight not only the enemy but also the miserable weather conditions. [There was] snow up to your hips sometimes, and you had to fight in it and live in it, day and night. It was hard, and I swore that if I got through it that I would never be cold or hungry again. Even if I had to steal or whatever, I would never be cold again.

There were so many dead bodies, German and American, left in the snow and freezing temperatures. They were frozen solid. The burial detail would come around and load them by the legs and shoulders and throw them into the bed of a truck. They made a loud noise, like you were throwing big pieces of firewood into the metal bottom of the truck bed. Sometimes the bodies would break open or the arms would snap off.

Christmas 1944, in the snow, in Belgium, they dropped us turkey, gravy, and dressing for Christmas dinner, but ours was nearly frozen when we got to it. Company I was in reserve at this time. We were deep in the Ardennes. There were huge, tall fir and evergreen trees covered with snow, and it looked like a Christmas card, but all the shelling had split them up and ruined them.

I found a mattress near a shelled-out house, slit it, and Sgt. Jack Elliot and I slid inside it like a sleeping bag to stay warm and to sleep. During the night, we heard someone walking near us. I didn't want to get out of the mattress because it was warm, so I just yelled something out. We heard something drop, and he ran off. Next morning, we found German machine gun ammo right near us where he had dropped it.

Not long after Christmas, my buddy Andy Downer and I were on outpost duty at night in the snow near Erria (Belgium) about one hundred yards in front of our lines. We each had some boys. Our job was to pass information on back to our lines behind us. Sometimes a German patrol would bump into an outpost, and we would have a firefight right there.

That night, German SS Panzer troops broke through the outposts and were overrunning our lines; the artillery and automatic weapon fire was real heavy. My boys wanted to get out of there bad. I told them we would have to have orders from headquarters before we could pull out. One boy said that he sure would go get them! He somehow made it back and said that Colonel Mendez told us to "get the hell out of there." He said he passed dead Germans on the way back to our outpost. We got out of there fast.

The regiment had to counterattack at night to take back Erria. We killed around two hundred Germans that night.

In Holland and at the Bulge, the German paratroopers would scare you to death before they attacked. They would yell and carry on loud, like the Confederate soldiers did. You knew they meant it before they attacked.

I was real scared. I was so awful scared that I could feel my heart beating in my ears. I thought the Germans could hear my heart beating, too. I thought, how much longer can I last, how lucky can I be to survive again and again. But you learn a lot after a while in combat. It's hard to describe the experience of combat except to another combat veteran.

We took a little town in Belgium near Thier du Mont ridge named Comte, I think, but then they pulled us out during pitch black night because we were sticking out like a sore thumb. Company I was in rear guard, and we had a tank behind us as we pulled out. It was armed with explosives and would blow up bridges and causeways after we had crossed. I remember hearing the loud BLAM! only fifty yards or so behind us each time they did this. Then, only about a week later, they sent us back to the same place, the same town. We came in and took the town again.

In Comte, a German had hidden out there in a house since we had taken the town the first time. He had apparently held a family hostage in their house for several days. One of my boys (Phillips) had found out, and he hid in a shed near the house, spying on the German. I think the German shot that boy in the leg through the same crack that he had been using to spy!

I told Sergeant Elliot, "[You] . . . take the back, I'll take the front, and we'll get him [the German] out of that house." Just then, I happened to kick out of the snow a British Gammon grenade filled with the plastic explosive composition "C." It had probably been there under the snow since the first time we had taken the town. It was an antitank grenade that exploded on impact, had no timer, and was three times stronger than TNT. I threw it on the roof of the house. It made a very powerful explosion. The German came to the door with his rifle. Sergeant Elliot was waiting there with his Thompson [submachine gun], and he unloaded it on him.

The family came running out of the house into the snow. Then suddenly a young woman with a baby in her arms ran out. She kicked, stomped, and screamed at the dead German lying in the snow while still holding her baby.

Some of us took up in a great big old house there with three floors and a big fireplace. We were on the ground floor, near the fire, while the family was building a coffin for a dead old man down in the cellar. You could hear the hammers and the saws. Then over us upstairs you could hear the women and the rest of the family crying and praying over the old man's body.

I remember thinking, "How strange to be here in the middle: happy to be warm, smoking, drinking wine, and cleaning our guns while they were crying and praying over that body, their grandfather, I think. And the men building a coffin below us in the cellar." I remember thinking, "What a place to be."

Cascio died at the Bulge. Brassie S. Cascio. I never knew what the "S" stood for. Cascio was really Italian: dark hair, pop eyes, pitted rough face, from Chicago. He died during the last offensive of the Bulge. There was a German machine gun in a house in a little small town. Cascio went to the door, and I guess the German surprised him there with that gun. He shot him up close, almost decapitated him. We got there real soon after. I turned the corner of the house and saw Cascio lying on the stone patio. There was his blood all over the stones, still steaming in the cold. They had already taken his boots. We later got a bazooka and shot that house to pieces.

After Christmas, and the Bulge was secure, we were pulled back from the front for a night of rest. Everybody wanted pancakes to eat for supper. We had just eaten a batch of them with syrup when I got sick and vomited all night. The next day we were to go back to the front to help another unit.

We were loading up when the platoon sergeant asked where I was. My buddy, Andy Downer, had told him that I was sick. The sergeant ordered me to the platoon doctor, who made me lie down, and then he punched around on the side of my belly. When he would let up, it really hurt. The doctor said that he couldn't get me to the field hospital now, but to go with my platoon's convoy, and when they unload to walk, to stay there and wait for him. His jeep would be the last in the convoy, and he was going to the field hospital. I could go there with him.

So I got off the truck and waited and waited, but his jeep never came. I didn't want to be out there alone, so I began to walk to rejoin my platoon. The snow was waist-deep in places, and the Germans were really shelling all around; we were about a mile from the front line. I finally got a ride with an old supply sergeant to some little town. There was still lots of shelling, and I found that my platoon had already pulled out. I waited until the shelling let up and then ran to a building with a big red cross on it. One of our doctors, Captain Klein, was there. He examined me and told me to go with the ambulance to another field hospital farther back from the front.

There the doctor told me to get on the table. They had tents with operating tables set up side-by-side, one table right next to another for nearly two hundred yards or more. . . . So, then they took out my appendix in a field hospital near Liege, Belgium.

After that, I was shipped through several Belgium towns and hospitals and on to First General Hospital in Paris, France. When I got there, I saw German medics who were POWs, carrying around American wounded. I was a little afraid of them at first, but pretty soon I figured out that they were glad to be there, too. They were always quick to offer a cigarette or a light.

Eventually I was shipped to a hospital in Southampton, England, via a hospital ship from Cherbourg, France. It was very nice, comfortable, and had good food. Here we were returned to good physical condition. Paratroopers were made—ordered—to run everywhere, not walk like the other soldiers. The sergeants said they were sorry, but they had been ordered to make us paratroopers run!

After the hospital, I was shipped back to Nottingham and then to an airfield at Chartres, near Paris. We then prepared to be ready to jump at short notice on a POW camp somewhere in Germany. We knew that the war was nearing an end and they were afraid that the Germans were planning to shoot POWs. This camp had many 82nd soldiers there. The planes were already loaded.

Then on May 7 some guys came through the airfield in a jeep and yelled, "[Do you] know the war was over?" The next [day], May 8, 1945, our colonel told us that General Eisenhower had selected the 508th Parachute Infantry Regiment to serve as his honor guard at Supreme Headquarters Allied Expeditionary Force (SHAEF) headquarters in Frankfurt, Germany.

We soon were moved into the best apartments in town after the army had given the residents three hours notice to move out. They had to leave most of their furniture for us to use.

Our regiment provided security for SHAEF headquarters and served as honor guards and [served in] . . . parades. We had to look our best and wore white silk parachute scarves and white gloves as part of our uniform. One of the things that we did was go to the Rhein-Main Airbase to meet all the dignitaries coming to SHAEF.

I remember waiting for review by President Truman, the secretary of the navy [James] Forrestal, the secretary of state James Byrnes, the secretary of war, and lots of others. I even saw Joe Stalin. I forget, there were so many. I also saw the famous figure skater Sonja Henie, who went up with us for a practice jump and was made an honorary member of the 508th.

I guarded General Eisenhower's office at SHAEF many times, both at the outer office and his own office door, and sometimes as sergeant of the guard at the gate. So many officers went in and out of there, we were supposed to salute only the generals! I saw many I recognized: Bradley, Montgomery, Smith, Patton, Taylor, and so many more that I didn't recognize!

Once I was sergeant of the guard at the gate with a trooper from Texas. We saw this officer come up in a strange, old-fashioned fancy dress uniform and wearing a colonial-style feathered hat, like Napoleon. My gate guard whispered to me, "What in the world rank is that, do you think?" We had never seen anything like this, and we had been trained to recognize the insignia of all the Allies. I said, "Don't worry, just salute him." Well, I found out later that this guy was an admiral, the commodore, and head of the whole French Navy!

Some of the regiment would get into the general's cognac, brandy, and other "supplies." I knew better than to drink while on guard. General Eisenhower told our colonel, "Tell your boys to take it easy on my liquor cabinet." That's all he ever said.

Once I was on guard in the general's office, and they were in there making a film. I remember the bright lights on his secretary, Miss Sommersby, as she was posing to look like she was taking dictation from General Eisenhower. His little black Scottie dog was there, too.

General Eisenhower spoke to us often and once asked me who would win the regimental football game that day. "Red Devils, Sir!" I said as I saluted. The 508th had the best team there. We only lost one game with that score being 6-0. Our games were something! Our team came running into the stadium with a loud cannon bang and streams of red, white, and blue smoke. It looked like the team ran out of this smoke and onto the field. Our regimental band would lead out. We also had a drum and bugle corps. General Eisenhower would come and sit on one side until halftime, and then he would go sit on the other.

Once I was taking down the flag outside of SHAEF with some of the other 508th guys, and Generals Eisenhower, Smith, and Bradley happened to come out of the building together. They stopped, saluted the flag, and waited for us to take it down and fold it. I was pulling at the rope when suddenly it came off the pulley and wouldn't slide. That flagpole was at least one hundred feet high. I had to force down the rope by literally jumping up at it and using my body weight to pull it down. Still it would barely move. It began to rain, and the generals still stood there, saluting and waiting. The rain finally wet the rope enough to help me get the flag pulled down. It was all I could do, though. The generals continued to salute, standing in the rain until we had folded the flag. Thank goodness that rope didn't break!

I regret not being able to march in the ticker-tape parade given in New York City after the war. In Europe, we combat veterans were anxious to get home and get jobs. Mostly green recruit boys without combat experience replaced us in the regiment. General Gavin knew about the big victory parade coming up, and he wanted to keep his combat veterans with the regiment in Europe so we would be the ones to march. But we didn't know this, and the high-point men were anxious to go home. So we were shipped from Frankfurt to Berlin, then all the way through France to Marseilles, and then shipped on home. A few weeks later, as I recall, the 508th represented the United States Army in a victory parade in New York City. Most of the combat veterans didn't get to march, just their replacements.

After I got back to the states, at Camp Myles Standish in Boston, we unloaded at night and got ready to walk to our barracks. They told us that we could put our bags on trucks they had there so we wouldn't have to carry them. I thought that maybe I should take my musette bag with me and not load it up. It had all my "contraband," French cognac and champagne, knives, a silver-plated German Luger pistol from an SS trooper in Holland, German insignia, some European currency, and other souvenirs that I wasn't supposed to have. But I figured that we would probably have to walk a couple of miles to quarters, and I was beat, so I handed it up to a recruit to load, along with my other bag. We had to walk two blocks. I never saw my musette bag again. They had stolen it.

Cpl. John Kline, U.S. Army

On December 11, the green 106th Infantry Division relieved the veteran 2nd Infantry Division in the quiet Schnee Eifel sector, a seemingly safe place to continue its training. A mere five days later, the massive German Ardennes Offensive exploded across the Allied front, and Corporal Kline and the other soldiers of the division were in a fight for their lives.

THE DRAFT PULLED ME INTO THE UNITED STATES ARMY, at the age of 18, one week after completing my high school education. After three months of infantry basic training with Company B of the 7th Infantry training battalion at Camp Wheeler, Georgia, I qualified as an "expert rifleman" with a score of 193 (the second highest score in the training battalion) on Toombs Range, July 2, 1943.

In September 1943, I went off to the University of Alabama, Tuscaloosa, for Army Specialized Training Program (ASTP), Civil Engineering. This was especially difficult schooling for me, for I graduated from a small high school near Terre Haute, Indiana, which had a very limited curriculum. My best subjects were basketball and girls. I was not good in math as a student in high school, and the pace was very fast at the level of training presented at this university. I felt honored to attend but . . . that my time was limited, particularly because of the math section. As it turned out, the war in Europe had depleted the human resources, and the army was now looking for replacements for shipping overseas for the D-Day landings. To do this, they drew upon thousands of men from existing stateside divisions. Along with many of my fellow students, we were destined to replace some of the men who shipped over as replacements. Our ASTP training ended, and the students went off to various infantry divisions throughout the continental United States.

I found myself transferred to the 106th Infantry Division located in Camp Atterbury, Indiana. I was initially assigned as a jeep driver to 2nd Squad, 1st Platoon, M Company, of the 423rd Regiment, which was a heavy weapons company equipped with 81mm mortars and .30-caliber water-cooled machine guns. I asked for a transfer from the motor pool to company and was assigned as 2nd gunner, 2nd Squad, 1st Platoon. Sergeant Smith was our squad leader. In October 1944, I received a promotion to the rank of corporal.

I arrived at Camp Myles Standish, near Boston, Massachusetts, the staging area for overseas moves, on October 16, 1944. We arrived at Glasgow, Scotland, Firth of Clyde, on October 22. As we neared the harbor, we received instructions to stand on the outside deck with our life belts on. This was the only time in crossing the Atlantic that we went on alert. They told us this is standard practice going into a harbor, where enemy subs could be lying in wait.

We left Glasgow by train late evening a couple of days later and rode all night. Breakfast was coffee, chips, and meat pie on the train. We arrived at Cheltenham, England, on October 25. The 423rd Regiment received billets on the grounds of the Cheltenham Steeplechase track about a half mile from town. We spent many hours in training marches, over the hilly countryside, while here. There was little physical evidence of the war, except the encampment area mentioned before. There were munitions stored along the roads in protective bunkers. During one of our many training marches, we came across the remains of a German bomber, lying scattered across a hilltop.

On November 28, after a heavy training schedule, we went by train to the port of Southampton for shipment to France. The next day we arrived in Southampton and boarded the *Duke of Wellington*, an English vessel. There were ominous signs all over the vessel, like DON'T PRIME GRENADES and KEEP WEAPONS UNLOADED. The English Channel was very rough. I understand that it is always choppy. The *Duke of Wellington*, pounding the waves with its bow, pitched and rolled like a roller coaster.

We were happy to reach the temporary harbor at Le Havre. The original docking facilities received heavy damage during the invasion. It was now made up of many old ships, cabled together to make the temporary harbor. We debarked and formed up on the docks. It was still light. The city was in ruins from the invasion, and little was still standing. I remember seeing a few German pill-boxes camouflaged to represent commercial buildings. There was a very heavy downpour of rain as we marched nine miles to board trucks late that night.

I arrived at Field J-40 (a staging area) near Rouen, France, on December 1. We joined other M Company members who brought along our squad jeeps. We used our pup tents for sleeping. The weather was wet and miserable. We could hardly keep the tent stakes in. As a consolation, the food was good.

On December 7, we left Field J-40 with our combat-loaded jeep. It was getting colder, so we had the jeep top up and the side curtains on. We kept warm by using our new liquid-fuel cooking stove. It was a small stove, enclosed in an aluminum canister about the size of a large thermos bottle. Some men used a can filled with sand and gasoline to keep warm. As we traveled along the French road towards Belgium, we came across miles and miles of German vehicles strafed by our aircraft. They were lying in the ditches, either completely burned or stripped for parts.

When we entered Saint Vith, Belgium, on December 9, the older, established troops gave us the normal "new kid on the block" salutations. They yelled at us, "You'll be sorry," and other similar phrases, some not so nice. We set up our bivouac in woods on the edge of town. The large pines, looking like huge Christmas trees, made the woods quiet, warm, and very beautiful. The silence and peaceful surroundings of the pines and snow was pleasant, especially after the week near Rouen, France, where we had rain beating on the pup tents and the hustle and noise of the motor march on the way to Saint Vith.

We left the woods near Saint Vith for frontline positions on December 11. Our destination was a defense line in the Ardennes forest atop the Schnee Eifel (Snow Mountain). The positions were inside Germany, twelve miles east of Saint Vith. A name we would learn to remember, Schönberg, was nine miles east of Saint Vith and three miles west of our positions. We were facing the German troops from emplacements on the East slopes (reverse slopes) of the German Siegfried Line, known as "The German West Wall."

We took over positions held by the 2nd Infantry Division and exchanged much of our new equipment for their old. The exchange went as quickly and quietly as possible. The 2nd Division was being transferred to Aachen, Germany, to participate in an attack on the Roer Dam area. My machine-gun position was in a log bunker with the field of fire obstructed by a dense forest. Conditions were quiet. Excellent chow came twice a day.

Postwar historians and military strategists now argue that the Schnee Eifel positions shouldn't have been occupied. They say that it was impossible to launch an offensive from there. They argued that the positions presented no defense against an assault from the east. This the Germans proved, on December 16, 1944, as they cut off our positions by attacking around the north and south ends of the Schnee Eifel. They, the crystal ball gazers, were right. A static defense line was not the answer for a thinly spread force. Any penetration through our lines would result in disaster.

M Company, 423rd Regiment, found itself assigned positions along the front line to support the rifle companies. A rifle company is equipped with 60mm mortars and air-cooled .30-caliber machine guns. Our duty was to support the various rifle companies of the 3rd Battalion, 423rd Regiment. They were I, K, and L Companies. Such was our deployment along the tree-covered ridge atop the Schnee Eifel.

We completed our changeover with the 2nd Infantry Division as darkness came. We had no time to become acquainted with the territory around our new positions. Because of that, and since we were new and inexperienced troops, our first night was unforgettable. We were facing, for the first time, an enemy that we only knew from newsreels and training films. It was a sleepless and anxiety-filled night.

I can personally confirm that a snow-covered tree stump will actually move—that is, if you stare at it long enough, and if you are a young, nineteen-year-old machine-gun squad leader peering, into the darkness, towards the enemy through a slit in a machine gun bunker. Every sound seems amplified. Every bush could be an enemy crawling towards you. Your eyes grow bleary from staring into the darkness. You are happy when the relief crew shows up. The next day, you take a good long look at the stump that moved during the night. You take note of all unusual objects, and then things start to settle down.

There were two gun emplacements (bunkers) for my machine-gun squad. One was higher on the hill, and the other, a couple of hundred yards down the slope. When we first moved in, our gun position was in the lower bunker. After the first night, we moved back up the slope, to the alternate bunker. For what reason, I don't know. We did appreciate the move, for the alternate bunker was much warmer and drier. As in the lower bunker, there were "trip lines" running from the bunker down into the forest and through the barbed wire. The lines attached to hand grenades and flares attached to tree trunks. If we detected movement in the area beyond the barbed wire, we could pull a trip line. This would cause a grenade to explode, and at the same time, a flare ignited to light up the area. Our field of fire was good but very limited. The 2nd Division had cut down a lot of trees and cleaned out the brush. However, the forest still offered the enemy excellent cover.

I remember one day finding myself convinced that I could see a vehicle, in the woods, several hundred yards down the hill. The contours of the hill and the thick forest were playing games with my imagination. When I looked at it from another vantage point, the illusion disappeared.

There was one rifleman to the left of my bunker. He was entrenched in a log-covered foxhole. According to members of the patrols, this rifleman was the last person between my machine gun emplacement and the 422nd Regiment, which was reported to be several hundred yards north on the Eifel. The two regiments sent alternate patrols across the unoccupied space each half hour. They reported very little German activity. The first days passed without incident. The most excitement we had in my bunker area was when a nearby .50-caliber machine gun started blasting away. The gunner had become bored and decided to kill a deer in his sights.

Our company commander set up his headquarters in one of the enormous Siegfried Line bunkers. The bunker was not completely demolished, as they usually were. The underground rooms were intact and accessible. He had taken a room several flights down. The command bunker was on a crest of a hill. The firing apertures faced west towards Belgium; the backside, towards the present German lines. There were steep slopes on either side, with signs and white caution tape warning of "minefields." There was a pistol belt and canteen hanging in one of the trees on the slope. Apparently, some GI had wandered into the minefield.

German activity was reported along our front on December 17 (the famous Battle of the Bulge started on December 16). The commander called me back to the command post. He informed me that I should be prepared to move my machine gun to his area to protect the command post. While visiting with him, I noticed that he was very nervous. His .45 Colt pistol was on the table, ready for action. Our master sergeant, who was also present, seemed equally concerned. Later I was to learn the reason for their anxiety. I suspect, in retrospect, that they were aware of the German attack, yet did not yet know the importance of the news.

As it turned out, my machine gun was not moved to the command post. During the night of December 17, we heard gunfire, small arms, mortars, and artillery. We also could hear and see German rocket fire to the south. The German rocket launcher was five-barreled and called a Nebelwerfer. Due to their design, the rockets make a screaming sound as they flew through the air. They carry high explosive warheads but [are] not very accurate; they can be demoralizing if you are in their path of flight.

On the morning of December 18, I was instructed to report to the mess tent for a briefing. As I was walking to the tent, I noticed two German prisoners being guarded by an American GI. They were sitting under a tree near the mess tent.

During the briefing, we found out that the Germans had broken through our supply lines. However, we were not told just how grave the situation was. The facts were that we were cut off from the rest of the division early in the morning of December 17. The artillery and rockets that we had heard to the south were sounds of the battle that was taking place at Bleialf, a small village on the road between Prüm and Schönberg. The 423rd Antitank Company, who had that defensive area, had been thrown out of Bleialf on December 16. They used all available troops in the area and pushed the Germans back out of Bleialf, only to be overrun again on the morning of December 17. They were overpowered by the tremendous numbers of German troops heading northwest up the Bleialf-Schönberg road. The Germans had closed the pincers behind us, at

Schönberg. We were like a boulder protruding from the middle of a stream.

We were told to eat a big breakfast because we were going to hit the road. We were then ordered to head west and join . . . the rest of the regiment. We, presumably, were to make our way to Saint Vith. The cook made stacks and stacks of pancakes. We all ate like it was our last meal. Little did we know that this would be our last decent meal for the next four months. We then prepared to leave our positions, taking only the bare necessities and as much ammunition as possible. Our personal gear was in our duffel bags, stacked near the mess tent. We left them there, thinking that we would retrieve them later.

We left our Schnee Eifel positions, heading west towards Schönberg. I was in my squad jeep with my driver and gunner. We were traveling between columns of troops that were afoot. At that time, I was not familiar with the names of the villages or towns in the vicinity. In my studies after the war, I read that we evacuated from the Schnee Eifel positions west through Halenfeld. Then we took a right fork at Oberlascheid to Skyline Drive [GI nickname]. Then near Radscheid we made a left then a right (northwest) onto a logging road leading into the woods overlooking Schönberg.

Our column did not come under enemy fire until we were near our destination, a heavily wooded area (Hill 504) southeast of Schönberg on December 18. As we approached the logging trail, near Radscheid, we were shelled by German eighty-eight. My driver drove the jeep into the ditch on the right side of the road. A bazooka-man had hitched a ride on the jeep over the right rear wheel. As we hit the ditch, his weapon fell apart. The rocket fell out and landed in the mud alongside of me, where I had fallen. Fortunately, the bazooka rocket did not arm itself. As I picked myself up, I noticed a pair of German binoculars lying in the ditch. I picked them up and hung them around my neck. They were probably left there by German troops who had been patrolling in this area. I have often thought, "What if they had been booby trapped?"

In the early morning of December 19, I received orders to position my .30-cal water-cooled machine gun in the edge of the woods overlooking Schönberg. I was high on a hill, several hundred yards from the town overlooking a slope leading into a valley. My unit was assigned to support L Company, a rifle company, who were preparing to enter Schönberg. They were advancing down the slope, attempting to enter the town along the Bleialf-Schönberg road, which was several hundred yards in front of my gun position, in the edge of the woods. The town and area were infested with Germans, but from my position, I saw no sign of them. I saw little, except the rooftops of the town ahead of us, and a few of our troops on the slope below us.

A rifle company to our rear, I Company, 423rd Regiment, was waiting on orders to proceed down the hill in support of L Company. It was about 0900 [9:00 a.m.] when we were suddenly hit by very heavy artillery fire. It seemed that all hell had broken loose. The shells were exploding all around us, on the ground and in the trees. Men were screaming for medics. I heard during the day that some officers had been hit. There was a terrible lot of confusion at that time. I thought to myself that the officers could be from one of the rifle companies. That was not so; it was our officers that were hit by the German artillery tree bursts. The very first German artillery bursts killed Capt. James Hardy, the M company commander, and the executive officer, Captain Wiegers, was blinded by a tree burst. Smitty, my gunner, was injured in the leg by an artillery fragment. I was struck on the back of my right boot on the same burst. My right overshoe and combat boot were ripped. I sustained a small wound in the area of the right Achilles tendon. In the excitement and trauma that followed, I did not realize I had been hit. It was not serious enough to prevent me from walking and eventually healed.

The first hostile artillery barrage, at 0900, was unbelievable in its magnitude. It seemed that every square yard of ground was being covered. The initial barrage slackened after forty-five minutes or an hour. I could hear the men from K and L Companies, on the slopes below, screaming for medics. Shortly after that, the shelling started again. The woods were being raked throughout the day by a constant barrage of small-arms and artillery fire. We remained pinned down in the edge of the woods and could not move. I found some protection in a small trench, by a tree, as the shelling started. It must have been scooped out by one of the riflemen the night before. The front of the trench, pointing towards Schönberg, was deeper than the back. My feet stuck up above the ground. I suppose that was the reason I suffered a leg wound. At one point during the shelling, I heard a piece of metal hit the ground. It was a large, jagged, hot, smoking piece of shrapnel, about eighteen inches long and four inches wide. It landed a foot or two from my head. After it cooled off, I reached out and picked it up. I don't think it was a mortar or an 88mm shell. It might have been flak from an antiaircraft shell.

We had very little artillery support. I learned after the war that the 423rd's artillery support, the 590th Field Artillery to the rear, was overrun by the Germans troops that were fighting westward towards Schönberg along the Bleialf-Schönberg road. They fought as "infantrymen," but, as they learned after the war, were not eligible for the Combat Infantry Badge.

On the Schönberg Hill, rifle companies, mortar [squads], and machine-gun squads were being pinned down in the woods. In the confusion caused by the demoralizing artillery fire, they were being separated from each other. The 422nd and 423rd Regiments lost track of each other. The day was going bad. There were no targets in view, at least from my point of view. The Germans were waiting for their artillery to neutralize us before they moved. With the ravaging artillery fire and no chance of counterartillery fire, we were literally sitting ducks. There was some action on the edges of the perimeter. From my position, I could see two German tanks. They were scouting around the area, in the edge of the woods near Schönberg. One of them threw out a smoke grenade. I was not able to identify any German infantry troops.

K and L Companies, in trying to push into Schönberg, were caught in the ditches and fields. It was their men that I could see and that I could hear screaming for help. They were being ripped to pieces by the tremendous artillery barrages. Unfortunately, my machine gun was placed too far back of the infantry company as they attempted to get into Schönberg. Normally, we would have moved forward, but the same artillery that was destroying L Company was also hitting us. At the same time, German troops coming up the road from Bleialf were hitting us from the rear. This trapped the reserve company (I Company) . . . [which was] preparing to come forward to assist K and L Companies.

I remember throughout all the shelling watching a tech sergeant, I thought from one of our mortar platoons, walking and running through the woods giving orders. He was trying to get troops moving. The mortar, antiaircraft, and artillery fire was fierce. Trees [were] flying through the air; shells were bursting everywhere. I hope he made it. He was a very brave soldier but was exposed to fierce, ravaging artillery fire.

At one point, as I looked to the right along the edge of the woods, I saw six or eight ground bursts, probably 88s. They hit in a small area along the treeline where several soldiers were trying to find protection. One of those men was hurled through the air, and his body was wrapped around a tree trunk several feet off the ground. There were continuous cries from the wounded screaming for medics. The woods and open areas on the slope leading to the road . . . [were] littered with dead and wounded. Some time between 1600 [4 p.m.] and 1630 [4:30 p.m.] an American officer, accompanied by a German officer, told us we were surrounded and cut off from the other battalion, the 422nd, and that our regimental commander, Col. C. C. Cavender, was ordering us to surrender.

The German troops surrounded us on all sides. They had mortars, antiaircraft guns, assault guns, plus artillery pieces, and were being reinforced by more and more troops from the southeast, and there would have been no possibility of reversing the battle situation. We disabled our weapons by breaking them on tree trunks or by taking them apart and throwing the parts in different directions. Then . . . the Germans led us to a clearing in the forest and directed us to throw down our equipment such as ammo belts, packs, hand grenades, and trench knifes. I quickly disposed of the German binoculars that I had found earlier.

We were led in a small column down to the Schönberg-Bleialf road in front of the rifle companies. There were Germans on one side of the road and Americans on the other. They had been facing each other, in a fierce firefight, from ditch to ditch. There were many dead, both Americans and Germans. The wounded were still crying for help. As we approached the Schönberg Road, it seemed that hundreds of Germans rose up out of the field.

There was a German truck burning in the middle of the road. Behind the truck was an American infantryman lying in the middle of the road. He was dressed like an officer, but with no insignia, as would be normal in combat. He was wearing his winter uniform, a heavy winter coat, [an] ammo belt, and [a] canteen. He was lying on his back, as if he were resting. The body had no head or neck. It was as if somebody had sliced it off with a surgical instrument, leaving no sign of blood. All my life I have had flashbacks of that scene, and I still find it hard to believe. I always wonder how it happened. He was the only soldier, either American or German, that I saw lying on the road. There were many wounded and dead in the ditches and fields [we passed] as we were led out of the woods.

The Germans then walked us in columns to Bleialf where they herded us into a church courtyard. It had turned dark, and the temperature was dropping. Most of us were without overcoats. We had only our field jackets and our winter issue of olive drab uniforms with long johns. I recall that I wore two pairs of pants, my long johns, and my field jacket. We had to sleep on the ground. I remember how nervous I was. Every little sound was amplified, and I wondered what was going to happen to us when daybreak came. We had had nothing to eat since early morning.

The Germans escorted us out of Bleialf the next morning, and we were on the road until 2300 that night. We had no water or food except for the snow from the ground. During the march, as we were going through a very small village, the Germans stopped us in front of some civilians. They made us take off our overshoes and give them to the civilians. That was when I discovered that my right overshoe had been ripped open on the backside by shrapnel. The shrapnel had cut through the back of my rubber overshoe, leather combat boot, and heavy sock. It had then cut around, but not through, my Achilles tendon. It was a small wound, but had it gone any deeper it would have cut my tendon, and I would have been unable to walk.

There was much evidence, in the area, that a large-scale battle had taken place. I remember [that] as we were leaving Bleialf there were German troops in American jeeps. They were opening ration boxes and meat cans. They were eating our Christmas dinner. My guess is that this had been our battalion supply depot. As we walked through the area, I was surprised to see my jeep with four Germans in it. I was positive it was mine. I had personally painted my son's name, "Teddie," on the jeep, and the name was there. There had been a real shootout, with hand-to-hand fighting. There were dead Americans and Germans lying in doors [and] ditches and hanging out of windows. The infighting must have been fierce, for some of the bodies were on top of each other.

We arrived in the city of Koblenz, Germany, on December 27. We received soup and bread served from a portable kitchen. Koblenz is a big city. It has taken a lot of punishment from bombings. We were walking in groups of about five hundred. I was on the left side of our column, next to the street curb. There was a uniformed German photographer taking pictures of our group as we walked by. I noticed he used a Leica camera. A civilian, dressed in a business suit, walked over to the curb near me. He made a loud remark and then hit me alongside the head with a brief case. The guards made him get back. They told us that the civilians were very upset because of the recent bombings. Maybe the civilian had lost some of his family. Later, I thought this might have been a staged protest for propaganda purposes. Why would there be an army photographer there with a businessman, alone, with a column of POWs marching by?

We arrived at Stalag IV-B, Mühlberg, Germany, on January 7, 1945. It was located thirty-two miles northwest of Dresden. We finally had a shower and had our clothes deloused. We were given some medication injected into the muscle area of the left chest. I never did learn what that medication was; possibly it was to prevent typhus or tetanus. We were billeted in small barracks. The sanitary conditions were deplorable. We were transferred a few days later to Stalag VIII-A near Görlitz, Germany. Görlitz is located about 70 miles east-northeast of Dresden on the Polish border, a few miles north of the Czech border and about 135 miles southeast of Berlin. Görlitz straddles the River Neisse in the territory of Lower Silesia, Germany.

In early 1945, the Russian Army's advance approaching the Oder River was the cause for the evacuation of prisoners from Poland and the Upper Silesia area. This situation caused cramped quarters in Stalag VIII-A, resulting in the camp food supply dwindling to very meager rations. To prevent the Russian Army from overrunning our prison camp and freeing us, the Germans decided to take all the occupants and send them westward on foot under armed guard. My group left the prison camp on February 14. We moved from one location to another until liberated by the U.S. Army on April 13, 1945, just a few miles east of the German town of Braunschweig.

We were then taken to a civilian general hospital in the city to wait for ambulances. I was so weak that I couldn't walk without help. They took us up to the second floor of the hospital, where they gave us a shower and deloused us. It is so nice not to be scratching every minute of the day. Those lice used to run races up and down my back.

The German doctors looked us over as if to diagnose our problems. Most all of us are diarrhea cases. The beds are nice and clean. It looks like the road home now! I hope so. It has been a long, terrible, humiliating four months.

Capt. Irvin Roth, U.S. Army

At the beginning of 1945, Captain Roth and his fellow company commanders of the 3rd Battalion, 114th Infantry Regiment, faced a crisis of conscience. Should they follow an ill-conceived order and attack to capture an indefensible position that was sure to result in serious American casualties when the Germans counterattacked, or refuse a lawful order in combat?

ON NEW YEAR'S EVE 1945, the 3rd Battalion of the 114th Infantry was dug in just east of Sarreguemines, Lorraine, France. Here we were entertained by propaganda broadcasts from the German lines, identifying our regiment and our officers, and promising our destruction in a new offensive. It was weird to hear the enemy greeting us and threatening our elimination. However, we felt secure, as the Battle of the Bulge was turning in our favor, and we felt we had the strength to hold our positions. But then, as promised, the German 17th SS Panzer Grenadier Division, howling and shrieking, attacked and forced the 71st Infantry and the 1st Battalion of the 114th back several thousand yards.

On Saturday, January 6, the 114th Infantry was ordered to attack and regain the ground lost. It was a cold and snowy day, but my company was confident, and we expected to continue the advance, which started on November 15. Our line was on the railroad tracks, which ran from Sarreguemines east to Enchenburg, and was held by the 71st Infantry through which we were to pass to the line of departure and into the Bleisbrucken Woods to our objective. I felt good about our preparations and confidently led the company through the foxholes of the 71st, across the railroad tracks, and into the woods. Soldiers of the 71st were in their foxholes and watched us as we moved forward. They were as silent as we were, but I could see they were relieved to see us attack through them. In leading Company I, I envied them their positions, but I steeled myself for the ordeal ahead.

Shouting encouragement, I urged my men forward. But we soon found ourselves in a veritable hell. Bleisbrucken Woods were very thick, and my vision was severely limited. I could see only a few yards to our front and to our flanks. German artillery fire was heavy, and because of the tree bursts, particularly destructive. We did not know where the enemy was, but the Germans knew our location and poured fire in our ranks with artillery fire and with automatic weapons and sniper fire. Here, we also became familiar with a new German weapon, the Nebelwerfer, nicknamed the "screaming minnie," a particular nasty rocket, which made frightening noises and carried a heavy load of explosives. We all tried to push forward, but when we got about one hundred yards into the woods, the intense fire and the inability to see very far either to the front or the flanks forced us back to the line of departure just south of the railroad embankment. [Feeling] . . . frustrated, angry, and . . . helpless, . . . I was hit by a piece of shrapnel, but so keyed up was I that I did not realize I had been wounded, but I realized that in order to keep my company intact and continue to be effective, we had to retreat and regroup. I discovered that all the officers were wounded, and we had casualties among all platoons. I kept the unit together, organized the men, and established a new defensive position on the old line of departure, about two hundred yards south of our deepest penetration into the woods, utilizing the foxholes of the 71st. I was charged up, tense, frightened, and discouraged. It was the first time Company I had failed to capture its objective.

Once I had established a new defense line, I moved to our left flank to contact Capt. Francis Mitchell, the commander of Company M, the 3rd Battalion's heavy weapons company, to tie in the heavy machines guns and mortars with our lighter weapons and to coordinate our defenses. I was standing next to Mitchell when a shot rang out. Instinctively I dropped to the ground, seeing as I did that Mitchell was falling sharply to his left, and as he collapsed, he cried, "Roth, I've been hit!" He fell to the ground, unconscious, mortally wounded. I ordered the rifleman around us to fire into the woods to keep the Germans down. Several men helped me to move Mitchell to the rear. He was now comatose, and I knew he would soon die. Later I realized that I was only a foot away from being killed. Fate had picked him, not me. I was sweating and [trembling] . . . but was able to continue organizing the defenses, and when I felt that we could now hold the ground, I returned to the Wolfing railway station, which was my command post.

The company headquarters were gathered in the half-ruined station together with Maj. Joseph Novellino, the battalion executive officer. I was shaking, nauseated, covered in cold sweat, and agitated. I felt I had failed and that I was losing control of myself. Major Novellino saw my condition and tried to reassure me, but I felt at the end of my tether and that I was falling apart. I quickly left the CP [command post] giving the impression I was going to the latrine, but as I reached the side of the station, I collapsed, sobbing, my body shaking, my nerves shattered. No one followed me out, so I was alone. Soon, I started to recover. I felt better. The collapse had acted as a catharsis, and after a short while I realized that I had taken control of my body and that I could continue to lead the company. I returned to the CP, thinking no one had noticed my condition, but I later found out, at one of our postwar reunions, that everyone knew about my collapse but no one mentioned it. In a very important way, this collapse and recovery strengthened me and, I believe, gave me a reputation among the members of my company that I could not be conquered and that they were in good hands. Major Novellino, seeing my bleeding wound, my condition, and the defense I had set up was impressed enough to recommend that I be awarded the Silver Star Medal, which was done.

That evening our battalion commander, an ineffectual leader, called the four company commanders to his CP, (he always had us come back to him; he never came forward to us, where he could actually see the terrain) and ordered us to attack again the next morning. Again, we moved out in the freezing weather of the German winter, entered the woods, and immediately came under heavy artillery fire. As in the first two attacks, we could not advance and stalled just inside the edge of the trees.

When the battalion commander called us back to his CP the next evening, the four of us agreed to a showdown. I felt the battalion commander did not realize the reality of our situation, so I determined to tell him "like it really was." With the other company leaders, we pointed out that the objective as marked on the map was in a gully downhill from us, so if we did succeed in capturing it, we would be subject to fire from the hills in front of us, our flanks would be hanging in the air with no security on either side, and the casualties we would suffer were too great a price for no apparent advantage. We four decided that to preserve the combat efficiency of our companies for future, better, well-thought out offensives, we would refuse to attack, even if it meant we would be relieved and court-martialed. When I finished, my heart was beating rapidly, and I felt very hot, but I was relieved that I had spoken up. The colonel seemed unsure of what to do, but since he had received orders from Col. Robert Martin, the 114th Regimental Commander, a regular army officer, he contacted him. Colonel Martin came down to the battalion command post. We explained our position and showed him the map marked with our goal, a creekbed at the bottom of a gulch. Colonel Martin then contacted the 44th Division Commander, Maj. Gen. William F. Dean, [who was] captured and wounded during the Korean War and later received the Medal of Honor. He was an excellent leader, knowledgeable and concerned, and often seen at the front. He came down to the battalion CP and listened patiently to the four of us. He then told us that he had been ordered by corps to continue pressure on the Germans along our front and showed us on his map that the 114th was the only unit that he could use. Since the conventional attacks, as envisioned by our battalion commander, were counterproductive, he suggested that instead of battalion or even company attacks, we send combat patrols into the woods to harass and worry the enemy, to keep them nervous, threatened, and confused. His plan proved successful; he had shown leadership and satisfied all the officers present, particularly the four company commanders and most particularly me.

The Germans retaliated by sending their own combat patrols into our position and harassing and worrying us. But we were fortunate in having a railroad signal tower by the railway station. It was two stories high and offered a bird's-eye view over our entire company front, and [from it] . . . we could observe the cleared area between the woods and the railroad. We destroyed several patriots, which had dared to come into our zone of responsibility. Neither the Germans nor we had the capability to force the other to give up territory, so what was to be a short and successful attack hardened into a static defensive line, which left us in place for over two months. It was not until March 15 that the Americans mounted a series of attacks, which led to the end of the war in Europe. On that day, we went into reserve after 149 days of combat.

For a week, we enjoyed a pause from combat, although we continued our training. Our rest was short-lived, because on March 26, we were ordered to cross the Rhine at Worms where the 7th Army had made a strong beachhead. What an exciting experience that was! I was in my command jeep leading the company, which was packed into quartermaster 6x6 trucks, over a pontoon bridge, moving into the heart of Germany. Our objective, Weinheim, was captured after a short one-hour attack. We then turned south toward Heidelberg, about ten miles away.

The quick victory at Weinheim gave me new confidence, and when a tank was attached to the company, I thought our advance would be a walkover. We did meet sporadic resistance at several road junctions along the railroad embankment, which ran from Weinheim to Heidelberg, but we kept moving until we reached the intersection of the railroad and the main street of Lutzelsachsen, where a machine gun behind a building on the left side of this junction stopped our lead scouts. I ordered the tank to go to the crossing to take it out. When the tank moved past the side of the building, it was hit by a Panzerfaust (a hand-held antitank rocket), which penetrated the side armor and exploded in the interior. Most of the tank crew escaped on the right side of the tank, but one crew member leaped out of the escape hatch on the left and fell into the shallow ditch about ten yards in front of me. Without thinking, with no hesitation, I jumped into the ditch, where I dragged the tanker, who had been wounded in the leg and was unable to move, back toward the head of my company. The German machine gun continued to fire, its bullets bouncing on the rails just a few inches above my head. The gunner was unable to depress his weapon low enough, so I was able to pull the wounded soldier back where some Company I men could move him to safety. For this, I was awarded an oak leaf cluster to my Silver Star. In retrospect, this was a foolish thing to do. My duty was to lead Company I and not risk getting wounded or killed doing something which was not part of my mission.

We were now about five miles north of Heidelberg, but when we continued, we suddenly came to an open field about 250 yards from some woods where we were met with heavy artillery fire, machine guns, and a particularly vicious weapon, quadruple-mounted 20mm antiaircraft automatic weapons. It seemed impossible to get close enough to the German entrenchments with all that open, level ground. But I did have a forward observer from the division artillery, Lt. Frank Gabine, and he and I derived a way to get over that exposed area. He would have our supporting artillery battery fire over the heads of Company I and into the enemy's front line. As soon as we heard the guns fire, we would jump up and run like hell toward the German lines. When we heard the shells land, we [would then] fling ourselves on the ground and fire our small arms, light machine guns, and 60mm mortars toward the Germans. We would repeat this, moving forward each time. Later, an officer from a reserve unit behind us told me it was like a choreographed dance—a wave of advancing men, a barrage, a falling down, a rising up, a move forward—beautiful to watch. I was charged up, moving Company I forward, each volley advanced us some yards toward our objective. I felt that each yard gained was a yard closer to victory, a yard closer to home.

This necessitated a constant movement, so when I saw one of my men laying prone and not moving while the guns were firing overhead, I shouted at him to get moving, which he did a little later as another opportunity opened up. I found the same soldier, not moving and looking as if he would stay there. I lost my temper, and pointing my rifle at him, I screamed, "Get up you SOB and start moving, or I'll blow your bleeping head off!" I must have looked and sounded as if I would do so, so he jumped up and continued forward. Immediately I realized that I had made a mistake—what if he had not moved? Would I have isolated groups, scattered and confused, fighting with varying degrees of resistance?

Company I continued southeast and, on the evening of April 28, crossed the Austrian border at 1930, the first company of the 44th Division to do so. A few days later, German radio reported the death of Hitler, and on May 5 German resistance ended in all of Austria.

The news of the end of hostilities brought no shouting or cheering, only a feeling of relief, a sense of peace. We had survived. I felt wonderful. I had led Company I to victory and contributed to bringing peace to Europe. This was tempered by the realization that we were still at war with Japan and that we had to face that.

When we entered Germany, which at that time included Austria, general orders were issued prohibiting contacts with Germans. The order said, "Specifically, it is not permissible to shake hands with them, to visit their homes, to exchange gifts with them, . . . or to accompany them on the street or elsewhere." This order could not be enforced. American soldiers are naturally friendly, and with money, candy, cigarettes, and with a long absence from female companionship, [they] could not be kept away from young German women whose male friends were away in the Wehrmacht or were too young or too old. The order was a failure and soon abandoned.

But while it was still in effect, I enforced it, not actively, but if I came across violations, I could not ignore it. It was something like our present "Don't ask, Don't tell" [policy].

Just before the end of the month, I was in my jeep cruising along the shores of Heiterwangsee, a resort lake near the town in which we were stationed as occupation troops, when I saw two Company I men with two young women on a bench on the beach. Since they had seen me, I could not just drive away, so I steered toward them. They jumped up and ran; the girls ran the other way. The two soldiers ran along the shore, through the water, and got their boots and bottom of their trousers wet. I did not continue the pursuit, and they thought they had gotten away, but I had recognized them.

On the first of the month, I had the company assembled for their pay. During the war, we paid monthly in cash personally to each. Here I paid in marks, which were pegged at 10 cents to 1 mark. On payday I sat behind a table, money organized and stacked for each man. When one of the soldiers involved at the lake came for his pay, he saluted. I counted out his pay, then leaned over the table and looked down. "Are your boots dried up?" I asked as I returned his salute. He reddened but did not speak as he left. Later, as I hoped, the story went around the company. "You can't fool the Old Man." I was twenty-five.

Sgt. Robert Palassou, U.S. Army

What is it like for a soldier to take an enemy's life, to see a soldier in the sights of your rifle and pull the trigger? In the rugged hills of Italy, Sergeant Palassou discovered his personal answer to this question.

I SERVED IN COMPANY L, 363rd Regimental Combat Team, 91st Infantry Division, in Italy, going into combat early in July of 1944, north of Rome and against the German Gothic Line, manned by their 12th Parachute Regiment entrenched on high ground.

The initial battle to seize Mount Vaso, not quite four hundre to five hundred feet high, proved to be one of the toughest of the campaign. Few of L company remained after the third day on the line. My memory of those events is remarkably vivid!

After we took Mount Vaso, Capt. Tom Draney was the only officer left in the company. Our first sergeant was the only non-commissioned officer, and only nine other men could be located. At that time, we believed we were the only survivors. Such a calamity would have been a terrible enough experience for veterans, but this was only our third day of combat, and the dreadful experience was devastating.

Company L had advanced three miles ahead of flanking units, thus our heavy casualties. We were reorganized, filled with replace-ments, and I became platoon sergeant. We went on to capture Leghorn, Pisa, and positions along the south bank of the Arno River. On one patrol, I was a half-mile behind the German lines when I came face-to-face with a German armed with a machine pistol. I fired first, but the bullet went between his legs, and my gun jammed! We were on the side of a steep hill, so I jumped down the bank as the German fired. My buddy protected me with his M1 rifle while I was in the air! I never carried a Thompson submachine gun again!

Following that, I had a problem with the second lieutenant, a former police officer from New Jersey, the only officer I ever had a problem with. He was briefing us about a forthcoming attack on the Gothic Line. We were all sitting on our helmets, being shown aerial photos of the German positions that had been marked in red to show fields of fire. They appeared so formidable that at the time I didn't think any of us would survive the assault.

When the lieutenant said, "I want to change some assignments in the platoon," I became apprehensive. He knew I hated the Thompson gun and was now armed with a sniper rifle. He said, "I want the best man possible as the platoon first scout," and of course he designated me!

He had the right to assign me to this position, but when he said, "I don't want our sniper rifle to fall into the hands of the Germans," I knew for sure he wanted me eliminated because I had embarrassed him earlier in the patrol action. He told me I was to carry a Thompson and wanted to take away my sniper rifle. I got up off my helmet, jacked a shell into the rifle, and said, "Lieutenant, if you want this rifle, take it." I heard the men behind me scramble out of the way.

I was called to report to the captain and asked to tell him what had happened. He told me he could not leave me in the same platoon. Sergeant Bill Monooth, who had overheard the altercation, said he would take me into his platoon. I turned in my sniper rifle and took an M1. (The lieutenant later cracked under pressure of the attack and was killed in action.)

Deciding that I didn't want the responsibility of being a platoon sergeant after six weeks of fighting the 16th SS Panzer Grenadier Division, I became, instead, a runner for the platoon leader.

On the morning of September 16, two battalions of the 363rd were to cross the Sieve River and attack toward Monticelli. Our battalion was to follow in reserve. We crossed the river, turning south along its bank to our assigned area. The cold water soaked us up to our chests, and one could hear our boots squish as we walked. I was able to drain some of the water from my boots, but it seemed our men were making far too much noise, causing me to become jittery. We slowed down as we came to a small creek where the Germans had blown a bridge. The embankment to my left was about twenty feet high and covered with trees.

As I waited my turn to go down into the draw ahead of us, just behind me and to my left I heard the bolt being drawn on a machine gun. My mind raced as I tried to picture the possibilities. I thought perhaps a German had been awakened by our noise, but [I was] afraid to fire, for there were two hundred of us. None of the other men had heard the bolt, so I became apprehensive that the men of the 2nd Platoon were not on their toes.

We advanced about a quarter of a mile, then turned east and proceeded through a field of knee-high grass. Dawn was approaching, and the ground fog lay ahead of us, causing more worry. I came across a fresh pile of human waste with scraps of paper holding German script. I ran back to our lieutenant, reporting what I had found, but he was not impressed. The platoon seemed to be suffering from a false sense of security, since we were reserve with units ahead of us. But I was nervous, sensing trouble.

I continued to move from man to man, urging them to whisper, to be alert. The fog seemed to thicken, but I could see we were about to descend into a large draw. Within a few minutes, the sun would rise over the hill in front of us and most of our cover would be eliminated.

As we started dropping down into the draw, shots were heard behind us. Spotting a ditch about five feet wide, about twenty men, the lieutenant, and the platoon sergeant assembled in it, some relaxed, sitting down, some smoking. Being nervous, I paced back and forth with my walkie-talkie held to one ear. With the sun rising over the hill, I saw one of my comrades (Stewart) from the platoon from which I had been reassigned approaching a haystack near the crest. A few moments later, I looked back at him. He was relieving himself. Then I saw three men approaching his position; they were wearing raincoats with loops on their shoulders, and below their raincoats, their suntan pants were visible—the uniform worn by the German paratroopers!

I grabbed my rifle and climbed out of the ditch, pointing it at the three Germans. All the while, our lieutenant cautioned me that they were Americans. I caught Stewart's eye, and he quickly arose, grabbed his Thompson, yelled at the Germans to put their hands up. This was one of the funniest sights I have ever seen, as Stewart stood there with his pants around his ankles and his Thompson pointed at the enemy.

Two of the Germans dropped their guns and put their hands in the air. The third dropped to the ground and positioned himself as if to commence firing. I pointed my rifle at him and yelled, "Drop it, Kraut!" He swung his head around to look with his burp gun still in hand. I yelled at him again to drop it, and I knew he was measuring me. All the slack was out of my trigger finger, but after a long ten seconds he capitulated and dropped his gun.

We discovered we had captured an officer with a map case and two highly decorated sergeants from the 4th German Paratroop Division. Puzzled as to where they had come from (they, like us, were apparently confused and did not recognize us as their enemy), I looked to the right and saw over fifty men with their backs to us, walking away. I focused on the lead man. He was carrying his weapon over the back of his neck with each arm raised to balance it. He turned to speak to another. After spotting me, he reacted quickly, swinging his MG42 with bipod off his shoulders to the ground. A belt of ammunition was already inserted in the gun. I threw my radio and cigarette into the air, shouting "Germans!" and dove into the ditch to retrieve my rifle.

I whirled around to face the enemy, and although off balance, fired at the machine gunner. He slumped over his gun. The lieutenant yelled at me, "You're shooting Americans!" I ignored him and continued firing at the men on the hill who were now three hundred yards from us. I fired three clips (twenty-four rounds) before the platoon sergeant opened fire also. The lieutenant continued to yell, "You're killing Americans!" I continued to urge the other men to shoot because the Germans were nearing the top of the hill and would soon be gone.

When the last German disappeared over the hill, all was quiet except for the moaning of the wounded. I was cautioned to remain in place but soon saw a man from one of the forward attack platoons make his way back down the hill and stop where the dead and wounded Germans were. The platoon sergeant and I led some of our men up the hill to join him. The grass was high, so we were cautious. I found that I had killed six Germans and wounded six more; one had crawled away.

I wondered how I would sleep that night after my mind had a chance to absorb the happenings of the violent morning. The dirty work had fallen on my shoulders, yet if my initial shot had missed, that machine gunner could have made mincemeat of our platoon.

The trauma of the incident really had an effect on me. A few days later in a terrific mortar barrage, the worst I was ever in, I thought for certain that I was living my last day on earth. Lying on the ground as close as I could hug it, I had my M1 in one hand and my 536 walkie-talkie in the other. I suspected even a fly could not live with all the fragments and bullets in the air. The German paratroopers had plunged fire upon us, and we were completely at their mercy, which was nonexistent.

I made my mind up that no one was going to get me up and moving again. I concluded if I had to, I was going to play dead until it got dark. Then, for some reason (I never question my instincts) I believed that by holding my arms out with my rifle and radio I was going to lose my arms. I let go of both, placing my arms under my body. The man in front of me had his feet near my head, and the fellow behind me had his head near my feet. I felt a number of times the blast of the shells near me, giving me a throbbing headache. During breaks in the shelling, I would raise my head to see what was going on only to have the German riflemen fire at me, having seen the movement.

One time I raised my head and saw that my rifle was missing. When I raised up again to look for it, they fired at me again. I never did find my rifle!

During a break in the shelling, the man in front of me commenced screaming, and the man behind me complained of a wound in the shoulder. I wasn't aware at the time that I, too, had been hit by a fragment of shrapnel the size of a quarter in my right calf. I was lucky, as it hit me flat, yet [it was] hot enough to burn the flesh. Rising up again, I saw one of my best buddies, a medic, about a hundred yards up the mountain, rolling around in much pain. Without giving it a second thought, I went to his aid. I took him to the shelter of a building. Our lieutenant came in with a shattered knee. He gave me his carbine, which I carried for the rest of the action. Although I thought by carrying a lesser weapon I would be relieved from the agony of killing, I was obliged to use it in another action for which I received the Bronze Star.

Most of the time I carried the carbine, in firefights I gave more attention to caring for the wounded when I could. Saving a life was more important to me, I reflected, after having killed many men. I should have been a medic, I guess, for the wounded all trusted in me and believed me when I encouraged them that their wounds were not so bad.

Since the war ended, many people have found that I was an infantryman [and] have asked me my feelings about combat. I always tell them the same story:

I would never wish for my worst enemy to have to go through what I did. But, on the other hand, for myself I have considered what I went through an honor, as I had the opportunity to know those men that fought our war. To witness their bravery under fire was uplifting. For me to see friends in trouble and go to their aid gave me a feeling of justification. Many were to give up their lives in the process of this campaign. I knew many heroes firsthand; they all were first-class heroes in my mind.

Sgt. Gerald B. Cullinane, U.S. Army

In late February 1945, in the hills and mountains south of Bologna and the Po River Valley, the army was once again on the move after being in active defense due to shortages of ammunition, terrible weather, and heavy losses since the previous October. Near Mount Belvedere, Sergeant Cullinane discovers the truth of being scared out of your mind.

ON FEBRUARY 2, 1945, Company F of the 87th Mountain Regiment of the 10th Mountain Division stumbled down the steep slopes, which had been our home of the past few days or so, and boarded trucks which would take us much closer to the active front line. The 6x6 trucks had lined up on the narrow road in the valley near Lucca in front of a few Italian buildings, which may have been houses or shops. While we were sitting in the trucks waiting to leave, young Italian women came out of one of the buildings with flasks of rosso vino, offering some to the bored troops waiting in the trucks. Soon, many of us were emptying our canteens of water and filling them with the raw red wine we were buying from the poor local producers. It didn't take too long for our forty-seven-mile ride up into the Northern Apennines to become rather frolicsome. All this even though we knew we were going to the front for the first time. It was the result of years of training that eventually created a "don't give a damn" attitude, and anything that relieved the routine was welcome. So, we overdid our imbibing of Italian wine. It was really the first time we had been exposed to the availability of the homemade product that proved to be ubiquitous throughout our time in Italy.

Our trucks took us through the mountains that afternoon, past other army support units, the usual jeep and truck traffic, and finally to the town of Silla along the Reno River. From here, we disembarked, feeling the effects of our *vino* gradually beginning to wear off. By now, it was late in the afternoon with not a whole lot of daylight left. We didn't know it, but we were facing a long, arduous hike up icy, slippery roads toward the heights of the Monte Belvedere sector. With full field packs, rifles, helmets, rations, and ammunition, we started up. It was not much fun, and we knew we were getting closer to the serious part of the war in Italy. Our foolishness with the afternoon's wine left those of us who had partaken with monumental thirst and little or no water in our canteens. I can clearly remember grabbing handfuls of snow constantly on that eight-mile trek to Vidiciatico. The 2nd Battalion of the 87th made the move into those hill towns, while the 1st and 3rd Battalions would move up somewhat later. We arrived in Vidiciatico about 11:30 that night and relieved some unit of the 86th Regiment. I remember talking to a soldier from the 86th, and he, as young people sometimes do, acted as if he had been on the line since Salerno, referring to Jerry this and Jerry that, all very condescending to us greenhorns from the 87th.

I went out on night patrol with an expanded squad led by 1st Lt. John Benson, who was our platoon leader. It was the middle of the night, and like most nights at that time, we could hear the sound of gunfire sporadically in the distance. It was easy to identify "theirs" and "ours." The German weapons, [which included] burp guns [and] MG34 or MG42 machine guns primarily, fired at a much higher rate than ours, so we could tell who was firing. That night was the only time I ever carried a Thompson submachine gun. We were fortunate in that we did not make any contact with the enemy in spite of our wandering out toward what would be our objective in the attack soon to come. Patrols of necessity have to be as quiet as possible, so the night was dark and silent. But while on a patrol, the anticipation factor is pretty high. No one wants to be surprised.

By the afternoon of February 19, 1945, we had moved out of Vidiciatico to open fields just below Querciola as a staging area for the 2nd Battalion of the 87th. Over the past several days, there had been a lot of truck activity in the whole area as supplies and ammunitions were brought forward in anticipation of our attack. Along the roadsides we saw continual dumps of rations, artillery shells, boxes of ammunition, etc., all of which told only one story— that something big was going to happen very soon.

That evening, I think, we were able to get a little hot food from our mess crew. We were in a defilade area not too visible to the enemy, so were able to get some nourishment. During the evening, some German shells came whistling in and hit near our assembly area but did no damage that I was aware of. We had the usual boring wait, not knowing what the plan was. Finally, when night fell, it became very dark, and we waited to find out what we were to do next. I believe it was about 11:00 p.m. when we finally began to move out. There had been no artillery fire on our part, and I suppose the Germans did not have certain knowledge that we were going to attack when we did. At that time, units such as Company F did not know about Riva Ridge, but the Germans must have known. Anyway, in the dark, away we went. I don't know personally of anyone in my company that was acting in any other way than he had acted throughout our training. That is to say, all of our troops were highly trained to do just what we were setting out to do. Hollywood has never gotten this moment correct as far as my experience goes. With our field packs, rifles, and our combat equipment, we set off in the dark across the fields leading to Florio and what we called "Chocolate Drop," a sturdy steep hill in front of us that harbored German defenders well dug in.

As we slowly advanced, probing our way, we stopped from time to time. At one stop, my platoon was next to one of those conical-style Italian haystacks. I flopped down, leaning back into the hay along with my buddies, since we had been awake for many hours and it was cold. I found myself warming up in the comfort of the soft hay. Before I knew it, I was asleep. The next thing I remember is someone saying, "Come on! They've moved out." I felt, "My God! They will think I've deserted." I just remember grabbing my rifle and running full bore through the dark night to catch up to my company. I have often thought about how unconcerned I apparently was to allow myself to fall asleep on the night of my first attack against the German Wehrmacht. I must have been incredibly naive or so detached in a metaphysical way from reality that I was not aware of the significance of what was happening.

I soon rejoined my platoon, which was the 1st Platoon. Leading the company attack was the 3rd Platoon and the 2nd Platoon. As we came closer to the German line and contact was made, I saw and heard the machine-gun fire of the enemy. His tracer bullets carved lazy arcs through the dark night toward our positions. My platoon . . . had three Italian partisans attached, one of whom had a Browning automatic rifle (BAR). For some reason, our platoon leader, Lt. John Benson, had gone back from our position to get a medic or medics to bring forward, as a firefight had erupted ahead of us with the other platoons involved. Benson and a medic approached our position along a kind of ditch from the rear. It was still pitch dark, probably 2:00 or 3:00 in the morning, when I heard a blast from the BAR, which the Italian partisan was carrying. He was only a few yards to my left. The next thing I heard, almost instantly, was the cry, "Stop! You've killed the lieutenant." It was true. The partisan had mistaken Benson and the medic coming up from the rear as enemy, or else he wanted to be a hero and show that he saw them first and would get them. At that point either our platoon sergeant or the captain, I don't remember, told one of our Italian-speaking soldiers, I think it was Vincent Addeo, to immediately take the partisans back to the rear, out of our combat area, and disarm them. It was a very sad moment for us, as we had lost our platoon leader who had been with us since Camp Hale. Technical Sergeant Fred Frick took over command of the platoon until a replacement second lieutenant came up from the Repple Depple [GI slang for "Replacement Depot"].

Shortly after this episode, Captain Kennett came by my squad as we were holding our position behind the fighting of our other platoons and called upon us to build a base of fire out toward the German positions. It was then that I saw a muzzle flash from what I perceived to be a German position forward of where we were. It was still the dark of night, probably near 4:00 a.m. or so. I lined up my sights and fired off one clip of ammo at the spot where I saw the muzzle blast. That turned out to be the only rounds I ever fired at the enemy of the United States while I was serving as a soldier in Italy. In fact, it was the last time I fired my M1 rifle while in the army.

As dawn broke, the outlines of the ridge opposite and to our left (Riva Ridge) came into view as did the heights of Monte Belvedere off to our right. L [Company] knew that E Company was below us on our left and G Company was above us to our right. I did not know anything about Riva Ridge, nor did I notice anything going on over there. I had no idea where the other regiments were, and, as infantrymen have always said, my war was a few hundred yards all around me, with me in the center. Our 3rd Platoon could be now seen attacking the steep hill of the Chocolate Drop on top of which Germans were dug in. I remember seeing one of our guys clawing up the bare face of the objective, only to see him slip back down as German hand grenades were tossed. His was a very brave action and by itself worth a Bronze Star. I hope he got one.

The firefight continued sporadically as the 3rd and 2nd Platoons moved into and around our objective, while the 1st Platoon maintained close contact in reserve. By midmorning I moved up with my squad to the small farm buildings called Florio. Nearby we passed the first casualties of the attack. I clearly recall seeing one of the younger boys who had been killed, in rigor mortis, lying on his side with one arm sticking up into the air. Another, Leonard Wood, had been hit in the leg and couldn't walk. He just had his two army blankets sewn together into a sleeping bag, and when he saw me, he called to me to take them. I think I did, but don't remember, because I was to have no need of them.

I also recall seeing Sgt. Stanley Leszko of the 3rd Platoon come around the corner of the hill with three German prisoners in tow.

Stan was a good soldier, and I think he really enjoyed going after those Krauts. He went through the entire combat time without ever being hit. He also was awarded three Bronze Stars. One of them probably should have been a Silver Star. Later we worked our way up to the crest of the hill to the old German positions. The hills and slopes of Mount Belvedere were thinly covered with small oak trees, and under one of them, I saw my first dead German. He was lying flat on his back in the snow in his long gray German overcoat, with his cloth Wehrmacht hat on and round steel-rimmed glasses. There was no sign of his demise other than a small trickle of blood from under his hat. He looked so peaceful and harmless that I couldn't help feeling that he probably had been doing what he didn't want to do. So many of us were carrying out what fate had brought to us, and he had bad luck. He could have just as easily been on his way back to a nice, warm POW camp.

We settled in on the top of our little ridge that had been our objective. The success of it had made us all feel pretty good in spite of our casualties. I guess somehow we were conditioned to expect losses. But we always thought it would be the other guy, not oneself. As it turned out, in the days in combat, I think my company lost more replacements than it did of the old soldiers from Camp Hale days.

I was in a deep foxhole, or small dugout, with a few others of my squad. We had a German MG42 machine gun that had been taken along with the territory and the prisoners. We were a little naive and revealed our lack of experience by deciding to fire the machine gun. Each of us took a turn at squeezing off a number of rounds generally pointed to our front. I realized in later returns to Italy that there were probably no Germans in front of us, as they were all up on Mount Belvedere trying to keep from getting beat up by the 86th and 85th along with the rest of the 87th. The firing of the German machine gun could well have attracted fire toward us from our own troops thinking we were Germans because of the distinctive sound of the gun. I guess we were learning on the job.

During the day of February 20, we could hear the fighting going on farther up Belvedere. We saw the air support, mostly P-47s, and I thought I saw one go down. He probably was just diving below the line of the mountaintop from our vantage point. One P-47 did approach near our location. At that time, we didn't know there was not likely to be enemy strength directly in front of us, and apparently the pilot of the plane didn't either, because he went into a long shallow dive over an old Italian farmhouse about seven hundred or eight hundred yards out toward our front. As he neared the house, the pilot dropped his five hundred–pound bomb, which landed very close to the target with a big explosion. We never saw anyone run out or blow up or crawl out, so I think the building was deserted.

The afternoon wore on, and we began getting our position organized for the coming night. Frequent gunfire could be heard still from high up the mountain, so not everything was as peaceful up there as it was at our site. It must have been around 3 p.m. or 1500 hours when my platoon leader told me to take a few of our squad back to get our packs from where we dropped them in the middle of the night after making contact with the Germans. We started down the hill and out across the sloping land behind us. We crossed a small ditch and [went] up on the other side on a thin layer of snow. The sky was fairly clear, with a weak sun trying to burn through. Without warning, an explosion almost in my face spun me around from the effect of being hit by a German shell fragment in my right shoulder. I had not heard any sound at all before the blast, which caused me to believe it was a mortar shell dropping straight down. It seemed as though the shell hit not more than six or seven feet from me. The first thought that flashed in my mind was, "They got me!" and I dropped like a rock to the ground, thinking in nanoseconds "just like in the movies!" That move was both instinctive and from lots of training.

A couple more shells followed the first one, but fortunately for me, they spread out off to my right instead of in the same place. Obviously, I was terrified initially. As I hit the ground, I rolled a little to get a look at my right side. I pulled my pile jacket off my right arm to get a look and saw my shoulder inside my jacket smeared with blood. There wasn't much pain I can remember, but after seeing my shoulder, I began to get a reaction of light-headedness and hyperventilation. All of this was happening at the speed of light—to the sound of bursting shells. I was lying on a slope and turned around so my head was downhill to keep the blood going there. I didn't want to pass out. The shock of getting hit triggered such a biological reaction that my bowels told me I was in trouble. The old saying, "It scared the shit out of me," I found was based on fact. A monumental effort on my part kept me from soiling myself until the urge passed. Meanwhile, as the other shells had landed, I jumped up and ran the short distance into the ditch we had crossed a few moments earlier. By now, shock had settled in, and I was shivering and shaking. The group of four or five that I had been a part of had all taken off up the slope as soon as the initial shell burst, so I didn't see them again. I had been at the tail end of our group and the only one hit.

It wasn't long before my buddies began running down toward my location. Several along the hillside had seen what happened and came looking for me. Stan Leszko was one of the first and had his camera with him. Also, our medic, "Doc" Adams, came at the same time. Stanley took a photo of Doc kneeling alongside of me after he dressed the wound. Adams had pulled my right arm out of my jacket, taken his scissors, and cut my T-shirt across to around my shoulder. I remember being annoyed because I had put on a brand-new T-shirt that I had carried all the way from the States for the attack, and now it was ruined. Adams sprinkled sulfa powder over the wound and bound my shoulder in bandage material before pinching up the skinny flesh on my chest and sticking in a small tube of morphine. I don't think he did it for pain, as I wasn't in much pain, but I still had the shakes, evidence of shock, and he had been trained for such occasions. I can still remember the cool rush of the narcotic through my veins as I calmed down from its effect. John Lander came by to see how I was doing, as did others. There was no more mortar or artillery fire while my evacuation was discussed. Since I was alone in being wounded at that time, all the attention was on me. I told the others that I could walk back to Querciola to the battalion aid station, but they insisted that I stay put and ordered a jeep out to get me. The jeep arrived with a litter across the back of it, and I was soon loaded on the litter for the ride back.

By now it was late afternoon and getting darker. With poorer visibility, any German troops farther up Belvedere probably couldn't see us moving back to Querciola in the jeep. The battalion aid station was located in the church in the village, and the church is there to this day, albeit fully restored and rebuilt. I recall it being dark when I arrived there. The inside was dimly lit by a few lanterns, and medics were moving about treating the wounded and preparing them for their next move. The division medical troops really knew what they were doing, and it was evident all through the transition from the battlefield to the hospital. I was given a shot of penicillin and probably something else, but I don't know what. An identifying tag, as I recall, was placed around my neck. After a brief spell, I was loaded into an ambulance with others and driven down to Lizzano-in-Belvedere to the city hall, which had been transformed into the division clearing station. I believe wounded from here were sent to evacuation hospitals, field hospitals, or general hospitals, depending on the condition of the wounded soldier and also on the rate of flow of wounded from the battlefield.

The clearing station in Lizzano was rather well lit, with electric bulbs strung around the large room I was in. I had been placed on a table in fairly bright light, and I wondered what would happen to me next. The whole room was packed with wounded and medics rushing about trying to keep up. An ambulance later drove the fifty-plus miles over winding mountain roads from Lizzano to Pistoia, arriving at the 70th General Hospital probably around ten or eleven o'clock that night. I slept all the way, having not had any sleep for twenty-four hours or longer. And my wound fortunately wasn't that painful, but it prevented me from ever seeing combat again.

3 | KOREAN WAR
1950–1953

Pvt. Jack Clifton Burkett, U.S. Marine Corps

Intense cold. This is a recurring theme in the 1st Marine Division's epic fighting retreat from the Chosin Reservoir. Much has been written of the terrible combat experienced during this campaign, but what about the details of just staying alive during such extreme conditions? Private Burkett's simple retelling of his day-to-day life tells you what it was like.

WHEN I ARRIVED IN KOREA (the Inchon landing on September 15, 1950), I was a member of Weapons Company, 3rd Battalion, 1st Marines. The weapons company was attached to George Company. Once we got to Inchon, we spent several hours watching the strafing and the bombing of the invasion area from the deck of the ship. We were briefed on what was going to take place just up ahead. The naval ships in the area all had big guns. I do not know if any were battleships; most of them were probably cruisers and destroyers. There were a lot of landing ships in the area. My rough estimate is that there were at least a hundred ships near the harbor. It was an awesome display of firepower as we watched the shelling of the hills surrounding Inchon. We could hear the explosions of the large naval guns and the strafing of the fighter planes. I saw many of those fighter planes strafing the hills. Many were also carrying bombs.

After the capture of Seoul, we thought it was just a matter of time before we could go home. We moved into North Korea and had their army in full retreat. We took many prisoners. By this time, they were surrendering en masse. Most of the prisoners I saw were very frightened and quiet. I do not personally recall any that were belligerent, but I heard that some were. On occasion, I had to take some of them back to the rear, where they were being held. I remember one group in which one of them was so badly injured that he could hardly walk. I directed several of them to carry him. Even though this was the enemy, I saw no reason to be inhumane.

While north of Seoul, we received orders to return to Inchon. We had no casualties during this return. We rested at Inchon before leaving by ship for a port city on the east coast of Korea to make an amphibious landing at Wonsan. The enemy was retreating so rapidly that the town was under United Nations control by then.

The trip from Inchon to Wonsan, North Korea, took approximately a week, I think. I believe it was a Japanese boat that the United Nations leased from Japan for that purpose. I do not recall the name. (I do not believe I ever knew.) It was not a fancy troop ship by any means. I believe we heard that it was a large fishing boat. The crew all spoke Japanese, so we were not able to understand them.

Since this was to be a large-scale invasion, there were many ships in the convoy. The fact that there were not enough U.S. Navy ships available indicates that there were any ships there.

When we finally landed on October 26, 1950, we walked ashore without opposition. Other units (I think they were Republic of

Korea, or ROK, troops) had secured the area before we got there. The North Koreans were in full retreat. Our unit did not go directly to the reservoir area. We first moved from the Wonsan area to a place called Majon-ni. This was a strategic location for preventing the enemy's retreat north. We took many prisoners while in this area. Most of the enemy soldiers surrendered willingly, but we did have to fight off several attacks. I was up in the hills, where we were holding the high ground, therefore I was not close enough to observe the attitude of these enemy soldiers, who were basically rounded up on the road. I doubt if many were belligerent. They had been completely routed at this point and were pretty much on their own in their attempts to escape our entrapment. The prisoners were taken to the rear by other marines than those in our units. I believe the military police handled this job in general.

On November 10, 1950, I was somewhere south of the Chosin Reservoir and still with Weapons Company, 3rd Battalion, 1st Marines. I am not certain of the location, however, I remember that we had an excellent hot meal. I believe we also had a birthday cake, since it was the Marine Corps' birthday.

From Majon-ni we went to Koto-ri and then on to Hagaru. The 5th and 7th Marine Regiments were further north of us, having reached Koto-ri (which was about thirteen miles north of us) before we got there. It seemed like those in command (including MacArthur) refused to believe the Chinese would enter the war. We did not get the word that the Chinese had attacked the 5th and 7th Marines until about the time we left Koto-ri to move to Hagaru to reinforce the units there.

It was considered probable that Chinese troops were in the area, but we became certain of it when we were attacked. While moving north from Koto-ri to Hagaru, our column was ambushed by the Chinese. This battle became appropriately known as "Hellfire Valley," but the official name of this battle was Operation Drysdale, after the commanding officer, a British Royal Marine colonel. The Royal Marines were attached to George Company and suffered many casualties at Hellfire Valley. They were an outstanding unit and fought with considerable valor. They were always neat and well dressed compared to the marines, who were not. This is the only unit of another nationality that I was alongside in Korea.

We were able to keep moving toward Hagaru with the tanks leading the way. I remember it was late at night when we reached the roadblock at Hagaru. I could look back and see the destruction that was being inflicted on most of the column behind me. Many of the trucks were burning, and ammunition in them was exploding. Most of our equipment and vehicles were destroyed.

We reached Hagaru on November 29, 1950. Once we reached it, we were placed on the perimeter surrounding it. I was in the foxhole close to the road leading to Yudam-ni. Hagaru was in a valley surrounded by high ground. We were dug in near the southern tip of the Chosin Reservoir. We could see the engineers attempting to build an airstrip. They worked day and night using floodlights at night. This made them especially vulnerable to enemy small-arms fire. Because of the airstrip the engineers managed to scrape out of the frozen ground, we were able to evacuate many wounded by air. I do not recall if any dead were evacuated by air.

Hagaru appeared to be an especially desolate village. The cold winter weather made it appear even bleaker. We could only escape the wind by huddling up in the corner of a foxhole. We were under attack at various positions along the perimeter almost every night after reaching Hagaru. On several occasions, they broke through our defenses and into the village. The company suffered the most casualties attempting to take and retain a hill to the east appropriately called East Hill. It was a steep hill that made climbing up a difficult chore due to the mud and snow. This was, of course, even more so when the enemy was firing at us. It was crucial that we control this hill. If not, we [would] lose Hagaru, as well as the 5th and 7th Regiments attempting to retreat to Hagaru from Yudam-ni. (The regiments at Yudam-ni were involved in hand-to-hand combat.)

East Hill was strategically located because, by controlling it, the Chinese could fire on and harass the people in the Hagaru perimeter. If we had not controlled it, we probably would have lost Hagaru to the enemy. This would probably have resulted in the loss of the entire division, because the 5th and 7th Marines were still fighting their way out of Yudam-ni, and it was crucial that they be able to reach Hagaru to reorganize.

Even as much as we hated these enemy soldiers, one had to admire their courage. They kept moving forward toward our defenses even into almost certain death. I assume, however, that they would have been killed by their leaders if they had not. Their method of fighting was almost exclusively to sneak or crawl up to our lines in the dark and hope to overrun us in the confusion. They felt that this would terrorize us [because we would not know] where they were or in what number. They were willing to sacrifice untold numbers in order to make this method of fighting successful.

When we retreated from Hagaru, we passed the burned-out vehicles and many bodies of dead marines. One marine I knew well was a Jeep driver for one of the officers. He was sitting up in the driver's seat just where the Jeep stopped after he was shot. He looked like he had just pulled over to the side to rest. His body was frozen solid. One of the trucks carried mail. Our letters were strung out all over the area. I wondered if any of those letters were mine.

We could only control the road by controlling the ridges running parallel to the road. We had to leapfrog from one ridge to the next. We would hold a ridge until the column cleared, then move forward to the front. The Chinese toppled any structures they could by dynamiting them so that they would fall across the narrow and only road. For the most part, they stayed off the road and fired at us from high positions above the road. They attacked those on the ridges at night. The ridges running parallel to the road were steep and slippery. It was a tremendous burden to climb them. It was even a great burden just to walk under the weather conditions that existed. This was made even worse by the ammo and other equipment that we had to pull up with us. All of this occurred while the enemy was shooting at us. Snipers were always a threat. I recall walking behind a marine who was much taller than me and was presumably taken for an officer. He fell dead from a sniper's bullet, and I fell over his body.

I was in Korea from October to the following May. I did not see much of the summer heat. January and February were cold, but nothing like it was in the Chosin Reservoir. There, the weather was miserable, but we were too cold to expound on the temperature. We were just as miserable at minus twenty as at minus thirty. The wind seemed to cut right through our seven to eight layers of clothing. We had a high percentage of frostbite. The ground was covered with snow, but it did not snow all the time. It was fairly worn down in most places, but certainly deep on the surrounding hills. We had to eat the snow in order to get water, since all of our canteens or water containers were frozen solid.

I do not even recall having a cold while I was in Korea, in spite of the weather conditions. In the Chosin Reservoir we wore several layers of clothes. Starting from the inside we had thermal underwear, next a wool shirt, next a dungaree jacket, next a wool sweater (this created an air space which held body heat), next a field jacket, and finally, a hooded parka. We had thick mittens with a single trigger finger. We wore shoepacks that did not do the job. First, they caused the feet to sweat and then freeze. It was critical to keep the feet dry to avoid frostbite. I had four or five extra pair of socks between the layers of my clothing. Every chance I had, I changed to a dry pair. I believe this kept me from getting frostbite. In spite of this, it was still miserably cold in the twenty to thirty degrees below zero weather we faced in Chosin. Some people got to spend some time in tents with stoves, but I never had that opportunity.

The M1 rifles and especially the carbines froze up on occasion. Many of us tried to find single-shot rifles rather than trust the semiautomatic ones. The canned rations were frozen solid because it got down to thirty degrees below zero. When we could, we all had to chop the ration cans open with a bayonet, chip off a block, and put it in our mouth until it thawed out. The same applied to water. Obviously all of our canteens were frozen solid. [We could] . . . eat snow to get water or do without. The one food that was most available was the Tootsie Roll. We had our pockets filled with them. We could bite off a part of one and hold it in our mouth until it thawed out. The biggest problem was eliminating or urinating. It was impossible to do so without working through seven or eight layers of clothing and then risking the possibility of frostbite or freezing. Any vehicles that were not kept running continuously would not start. In the event that happened, they were pushed to the side so that they would not hold up the rest of the column. Most were destroyed so that the enemy could not use them.

The spirits of the marines were low. We knew that there was a chance that we would never be able to break through the numerically superior Chinese forces. If one was lucky enough to avoid frostbite on the nose or the feet or hands by keeping active, the biggest effect of the cold was becoming lethargic and sluggish. It was a burden to just move. I began to doubt that I would ever escape alive. I even envied those wounded that were being flown out to a warm hospital environment.

The weather affected air support, because if the pilots could not see the enemy, they could not support us. There were many days when this was the case. Air support was one of the main reasons we were able to escape the entrapment. If the enemy had had the type of air support we had, we likely would not have made it. We received airdrops of ammunition, rations, and medical supplies. They were life saving. Some landed outside of our perimeter and fell into enemy hands, some were damaged in the drop, and sometimes a parachute would not open. But those supplies we managed to receive were mostly usable.

The best way for me to describe my own personal experience in the withdrawal from Chosin is to describe a particular night that stands out in my memory. We were moving south out of Hagaru, and I was sent up to the top of a hill along with fifty or so other marines. Our units were in no particular place by now, and many were from different platoons or companies. The officers just grabbed whoever was available. We reached the top with about an hour or so of daylight still left. We formed a line along the top of the ridge with a machine gun on our right flank. There was a natural depression in the earth there. It was an ideal place for the machine gun.

We could not dig into the frozen earth and therefore had little protection from enemy fire. It was so cold there that it felt like our bones were going to crack like an icicle. The cold Siberian wind blew right into our faces. I knew we were going to be under heavy attack in a few hours. This hill was strategic, because if we lost it, the enemy could fire directly down onto the convoy on the road below. I was so hungry my stomach ached, but I could not eat since the food was frozen and also because of my fear of dying. I had not slept in several days but could not sleep for thinking about what lay ahead. It was truly one of the most miserable days of my life. As I lay there that night amidst all those miseries, I thought to myself that maybe dying would not be that bad. At least the misery would be over. But then I could see the pain that this would cause my mother. I was twenty years old and too young to die.

Shortly before midnight, I heard voices in Chinese. One of the words I heard sounded like "chongin." I have no idea what it means in Chinese or even if I am correct in the sound I thought I heard, but I will always remember it as that. I began firing in the direction of the voices. Soon all hell broke loose. We were all firing into the darkness where we thought the enemy was. Then the machine gun on the flank opened up. That machine gun never stopped firing until dawn. I kept praying that the barrel would not burn up. The ammo carriers spent the entire night hauling ammo up to that gun. It was located such that it could cover the entire rise at almost 90 degrees. I could hear enemy bullets striking the ground all around me and the cries of marines on both sides that were hit. It was the longest night of my life. There were many times when I felt in danger in Korea, but I felt in the most personal danger that night. None of us were sure we would ever get out alive, but we held together and defended that ridge.

The cold weather helped us in the sense that had the Chinese rushed our lightly manned positions when we first opened fire on them, they could have easily overrun us. However, they were as cold as we were, and they were likely unable to move fast enough to charge us. I lay there firing into the darkness for at least six hours. All this time the machine gunner continued to sweep back and forth across the rise that they were crawling up. Several of his assistant gunners were killed, as were several ammo carriers. Nevertheless, in spite of the enemy fire being primarily directed at him, he was never hit.

Dawn was a beautiful sight because the Chinese always began to withdraw when it began getting light enough for us to see them. I let out a sigh of relief, feeling that I had survived another day in that hell. As it became light enough to see the enemy casualties, the view was awesome. I had never seen that many dead in one place. I doubt if many people have. The count of the dead bodies was way up in the hundreds, my guess being at least five hundred. We had that machine gun and its gunner to thank for our lives.

I have no idea what hill we were on, and I have never since talked to any other marine that was there. I have never heard what the official count of enemy dead was, but that machine gunner must certainly have been among the top in enemy kills in the Korean War. The only thing I can remember for certain was that his name was Whitehead and he was from Louisiana. I always wanted the chance to thank him for my life, but never saw or heard from him since. There were many heroes in the Korean War, many of whom were never recognized. Private Whitehead was one of them.

An hour or so after the sun came up, we ventured out to see if there were any living Chinese. I could only see frozen bodies. On one of them nearest to me, and therefore one I could have killed since he was closest to my position, I saw a pocket watch. I took it from his body for a souvenir, and I still have it today. It has a Chinese inscription inside the front cover. Someday I intend to have it interpreted.

After we arrived safely in Hungnam, and when I had the chance to reflect on what I had just been through, I was sad and depressed to think of all the marines that were killed in the Chosin Reservoir. I wondered why in the hell we were in this godforsaken land in the first place. I was also unhappy with the thought that we had been driven back by the enemy. At that time, I would never have believed that this could happen to marines.

Pvt. Arthur Smith, U.S. Army

In November 1951, United Nations forces in Korea ceased significant offensive operations, opting for an active defense. The frontlines settled into positions that were reminiscent of the trench warfare of World War I, with opposing forces dug in on adjacent hilltops separated by a few hundred yards. When Private Smith got to the frontline in the fall of 1952, he discovered that his comrades in the 40th Infantry Division fighting and dying over the ground between "Heartbreak Ridge" and the "Punch Bowl" since February.

I ARRIVED IN KOREA IN EARLY September or October 1952 and was assigned to Able Company of the 224th Infantry Regiment of the 40th Division. My regiment ended up in the central part of Korea. When I first got there, we were picked up and moved to our units in trucks. Once we arrived, a captain came onto the truck and asked, "I don't suppose any of you know how to fire a machine gun?" This one dummy standing there said, "I do." It was me. I said, "I'm an expert." He said, "I have a place for you, son." I ended up [being] the company machine gunner.

There were two of us GI's to a nine-man infantry squad, with the seven others being South Koreans with no training. We were to fight and train them at the same time. Despite this handicap, they decided to send us to the front lines by truck. When we finally pulled up to a stop in our truck, we had no idea where we were. We could hear the firing of artillery to cover our move up to the front lines, when all of a sudden it turned out that the noise came from a quad of .50 [caliber] machine guns planted on a halftrack. It's what they used to shoot down aircraft in World War II, and it was sitting just above us. We didn't even know it was there until it opened up. We quickly went over the sides of our truck.

My new position was located between "Heartbreak Ridge" and the "Punch Bowl." We called our site the "Sandbag Castle." We had trenches . . . [and] a bunker, all built with sandbags. If the enemy broke through the Sandbag Castle position, they could pour in behind all the other units up and down our lines. Ours was the site that held it all together.

Before we took over responsibility for our new defensive positions, the Turks had been defending the area. While there, they had buried "Bouncing Betty" antipersonnel mines all over the place without leaving us any maps of the location of the mines. These antipersonnel mines were very nasty things. They had three prongs; you touch any one of the prongs, and the mine bounces into the air about six feet off the ground and explodes sending out steel balls.

More than once, we had to find a way through the Turkish-laid minefields to get to nearby Heartbreak Ridge. We lost the whole second squad while attempting that movement on one occasion. One of the men in that squad was a kid named Shrinner. He was from Hawaii and just seventeen years old. We heard an explosion off to our right, and then the screaming and crying started. It turned out to be Shrinner. It took four hours to get in there and get him out. He was screaming the entire time, knowing that he was going to die. The whole squad received wounds when he stepped on the Bouncing Betty. The squad leader caught a piece of shrapnel right between his eyes.

Finally, on the sixth night of my stay at Sandbag Castle, they allowed me to come down from my position for a break. Sadly, whenever they pulled me out of the Sandbag Castle, they would lose the position to a Chinese attack, and then we would have to counterattack it and retake it at great cost. Finally, I decided to stay at my position as long as possible. My squad and I wound up staying up there over 107 days and nights. No other unit had ever stayed up there that long.

At the farthest point, we were three hundred yards away from the enemy, and we took terrible losses in the fighting. We were down to approximately 60 men, at one time, from 250 men in the company. We would still send out nine-man patrols, because we didn't want the enemy to know how many men we were short. On the three-man outposts, we sometimes didn't have enough men to fill all the positions on the line, so we filled every other one.

I went through seven thousand rounds a day of machine gun ammunition and at least seven cases of bazooka ammunition. At nighttime, the enemy always took the bodies, so you had no idea how many you killed. That works on your nerves, too. You're firing out there; you know they're out there. One time they were so close that I pulled the pin on a grenade. You're supposed to let it pop, then go one, two, and three and throw it, because it goes off on five. I popped a grenade, and I went one, two, three, and four, and then threw it. Just as it cleared it went off, and I didn't hear any more over there; they were that close.

Korea is cold in November. It's sixteen to thirty-two degrees below zero, and we still hadn't gotten our winter boots. We were still wearing our leather boots. I was helping improve the bunker down by the command post one day and noticed that whenever I was working in one spot for a while, my shoes would freeze to the ground.

My feet began hurting so bad one day that I told the lieutenant I was going to take a break and get some sleep before I had to go back to my firing outpost. I went back to my bunker and crawled into a bunk and pulled my sleeping bag around me. I never crawled into the sleeping bag. I would keep my feet open and wouldn't zip it up. I'd hold it together with one hand, my .45 pistol in the other, because I didn't trust the fact that it might not open like it was supposed to. I woke up about fifteen minutes after I went to sleep with pain like somebody had taken a cigar and put it right in the arch of each foot. I leaped up, and I was jumping around the bunker trying to get some circulation going in my feet, but it was too late, they were frozen. It didn't look too bad at first, but I went down to the medics the next day.

The doctor said, "Oh, just put wintergreen on them. Wash them every day, and put wintergreen on them."

I said, "Where am I going to get the water? We don't have water, and the water we do have is for drinking." Besides that, we had to boil all the water we drank because of the dead bodies.

He said, "Well, get snow and melt it."

I said, "No, snow is on the north side of the ridge. What do I do? Say, 'Hold up fellows; I've got to go get some snow to melt to wash my feet in, and don't shoot me.'" He just told me to get out of there.

Two weeks later, I was hobbling around my position, and I decided to take my shoes and socks off. Much to my horror, I found that all across my toes [and] up to an inch across the rest of my foot the skin had died, cracked, and was bleeding, so my one trip to the doctor didn't help. I decided to go to the rear. I also had four teeth broken off, and I said I wanted to go see the dentist at regiment. So the lieutenant said okay, and the guys in my squad knew why I was going back, and they all said goodbye. I said, "What do you mean, 'goodbye'?"

They said, "You're going to the States."

I said, "No, no, I'll be back."

They said, "Uh-uh, you're not coming back up here."

I went back and into the bunker where the dentist was. He was an oriental guy sitting in the dentist chair reading a magazine. He said, "What do you want?"

I said, "Well, I have a few broken teeth." So he got out of the chair and threw his magazine down. I sat down, and he looked and said, "Yep, they are pretty bad, but we're too busy right now. In about three months come back." I got up, he picked up the magazine and sat back down in the chair, so I went over to the medical bunker, and hobbled in, and the guy said, "What do you want?"

I said, "I just want to show you something."

He said, "Okay." I took my one boot off and sock. He said, "My God, what happened?" I told him about being frozen and all, and he said, "Is the other foot like that?"

I said, "Yeah."

He said, "Get your boot and sock off," and grabbed the phone, cranked it, and said, "Quick, give me the regimental surgeon." And that's when I thought I was going to lose both feet.

The surgeon quickly came down. He looked over my feet, and then he asked what happened, and I told him about the other doctor suggesting wintergreen and having a very limited supply of water at the Sandbag Castle. He said, "Well, why didn't you change socks? It's your fault."

I said, "Wait a minute. You told us when we went on line to turn all our socks in; we'd get a fresh pair of socks every time we got a shower. We get a shower every fifteen to twenty days; I was up on Sandbag Castle for thirty-one days without a shower." So, they shut up pretty quickly about it being my fault. The winter boots were still back in the warehouse, not up on the line with us. So, they sent me up to battalion; I guess to keep me quiet.

The medical staff took my boots and started soaking my feet in a skin-toughener, then took a GI scrub brush to take the skin off twice a day, and I said, "Well, give me my boots."

They said, "Uh-uh, only if you have to go to the bathroom." They were afraid I'd go back up on line. So Christmas Day, or Christmas Eve, I'd been there almost a week, or maybe ten days. The white dead skin was gone, and it stopped bleeding. One night the enemy hit the Sandbag Castle hard, and I said, "You give me my boots."

The medical staff said, "What for?"

I said, "They need help."

I was at the bottom of the hill, and I knew my squad was in trouble. I said, "Give me my boots."

The medical staff said, "No."

I said, "They need help, and I'm a machine gunner."

He said, "We'll call up there." So they called up, and they said, "If they need you, they'll call us, and we'll send you up; get back in the medical bunker." So the next morning, they decided to let me loose, and I went back to my squad. Thank God! They had managed to throw back the enemy attack.

I then went back to my company and got with the platoon. The platoon leader we had came out and said, "Oh, I wanted to meet you two guys. How would you guys like ten to fifteen days R&R (rest and recreation) in Japan?"

"Oh great! What do we have to do?"

He said, "Get a live prisoner. This regiment has never taken a live prisoner, or got back with a live prisoner." They usually run and get shot. "We want you to go out with a patrol, then we'll leave you, and when one of the Chinese comes down, knock him out and drag him back to our positions."

I said, "Okay, how long will it take to get it coordinated?"

He said, "What are you talking about?"

I said, "The other companies and our people all know when we're going up there."

He said, "Oh, we aren't doing that."

I said, "Why?"

He said, "We aren't going to tell anybody up here."

I said, "You've got to be nuts." Anything that moves out here gets killed. I said, "I want support. I don't want to be shot and killed by my own people. No, hell no, would I do that."

Well, that started it. I was sent out on an outpost or a patrol the next thirty days in a row. I suppose it was a sort of punishment for my attitude. On the thirty-first night, I didn't get sent out. At midnight, I finally laid down because I was worn out. No sooner had I laid down when the guy on the phone said, "Smitty, he [the platoon leader] wants you." I literally exploded. I came out of that bunker, I picked up an M1 rifle, I stepped outside, I emptied it, made sure it fired, and I stepped inside, and I threw a full clip in. I said, "You tell that son of a bitch I'm coming." I guess I gave it away, the way I said it, because I went down there, I kicked the safety off, flipped the curtain back on the bunker. If that man had been sitting there, I would have emptied it. The sergeant was sitting there with a radioman, and their eyes were about as big as silver dollars. They looked at me and the M1; they looked at the trigger housing, back up at my eyes, and I said, "Where is he?"

"Well, he doesn't want you now, Smitty; its okay, you go on back."

I said, "No, it isn't okay. He wanted me, and I want him. Where is he?"

"We don't know."

I said, "You sure?"

"Yeah, he's gone." So I went up and down the line at nighttime; it's a wonder I didn't get shot by my own people, yelling his name.

Finally, I went back to my bunker, and when I walked in, they said, "Hey, Smitty, guess what?"

I said, "What?"

They said, "You get to go back for twenty-four hours R&R."

I said, "How about that." Thirty-one days and nights without a shower or a change of clothes, and all of a sudden it's my turn, and I wonder why. So the next morning, I walked off the hill, and our hill was so steep you had to zigzag. You walk down this way, and then you'd zag back across. I started down, I looked, and there was a platoon leader and a runner standing there, and the lieutenant was standing behind them, peeking over their shoulders as I walked down. If I'd go to the right, he'd pivot back to the left, keeping men between me and him. And when I came back up on the hill after I spent the night, got a shower, and went to my bunker, they said, "Grab your gear."

 I said, "What?"

They said, "Yeah, you're transferred to 3rd Platoon."

I said, "Why?"

He said, "You know damn well why; you get out of here."

The endless combat and death of the young Hawaii kid Shrinner worked on me more than I realized. All of a sudden, I doubled over like I had appendicitis. If I tried to straighten my legs out, it was like tearing my guts out. So I started crawling on my hands, and I crawled, oh, about seventy-five to one hundred yards down to the medical bunker, and I knocked on it and yelled, told him who I was so he wouldn't shoot. Yates, this black medic, opened it up, and he saw me laying there staring him in the eye. He said, "What's wrong?"

I said, "I think I got appendicitis." So he really hurried, got some help, and got me on a stretcher. We had a truck that we sent food and ammo up the hill. He got me on it, and they met me with an ambulance or a jeep; they put the stretcher on the jeep and ran me back to regiment. When they were carrying me in, my legs were still drawn up; I saw a nurse, the only nurse I saw. I heard her say [that] yeah, she was brought up for the special operation they had to do. They were usually kept back.

I wasn't the special operation. My problem was not that drastic. I fell asleep; it was nighttime, and I was still lying there. So I fell asleep, and when I woke up the next morning, I squeezed my right hand where I usually had my .45 when I went to sleep, and there was nothing there. I didn't know where it was. I cracked one eye, and I saw this big bottle. What the heck is this? I saw the tube, and I followed the tube down out of the bottle, and it went in the arm of the guy next to me. Then I realized I was in the hospital, and I could straighten my legs out then. They told me I had battle fatigue, and that's why I doubled up like that.

I went down to the chow line, and the first sergeant was down there. I said, "You got a good rear echelon job?"

He said, "Smitty, how many points you got?"

I said, "I don't know, thirty-eight, maybe thirty-nine or forty."

He said, "There isn't anybody in Korea with that many."

 I said, "I know one guy who does."

He said, "I'll check." So I had my dinner and went back to my squad, and he said, "Get your gear." I said, "What?" He said, "You're going to the bottom of the hill; you're not even supposed to be up here." Most guys rotated on thirty-two points, and I had almost forty. So they sent me to the bottom of the hill to do me a favor, and that's the last time I saw combat.

4 | **VIETNAM WAR**
(1965–1975)

Capt. Roy D. Martin, U.S. Army

Manna from heaven. . . . *Just as welcome for company commander Roy Martin and the troopers of B Company, 8th Cavalry, was a resupply of ammunition falling through the trees, although some of the soldiers were almost hit by the flying ammo. It had been a "tough day at the office" for Captain Martin and his men, and there was still a Viet Cong machine gun that needed to be eliminated.*

MAY 20, 1966, 1600 HOURS: The first of three CH-47s lifted off from our base camp in An-Khe, Republic of South Vietnam. Each aircraft carried forty combat-loaded paratroopers assigned to B Company, 1/8 Cavalry, Airborne, Airmobile. The pilots climbed to an altitude of nine thousand feet. At this altitude, the air is fresh and cool. The day is clear with the exception of little white clouds at an altitude of six thousand feet.

My command group consists of two radio operators, Spc. 4 Jerry K. Brown, a young trooper from Indiana, and Spc. 4 Carroll B. White of Baltimore, Maryland; the artillery noncommissioned officer; and last, but not least, the senior medic. The 1st Platoon leader, Lt. Robert Crum Jr., and his platoon make up this load.

Many of these men have fought in every battle from Bong Son to the Ia Drang Valley. Today they have that faraway look in their eyes. Every man is busy with his own thoughts and feelings. They are good, battle-tested men who know their job. Two months earlier, it had been suggested that I rotate to another position, since I had completed my company command time. Fortunately, I had convinced the battalion commander to leave me with the "Bravo Bulls."

I loved and respected these men and felt safe with them. In my mind, soldiers are trained to fight. The major reason for my decision was that I had no desire for staff duty. These were battle-tested men, and there was no doubt in my mind that they were up to the battles that we are going to face.

I moved to the front of the aircraft, so I could observe the terrain and get a look at the landing zone (LZ). We are flying in a north-easterly direction. I can see a stream flowing out of the mountains. Far below, I can see a small Army of the Republic of South Vietnam (ARVN) Special Forces camp. At this point, we make a turn to the east. I can see the jungle rise to meet the mountains. There is a beautiful waterfall coming out of the mountains. Then we start to descend very rapidly. We are approaching a small LZ with tall elephant grass and a stream flowing through the middle. The LZ is less than a fourth of the size of a football field. It is surrounded by hills. Approximately a half-mile east of the LZ, I can see smoke from cooking fires. I know that this area is infested with Viet Cong [VC] forces.

The CH-47 hovers at about ten feet, only long enough for forty combat-loaded airborne/air assault warriors to dismount. The entire procedure took less than ten seconds. During the past six months, the battalion had been led by Lt. Col. Kenneth D. Mertel, but at this time, Lt. Col Levin B. Broughton led the battalion. These officers were the finest leaders in the division. The two commanders differed in one important respect, though. Lieutenant Colonel Mertel relied heavily on his company commanders—the bottom line is that he demanded perfection—while Lieutenant Colonel Broughton put more responsibility on his staff officers.

At the time of this battle, the "Jumping Mustangs" had been in the country more than eight months. We had fought on the east coast and in the central highlands. B Company had served as the reaction force for the Ia Drang Valley operation. We had fought in several major battles, and we had lost very few men, considering the battles that we had fought. We had learned to travel light and fast; in order to close with and kill or capture the enemy, we had to be smarter, faster, and better than they were.

The average load consists of basic weapons, a compass, a steel pot, a pistol belt supported by suspenders, two canteens, a first-aid packet, . . . ammo pouches, and a poncho on a belt, with one set of toilet articles per fire team, one toothbrush, one pair of extra socks, [and] . . . C rations. Other gear consisted of tactical radios, grenades (fragmentation, concussion, and smoke), special equipment as needed, and lots of ammunition. Note: We had learned early on that personal items like commercial radios, magazines, etc., were luxuries that could become health hazards. I had long since abandoned my camera in order to carry more ammunition.

B Company closed into the LZ at dusk. Weapons were cleaned; equipment [was] checked and readied for the following day's operation. I reported to the battalion command post, where the order was issued. At daybreak, tomorrow, May 21, 1966, two rifle companies will move to the northeast along a stream. With B Company on the right and C Company on the left, the two companies will

maintain contact insofar as possible. The enemy has been identified as the 2nd VC Regiment, reinforced by C-14 Company and the
32nd Artillery Battalion. Our mission was to find and destroy or
capture the enemy. We were to have the usual artillery, gunships,
and tactical air support. Supplies and ammunition would be air-
dropped on request. I returned to the company area and issued the
order to the platoon leaders.

The second platoon, commanded by Lt. William L. McCarron,
a second-generation Scotsman from Virginia, would move first,
followed by the company command party. The first platoon, commanded by Lt. Robert Crum of Houston, Texas, would follow, with
the responsibility of securing the right flank of the company. First
Sergeant Ray "Top" Poynter, a World War II veteran with jungle
warfare experience, was a seasoned combat soldier. His on-the-spot
training had saved many lives. He and I had been platoon sergeants in the 503rd AIR at Fort Campbell and later in Germany.
We were like brothers. I did not have to worry about the logistical
welfare of the men, because he would see to that. The third platoon, commanded by Lt. Jared East from Louisiana, would bring
up the rear, with the responsibility of rear security and company
reaction force for the operation. The platoon leaders were brave
men, always ready for a fight. They had earned the respect of their
men and were supported by experienced platoon sergeants.

Morning came with a hot blazing sun. There was no wind, and
the air was humid. We moved into the thick undergrowth on the
edge of the jungle along a well-used trail and guided on the stream
as planned. After moving about two hundred yards, we moved into
the jungle. The trees were tall and the boulders, big.

At 1100 hours, the 2nd Platoon came under automatic weapons
fire. The fire was returned immediately, and the enemy fire ceased.

The point man, Spc. 4 Milton Parks, was wounded. We had come up on the first outpost. The nearest LZ, for evacuation, was the one that we had landed on the day before.

I ordered the forward observer (FO) to place fire on suspected enemy on the south flank. This was accomplished with care, because we did not know the exact location of "C" Company. A litter was hastily designed from two poles and a poncho. We had done this many times, so it only took a few minutes. Lieutenant McCarron designated a squad to evacuate Specialist 4 Parks.

The company proceeded to guide on the trail and stream with caution. The farther we moved into the triple-canopy jungle, the more signs of enemy activity we observed. The trail was heavily traveled, and there were recently abandoned enemy campsites. We recognized the smell of enemy campfires. Apparently, this was the source of smoke that I had observed yesterday. At this time, we had not made contact with C Company. This caused me some concern, since we needed to know their location in order to coordinate supporting fires. I called Captain Mozey and arranged to meet him.

At approximately 1400 hours, the company formed a hasty defensive position. While checking the perimeter, I noticed well-constructed bunkers on the end of a finger of land that ran to the bend of the stream. This hill was the commanding terrain, above and overlooking the stream. They were to our immediate front and on the opposite side of the stream. This gave me reason for worry. On closer inspection, I saw that they were empty, but had been recently used.

I met Captain Mozey, C Company commander, at the stream on the north side of our perimeter. He and I had met and developed a friendship in the advanced officers training class. His combat savvy and outstanding leadership is the finest. We shared a can of jelly that he had. He made a small joke about something. I felt good knowing that we were together on this operation. We discussed the bunkers. Since they were on the C Company side, Captain Mozey said that he would occupy them immediately. He would hold these while B Company passed to the south. We knew that there was going to be a big fight. His company had killed four VCs earlier this morning. We reckoned that there was a battalion-sized VC force in this immediate area. The ashes from the cook fires were still hot, and numerous trails were found. These prepared bunkers indicated that the enemy had been here for several days and planned to stay. We were in the VC house.

I asked the artillery FO to place fire on what appeared on the map to be a hill to our front. He informed me that he could not, because the 105th Battery was moving. We had no choice but to move, because we were in an exposed position. McCarron reported three VC moving in a northward direction to our immediate front. Normally, Sergeant Poynter would have joined the 3rd Platoon. Fortunately, he did not get the word. The 2nd Platoon had just passed the enemy bunkers that were now occupied by C Company. The B Company command party, moving at the tail end of the 2nd Platoon, was moving through a defilade position to the front of the C Company bunkers.

At this time, a heavy volume of automatic weapons fire, including .30- and .50-caliber machine guns, opened fire on the 1st Platoon. This was coming from my right rear and about fifty yards up the hill. The command post was also taking a high volume of fire. Fortunately, we were in a defilade position, and the enemy fire was going over our heads in the direction of C Company. The 1st Platoon leader did not answer his radio. However, someone from the 1st Platoon was returning the enemy fire.

Lieutenant East, 3rd Platoon leader, reported that he was taking a heavy volume of fire. I asked him if he could flank the enemy positions. He reported that he could not, because he was pinned down. I asked the 2nd Platoon leader, Lieutenant McCarron, if he could move to flank and assault the enemy positions. He reported that he would try. The artillery FO stated that calling artillery and ARA on well-constructed bunkers would kill us and leave the enemy unharmed. I asked him to direct the artillery on suspected enemy positions and communication routes. This would discourage reinforcement and ensure that it did not kill us. I asked the platoons to pop smoke, so Captain Mozey could see our forward positions in order to provide supporting M60 fire. I asked him if he could place M60 fire on the snipers that were keeping us pinned down.

Sergeant Gerald Hoover, one of the squad leaders from the 1st Platoon, came to the CP [command post] to report that Lieutenant Crum had been killed and that all of the 1st Platoon was pulling back to the hill where C Company was located. I recognized the snap of a bullet passing my left ear. The VC bullet hit Sergeant Hoover, in the chest, and he died before he hit the ground. I swung around just in time to kill the VC, who had advanced to within ten yards of our position. Out of the corner of my right eye, I spotted three more VC closing on our position. I dropped all three, beginning with the last one first. They fell into a ravine directly to our front. I had modified the sling of my M16 so that it came over the top, thereby ensuring that the barrel always pointed the same direction that I was looking.

Based on the information provided by Sergeant Hoover, I knew that the 1st Platoon had withdrawn, leaving a gap between the 2nd and 3rd Platoons. The command group was in that gap. I called

Captain Mozey, who was taking heavy automatic weapons fire, and asked him to please send a platoon to cover the position that the 1st Platoon had evacuated. He stated that the trees must be rotten over here; chips are flying all over the place. As a matter of fact, the trees were literally being shot up by the enemy automatic weapons, which were located on the opposite hill. I could hear the crack of the bullets as they passed directly over our position. However, this did not bother Captain Mozey. He continued to move about his unit giving orders and maintaining control of the battle. He immediately attached Lieutenant Vavrek and his 3rd Platoon to B Company for this mission.

East reported that a platoon-sized force was moving behind him. He stated that they had killed five NVA [North Vietnamese]. He estimated that a platoon-sized force was moving up the stream toward C Company. Shortly afterward, Lieutenant Vavrek encountered and engaged this group in a fierce battle. At first contact, two of his squad leaders were wounded by a well-entrenched .30-caliber machine gun spitting from a heavily sandbagged bunker. Specialist 4 Michael G. Vinassa, a grenadier in the 2nd Squad, crawled forward despite the heavy enemy fire until he reached the left lip of a draw, where he began lobbing grenades among the enemy positions with telling effect. One by one, he silenced the VC gunners.

But the 2nd Squad was bogged down. Deadly fire from the .30-caliber machine gun sprayed the area, and the squad leader, Sgt. Harold Kovolenko, was showered with dirt from the enemy's bullets, which chewed the ground only inches from his face. Specialist 4 Jimmie Sampson popped up from his cover and squeezed off a series of bursts from his M16 aimed at the machine-gun position, drawing fire away from Spc. 4 Dennis M. Harley and the other members of the squad. The VC pair behind the machine gun swung their weapon in Sampson's direction and chopped him down. Luckily, he was not seriously wounded.

But it was Vinassa who saved the day when he shouted, "I'll get the gun!" and dashed from the lip, into the draw, and up the slope straight at the bunker, while the machine gun continued to fire on Sampson's position. Pulling a grenade from his harness, Vinassa bent low and hurled himself across the last thirty feet into the machine gun's muzzle. It swung in his direction just as Vinassa chucked the grenade in an underhanded throw through the firing aperture. The muzzle was aimed right at the heroic grenadier, and he caught the blast in the chest. A moment later, an explosion erupted within the machine gun position, then smoke and dust burst from the bunker. Specialist Vinassa was dead when the troopers of the 2nd Squad reached his side in their rush up the hill. Two VC machine gunners lay slumped across their weapons in a bunker jammed with full ammo belts.

Further up the hill, First Sergeant Poynter, who had been following the 1st Platoon with Platoon Sergeant William Robinson and a couple of riflemen, found [himself] in the path of several VC that were following Private [David] Dolby and other withdrawing members of the 1st Platoon. Specialist Robinson took a VC round in the magazine of his M16. First Sergeant Poynter fired into the advancing enemy, killing several VC. One VC dropped his weapon and ran back up the trail. First Sergeant Poynter next stopped Private Dolby and directed him to place fire on the enemy positions. Unfortunately, Private Dolby continued to withdraw and joined C company. First Sergeant Ray Poynter's combat experience, combined with courage and fast action, saved the withdrawing members of the 1st Platoon. He would hold the position until later that night, when Lieutenant East's platoon closed on that location.

At this time, a resupply drop that had been ordered by Captain Mozey came falling through the jungle canopy. It landed between the position held by Poynter and the bunkers occupied by Mozey. The resupply drop was timely, in that we were running out of ammunition. Some of this came close to hitting some of the men. Sergeant Robert E. Speakman states that Dolby and some other members of B Company picked up some of the ammunition and moved to the C Company perimeter and joined them. Captain Mozey states that he placed Dolby and the men with him in a position vacated by his 3rd Platoon.

Lieutenant McCarron returned with the 2nd Platoon and reported that he could not flank the enemy positions because he encountered heavy enemy fire from the front and the left. He further stated that he had not received any fire from the right and that there may be a gap in the enemy positions. I told him, "Follow me. We are going to attack." Only half of our mission had been accomplished, the "close with" part. We had killed some of them, but not nearly what we were going to kill. Lieutenant East's platoon, Lieutenant Vavrek's platoon, the action of Sergeant Poynter, and the supporting fire provided by Captain Mozey, combined with the fact that he occupied the positions that the VC had planned to be in at this time; presented the perfect conditions for us to attack.

Based on Lieutenant McCarron's report and what I saw, the weakness in the enemy defense was a draw and the steep side of the hill. We would crawl up the side of the hill, under the cover of the supporting fire, and break through the bunker line. At about this time, the Battalion S-3 wanted to know what we planned to do. White answered, "Six says we are going to attack." This RTO [radio-telephone operator] had learned to read my mind. Fortunately, the rain was falling hard and darkness was coming. This, combined with Captain Mozey's covering fire, enabled us to crawl up a steep hill. We crawled through the first line of bunkers unnoticed.

I asked Captain Mozey to raise the M60 fire to the top of the hill. We continued up the hill until we were well above the enemy defensive positions. We discovered several communication wires running down the hill to the bunkers. Platoon Sergeant James L. Johnson cut these wires. He and Sgt. Arsenio D. Lujan would provide rear security, while the remainder of the 2nd Platoon and command group attacked the bunkers.

I asked Captain Mozey to cease fire. It was getting darker, and we could barely see. C Company's artillery FO was adjusting flares fired by his unit. In addition, he called for a flare ship. I saw an AK-47 pointing around the left side of a tree, an indication that the owner was left-handed. I pulled the pin of the grenade that I was holding to throw into the bunker that he was guarding. I counted one thousand, two thousand, then lobbed the grenade. It exploded just as it passed his head. The explosion blew him clear of the tree; he appeared to be very small and very dead. I rushed the bunker before the enemy had time to react and tossed a grenade through the door. Following the explosion, I heard moaning and scuffling sounds coming from the bunker.

Off to my left, a VC machine-gun crew opened fire on Lieutenant McCarron, hitting his RTO, Spc. 4 Allen Ritter. McCarron charged the position, firing his M16 and killing the gunner, his assistant, and the ammo bearer. He charged the bunker, destroying it and killing the remaining occupants with a grenade. I did not hear any more firing after this. Aided by the light provided by flares, we moved from bunker to bunker, killing the occupants with well-placed grenades and carefully aimed M16 fire.

When we destroyed the last bunker, we joined Johnson and Lujan back up the trail. The silence after a firefight is awesome, and the feeling is unexplainable. I heard a VC chattering as he came up the trail. A flare drop exposed him, and he was headed straight for Sergeant Lopez. My M16 was jammed. Lopez killed him with one shot. The VC was carrying one of our old .50-caliber machine guns, no doubt captured from one of the ARVN outposts. The flare ships remained on station, and the artillery FO continued to drop flares for much-needed light. By this time, it was very quiet. The smell of grenade and gunpowder filled the air, and it continued to rain.

I asked Lieutenant McCarron to provide security, while I searched the area for any wounded or missing. Since the position held by C Company provided the best terrain for security, and [because of] the fact that my 1st Platoon, including the dead and wounded, had closed into that position three hours ago, we decided to close into his position for the night. We moved down the hill where we met First Sergeant Poynter, Lieutenant Vavrek, Lieutenant East, and their platoons. I ordered Lieutenant Vavrek to take his men and move up the step slope and join C Company. East and his platoon would follow. Lieutenant McCarron and his raiders would cover the movement. We closed into the position at 0100 hours, May 22, 1966.

The medics were treating the wounded under the watchful eye of Captain Mozey and Lieutenant Jon Williams. The credit for evacuating the wounded goes to Lieutenant Williams' platoon. They had been evacuating the wounded during the entire firefight. They did this under fire and with bravery and compassion found in few men. Unfortunately, they were never given the credit that they deserved. Private David McCallum, a medic attached to C

Company, deserves special recognition for his untiring efforts to treat and comfort the wounded. Captain Mozey met me as I came to his perimeter and guided me to the CP, where I found First Sergeant Poynter. I was totally exhausted. We had fought the good fight, and we had defeated the enemy in his own house. The few remaining VC had gathered some of their dead and retreated. We took roll call and found that Lieutenant Robert Crum and Private Angel Rodriguez were missing. Since they had been reported KIA [killed in action] and I had personally searched the area where they were last seen, we decided to recover the bodies at first light.

There was no further enemy activity this night. At first light, Lieutenant Vavrek's platoon and Pvt. David Dolby, with his buddy, Pvt. Kenneth Fernandez, recovered the two missing troopers, Lieutenant Crum and Private Rodriguez.

A chain saw was lowered through the jungle canopy and used to clear a small opening to evacuate the wounded and dead. The casualties were hoisted up to a hovering CH-47, using a basket designed for this purpose. The wounded were evacuated first, followed by the dead, then the enemy weapons and equipment that may have intelligence value. This action took most of the morning. Thanks to the CH-47 crew and modern extraction procedures, many of the wounded are alive today.

C Company moved out to sweep the battle area and continue the attack. Captain Mozey reports that he counted fifty-eight VC bodies and bloody trails where some of the dead or wounded had been carried away. He reports that he found the fully dressed body of a high-ranking Chinese officer in the command bunker. He also found several other bodies of NVA officers buried in shallow graves. His report provides proof that the VC forces had been severely beaten, since they never leave their dead behind, especially officers, unless they do not have the ability to evacuate them. The VC had made a hasty retreat leaving behind more than fifty-eight bodies and numerous weapons, including three .50-caliber machine guns.

We shored up our defense, regrouped, and continued to evacuate the enemy weapons and equipment. These activities took most of the day. The company remained in this position overnight, because it was a good defensive position, and we would move to support C Company if they needed our help. The VC survivors had broken contact, and there was no more action in this area The following morning, we moved to the LZ and were airlifted to another firebase.

Maj. Joseph B. Mucelli, U.S. Army

When we think of Vietnam we tend to think of "America's war" and the names on the Wall. In late February 1967, however, Major Mucelli was a senior advisor in Lam Dong Province in the southern Central Highlands. He experienced combat just as brutal as that experienced by any American during the war, having gone into battle with the 407th Montagnard Scout Company and the 345 Regional Force (RF) Company.

On the morning of February 24, 1967, the radio room of Advisory Team 38, which was located in Bao Loc, Lam Dong Province, received a message from Maj. Don Graney, Dilinh District senior advisor, concerning a roadblock on Provincial Highway 20. The Viet Cong had established this roadblock in the vicinity of AN764803. Typically, such roadblocks were used to distribute propaganda to occupants of the buses, Peugeot taxis, and trucks that traveled this important route between Saigon and Dalat and to collect taxes before any goods or people could transit the area.

Major Graney indicated that he and Capt. Paul Van Hoose, his assistant district advisor, were accompanying the district chief, Captain Hoi, with elements of one Regional Force (RF) company, plus some district security troops into the area. The force, which totaled little more than a reinforced platoon, [was] to attempt to clear the roadblock. Apparently, the plan was to move on a route north and parallel to Highway 20, and then turn south towards the roadblock.

I monitored this information with Lt. Col. Earl Sharp, the province senior advisor. Frankly, I had misgivings about the possible outcome of this operation, because the movement had begun before any of our forward air control (FAC) or army "Bird Dog" pilots were airborne to observe and cover the area. Also, Major Graney had only recently taken over his position and had no prior combat experience, having served several months at the province level, and Captain Van Hoose was a new arrival. I later found out that Captain Hoi had been resistant to moving out with what he considered an insufficient force, with no immediate backup, but caved in to pressure from the advisors.

In any case, the friendly troops were en route, and the only thing we could do at this time was . . . get some airborne observation over them and alert any other forces for possible employment. A short time later, we received a message from Captain Van Hoose that their elements were in contact with an unknown-size enemy force, somewhere to the east of Bobla hamlet.

Only moments later, Capain Van Hoose sent a panicked message [informing us] that the district chief and Major Graney were hit, and to get air strikes. That was the last message received from either the advisors or the Vietnamese maneuver units. Due to the urgency of the situation, with two advisors and the district chief's fate in question, the decision was made to cautiously move additional forces into the area to attempt to regain contact with any members of the previously committed units. I notified interpreter Sgt. Nguyen Tan Lai that we were going out on a high-risk operation and to get all his stuff, plus a radio.

I had worked with Lai since March 1965, and he was an utterly reliable, aggressive individual who should have been an officer in the Vietnamese army. He was like a brother to me, and I usually addressed him by the familiar "Lai-uy." My faith in him was proven to have merit in the next few hours. We saddled up and took a helicopter to Dilinh and picked up Sgt. Hamilton Henry from the district team. Henry was an experienced senior noncommissioned officer (NCO) who I had worked with in several past operations, and he struck me as the type of guy who would be reliable if the world turned to ca-ca. We then moved by helicopter to the area west of Bobla hamlet (AN764805), where we joined the 407th Montagnard Scout Company and another RF company, which I believe was 345 Company. I briefed the company commanders on what we knew of the situation and recommended extreme caution due to the uncertainty of the number of enemy troops we might encounter plus the fact that we could not deliver any preparatory fires due to the missing advisors and district command group.

I had total faith in the combat effectiveness of the 407th Scout Company and their commander, Captain Tai, as I had worked with them for almost two years. Captain Tai was a former NCO in the French Army, a White Tai tribesman who had operated on the Vietnam/China border, and a professional in every sense of the word. I remember sitting with him in a bunker one night during a "cease-fire" and passing a bottle of Johnny Walker Red back and forth and not thinking it was corny when he said, "This is not much of a war, but it's the only one we've got." Less than a year after we set out on this operation, Tai was to lose a leg in the same general area.

The RF company was less capable in maneuver-type operations against a determined enemy force, though three of the fourteen RF companies in Lam Dong were the equal of any similar-size force in any army. This unit was a competent one, but not flashy. The 407th had about seventy troops, and the RF company about sixty-five. Both units only had one M1919A6 machine gun and one 60mm mortar each, with the rest of the troops armed with M1 rifles, M2 carbines, Browning automatic rifles (BARs), and Thompson sub-machine guns. I had an M16 rifle with a scope sight, and both Sergeant Lai and Sergeant Henry had M2 carbines.

We passed by Bobla hamlet, which was a fenced-in Montagnard village, and the occupants could only say that there had been a roadblock on the highway and the sounds of an extended firefight to the east. We moved on two parallel routes to the east, with the 407th Scout Company on the right, and the RF Company on the left.

I accompanied the RF Company with Sergeant Henry and Sergeant Lai. The 407th was guiding towards a copse of trees at approximately AN768804, and the RF company moved towards the house of a French tea plantation owner, about 150 meters to the north. We briefly halted both units while I talked to the plantation owner, whose name I cannot recall, and asked him if he had any knowledge of the situation. I might add that there was no visible evidence of any combat action in any of the areas we had so far traversed.

The plantation owner was standing on a small balcony and was visibly disturbed. On being asked if he had seen any enemy troops

157

in the area, he said, "No, no" loudly and shook his head. It was obvious to me that he meant the opposite and that their presence was very close. In retrospect, I believe that it was possible that he was under direct observation when I talked to him and that there may even have been enemy troops in his house.

I indicated my suspicions of an immediate enemy presence to the Vietnamese, and we continued cautiously eastward in a line formation, with the 407th moving along with us on the right, through the tea fields. The tea bushes were about four to five feet tall and afforded excellent concealment from aerial observation. At this time, we had Capt. Darryl Westby, USAF forward air controller (FAC), overhead in his O-1 aircraft. We had only moved about one hundred meters eastward when both companies received heavy rifle and machine-gun fire and went to the ground.

What was evidently an overwhelming enemy force assaulted to the west and proceeded to attempt to encircle both companies. Later intelligence indicated that the enemy force consisted of the 186th Main Force Battalion, the 840th Main Force Battalion, and the C210 Company, with a combined strength of about one thousand troops. These units were armed with AK-47 and SKS rifles and RPD machine guns as well as 60mm and 82mm mortars. Additionally, the 186th MF Battalion had two German MG42 machine guns, whose cyclic rate of 1,200 RPM [rounds per minute] could saw a man in half. Their presence in the fight was immediately apparent to me! After being unsuccessful in turning the right flank of the 407th Scout Company, they drove a wedge between the RF Company and them and decided to concentrate on the left flank unit. Captain Tai successfully disengaged and moved back westward in good order, even capturing nine rifles and a machine gun in the process. He withdrew to the vicinity of the original roadblock to await further reinforcement.

In short order it was apparent that the RF company, with the exception of a few individuals who broke out or were bypassed unnoticed, was encircled and being rapidly annihilated. At this point, Captain Westby had TAC air (tactical air, or fighter planes) on station, and we proceeded to direct their strikes as close to the diminishing perimeter as possible. The blast effect of the large bombs produced a ripple effect on the ground that literally lifted us off the ground.

While the TAC air slowed down the enemy assault, it in no way provided an avenue of escape. The point was reached where Captain Westby had TAC air assets stacked up, as virtually everything in Southern II Corps was diverted to my support. In any periods where TAC air wasn't immediately available, artillery fire was delivered in the area of Hill 955, at AN776803, as it seemed that the greatest volume of antiaircraft (AA) fire was originating from this position.

My communications with the FAC aircraft were made difficult at first by a bogus radio transmitter, who used my call sign and tried to confuse Westby, but it was not successful because we had worked together long enough that he knew my voice. The transmitter was definitely not Vietnamese, as was confirmed later. Most of the time when strike aircraft were delivering their ordnance, I was flat on my face, but on several occasions, I saw what looked like 20mm flak bursts around circling aircraft, so there must have been other enemy units in the area that had a sophisticated AA capability. I don't know how they never succeeded in knocking down Westby's flimsy, low-flying O-1 aircraft. Incidentally, in the process of pulling a map out of my pocket, about nine hundred dollars in cash came out with it and blew down the rows of tea. The money was the result of being paid the day before by a finance officer from Nha Trang. Normally,

I only received about fifty dollars a month with the rest going to a bank, but a lazy finance clerk in IFFV (First Field Force, Vietnam) didn't renew my allotment request. I would have no sooner tried to retrieve this money than if it were used toilet paper under the circumstances, and some Viet Cong soldier probably profited from the day's actions. I hope he lived to spend it.

I don't know how long the morning's activities lasted, but I was later told that a total of thirty-three air strikes were delivered that day. We eventually were reduced to a group of nine survivors: myself, Sergeant Lai, Sergeant Henry, and six Vietnamese soldiers, of whom five were wounded. The wounded were all relatively mobile, but one lieutenant had his arm blown off at the elbow. Some of the others could crawl a little or had to be dragged. Lai and I used all the available field dressings and then tore up our T-shirts to use as bandages. We constantly moved around in the tea bushes, but finally moved to the edge of a road that had drainage holes about the size of fifty-five-gallon drums dug along its perimeter. They made outstanding foxholes and protected us from the air ordnance, which was being delivered ever closer. At this point, the large enemy force was being hit by everything we could deliver, but only a small portion of them knew exactly where we were, which was the source of the fire control. I had long run out of the colored smoke grenades, used to mark my location, and was relying on Westby's ability to identify our position by verbal guidance.

Inbetween air strikes, the enemy immediately around us would creep or rush ever closer. Sergeant Henry by this time had been shot three times and lay at my feet in the bottom of our improvised foxhole. I brought the air strikes even closer, to the point where we could see enemy bodies and parts of bodies flying over our heads as the bombs impacted. Some of the body parts were burning as

▲ Three American soldiers smile for the camera behind their French-supplied machine gun. The M1917 steel helmets they wear are American-made copies of the standard British Army World War I helmet, designated the Mark I. *National Archives*

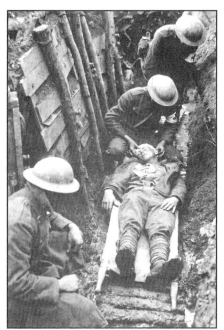

◀ Artillery was the biggest killer of infantrymen in World War I on all sides. Pictured are stretcher bearers tending to an American soldier with a head wound. One of every three casualties died of their wounds in World War I. *National Archives*

⬆ American soldiers stand ready to fire a 37mm cannon from behind a barbed wire barrier. In May 1918 there were upwards of five hundred thousand American troops in France. By the end of World War I, that number had grown to two million. *National Archives*

⬆ American soldiers in France are hurling their hand grenades at the enemy from a hastily built trench. The American military lost 50,000 dead in World War I and another 230,000 wounded. *National Archives*

◀ French citizens wish the best to a couple of U.S. Army soldiers during World War I prior to their departure to the front lines. The American soldier on the left has a French machine gun strapped to his shoulder. *National Archives*

◀ A U.S. Army soldier points his water-cooled .30-caliber M1917A1 Browning machine gun skywards during a training exercise in 1940. He wears an M1917A1 helmet, an improved version of the helmet worn by American troops in World War I. *National Archives*

▶ An American soldier poses with his new M1 Garand rifle tipped off with an impressive-looking bayonet. He also wears the new M1 helmet, introduced into service in 1942. Twenty million M1 helmets came off the production lines during World War II. *National Archives*

▲ A U.S. Army soldier demon-
strates the proper manner in which
to throw a hand grenade during
a training exercise. The standard
American military grenade in use
during World War II was the 1.3-
pound fragmentation grenade Mark
IIA. *National Archives*

▲ Looking over the bodies of two
dead Japanese soldiers is a U.S.
Marine infantryman. Unburied
corpses left a nasty odor on the
battlefields of World War II that few
soldiers will ever forget and posed a
serious disease risk.
National Archives

▶ A shortage of winter camouflage
uniforms during the Battle of the
Bulge led many U.S. Army soldiers
to make their own, as shown, from
confiscated bed sheets. The Battle of
the Bulge cost the American military
over eighty thousand casualties.
National Archives

▲ A U.S. Army soldier is pictured with the battery-powered SCR-536 Handie-Talkie (HT) AM radio. This short-range portable radio had a range of about a mile and served with the American military from World War II through the Korean War. *National Archives*

▲ Being loaded for use is the original M1 2.36-inch rocket launcher, best known to most as the "bazooka." The weapon entered into use with the U.S. Army in 1942 and later saw use with the marine corps during World War II. *National Archives*

▲ A group of weary U.S. Army infantrymen takes a break. The losses among the infantry divisions in the European theater of operations were terrible. While they represented only 14 percent of the army's overseas strength, they suffered 70 percent of the casualties. *National Archives*

▲ As in World War I, German machine guns posed a serious and constant threat to American infantrymen in World War II. U.S. Army soldiers fire a captured German MG34 machine gun in this photograph. *National Archives*

▲ Two marine infantrymen operate an air-cooled .30-caliber Browning M1919A4 machine gun on a World War II Pacific beachhead. The machine-gun loader and gunner also have M1 Carbines, which weighed five pounds. *National Archives*

▲ Marine infantrymen hitch a ride on an M3 halftrack armed with a 75mm gun. The terrain and the climatic extremes in the Pacific took a heavy physical and mental toll on the Marines that served in that theater of operations in World War II. *National Archives*

▲ U.S. Army soldiers man a machine-gun position on a Korean hilltop. The Korean War started on June 25, 1950, when ten divisions of North Korean troops, supported by Soviet-supplied tanks, invaded South Korea. *National Archives*

▶ An American soldier huddles in his poncho to ward off the cold. The temperature in the Korean winters could plunge to forty below zero. The U.S. Army provided the bulk of fighting troops during the Korean War. *National Archives*

▲ An American soldier during the Korean War attempts to comfort a comrade in his time of need. U.S. Army psychiatrists found in World War II that poor precombat training and excessive physical fatigue were leading causes of psychiatric casualties. *National Archives*

▲ U.S. Marine Corps riflemen take aim at enemy snipers during the Korean War. The Marines suffered over 30,000 casualties during the conflict, which included 4,262 killed in action, 244 nonbattle deaths, and over 26,000 wounded in action. *National Archives*

▶ Many of the U.S. Army infantrymen who fought during the Vietnam War rode into battle on the M113 armored personnel carrier. It was a boxlike, aluminum-armored hull vehicle, which could carry an eleven-man infantry squad. *Patton Museum of Cavalry and Armor*

▶ The U.S. Army made widespread use of helicopters in the Vietnam War to transport infantrymen quickly to the battlefield. The workhorse army helicopter of that conflict proved to be the UH-1 Iroquois, nicknamed the "Huey." *Department of Defense*

▶ Operation Urgent Fury was the 1983 American military invasion of the island of Grenada, located in the Caribbean. Pictured is an M151 light utility vehicle of the 82nd Airborne Division just before loading on a plane for a trip to the island. *Defense Visual Information Center*

▲ Two Cuban Army BTR-60 wheeled armored personnel carriers sit at the side of a Grenadian road after suffering destruction at the hands of American military forces during Operation Urgent Fury. They featured turret-mounted machine guns. *Defense Visual Information Center*

◀ The American force that invaded Panama in 1989 consisted of combat elements of the XVIII Airborne Corps, the 82nd Airborne Division, the 75th Ranger Regiment and the 7th Infantry Division (Light), some of whose soldiers appear in this photograph. *Defense Visual Information Center*

◀ Operation Just Cause was the 1989 American military invasion of the Central American country of Panama. Pictured are American soldiers with a captured Panamanian Defense Force antiaircraft gun. Twenty-three American military personnel died in combat during the invasion. *Defense Visual Information Center*

◀ Two American soldiers stand guard from a slit trench during Operation Desert Storm. Due to the fear that the Iraqi military might employ chemical or biological agents during the conflict, the troops wear protective gear. *Defense Visual Information Center*

▲ A Marine Corps infantryman, armed with an M16A2 rifle, pauses during a training exercise prior to Operation Desert Storm. American military combat losses were 148 dead, while Iraqi military losses were around 26,000. *Defense Visual Information Center*

▲ An insurgency as faced by the American military in Iraq calls for constant patrolling. A U.S. Army infantryman pauses during a patrol with his 7.62mm M240 medium machine gun. The M240 weighs about twenty-four pounds. *Defense Visual Information Center*

▲ U.S. Army infantrymen in Iraq search for enemy insurgents. Different weapons appear in the picture, with the soldier on the right and center of the picture equipped with M4 carbines, while the soldier on the far left has a shotgun. *Defense Visual Information Center*

▲ To move its mechanized infantrymen around Iraq, the U.S. Army relies on the M2A2 or M2A3 Bradley. Additional protection for the Bradleys serving in Iraq comes in the form of reactive armor tiles on the vehicles' turrets and hulls, as seen in this picture. *Defense Visual Information Center*

▲ A new addition to the U.S. Army's fleet of armored infantry carriers is the eight-wheel Stryker, which, like the Bradley, has seen extensive service in Iraq. Added protection for the vehicle comes from its standoff bar armor. *Defense Visual Information Center*

▲ While production of the 7.62mm M14 rifle ended in 1963, combat experience in Iraq has seen an updated version of the weapon, reissued in limited numbers with a scope and fiberglass stock, as seen in this picture of a U.S. Army infantryman. *Defense Visual Information Center*

◀ Pictured are U.S. Army infantrymen in Iraq searching for enemy insurgents. The 5.56mm M16 series rifles they use first appeared in service during the Vietnam War. They are gas-operated weapons and currently come with thirty-round magazines. *Defense Visual Information Center*

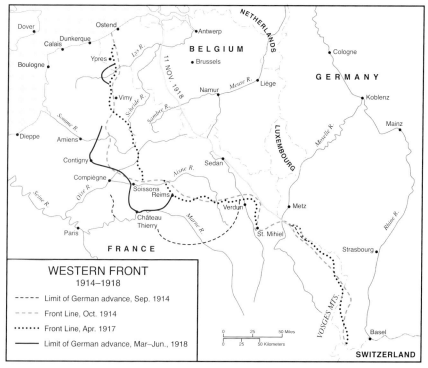

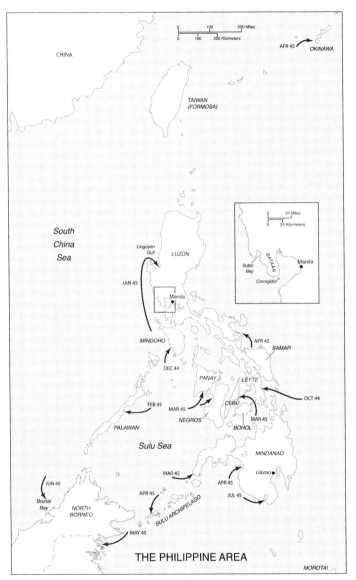

CHINA

0 100 200 Miles
0 100 200 Kilometers

APR 45 OKINAWA

TAIWAN
(FORMOSA)

South
China
Sea

0 25 Miles
0 25 Kilometers

Lingayen
Gulf   LUZON

BATAAN

Subic
Bay   Manila

Corregidor

JAN 45

Manila

MINDORO

DEC 44

APR 45
SAMAR

PANAY   LEYTE

FEB 45   MAR 45   CEBU

NEGROS

OCT 44

MAR 45
BOHOL

PALAWAN

Sulu Sea

MINDANAO

MAR 45

Davao

JUN 45

APR 45

APR 45

JUL 45

Brunei
Bay   NORTH
        BORNEO

SULU ARCHIPELAGO

MAY 45

THE PHILIPPINE AREA

MOROTAI

▲ This map shows the various islands of the Philippines and the dates upon which an amphibious invasion took place by American forces in order to rid them of a Japanese military presence during World War II.

a result of their fat catching fire from the heat of the explosions. The tea bushes over our heads were on fire as a result of napalm strikes less than fifty meters from our location.

At one point, before we had dragged ourselves into the drainage holes, I looked up after an F-4 made a bomb run and saw an enemy soldier who appeared to be about thirteen or fourteen years old, with an SKS rifle, laying less than two feet in front of me. He was trembling uncontrollably and seemed to be totally unaware of anything going on around him, even though we were looking into each others faces. I pressed the muzzle of my M16 into his neck and said, "Dung Lai," which means "don't move." The second F-4 flashed over us as it released its bomb, and I buried my face in the dirt. When I looked up again, he was gone.

After we had fixed our "last stand" position in the drainage holes, it was a matter of using our rifles inbetween bomb drops, but eventually the only people left that could shoot were Sergeant Lai, in a hole somewhere to my right, myself, and a Vietnamese BAR man in the hole on my left. I heard him yell in K'ho Montagnard that he was out of ammunition, so that brought the rifle strength down to two people. At this point, we were receiving machine-gun fire from across the road and showers of grenades. Suddenly I felt a terrific impact on my back, and it drove me face forward in the dirt, with my mouth open. (I finally found out what was meant by the term "he bit the dust.") I fell backwards and looked up at the sky and the clouds passing overhead. It seemed like I was back in rural New York State, on a hill in the middle of the summer, watching the clouds roll by. I heard what I thought was a screen door slamming, again and again, and then my mother's voice calling, "Joey, Joey." In my dreamlike state, I wondered what she was calling me for, when I suddenly realized that I wasn't hearing a screen door slamming, but the sounds of rifle fire! I awoke from my dream with a start and fell forward on the edge of the hole. I saw three Viet Cong soldiers less than fifteen feet away, approaching. One of them was raising a PPK submachine gun. I saw something moving from my left, which turned out to be the Vietnamese BAR man. This man, whose name I didn't even know, simultaneously pitched his empty BAR at the three men and then literally threw himself over me, to shield me with his body. I actually heard the thump of bullets hitting his flesh, but fortunately, the relatively low-power 7.62 Tokarev rounds failed to penetrate his body. He rolled forward, and the three VC made the fatal mistake of not taking further action. I managed to shoot all three of them down before they could react.

With the assistance of a Colt 2 1/2–power scope on my M16, I killed twenty-two enemy soldiers with twenty-seven shots on that day, not including one individual who I observed bayoneting wounded Vietnamese soldiers. In his case, I shifted the cross hairs of the scope and blew his lower jaw off. After this encounter, I decided to relocate again, so Lai and I pulled and dragged our six companions out of the holes and crawled eastward down the rows of tea. At first, I thought I was seriously wounded, because when I reached to my back I came back, with a handful of semicongealed blood, but later [I] realized that it was Sergeant Henry's blood. Henry was holding up pretty well emotionally, perhaps encouraged by my repeated message that "I don't know how the hell I'm going to do it, but I'm going to get you out of here, Henry!"

My last act, as we went into the tea on our last shuttle, was to spray one twenty-round magazine, full automatic, laterally along the tea, across the road, about six inches off the ground, to convince anyone else not to follow us. Lai was carrying the radio on his back and at this point was the only one of us who was unwounded, though he had a big piece of shrapnel sticking in the sole of his boot. Fortunately, he was able to pull it out.

During all these incidents, we were in contact with Westby, whose radio call sign was Walt 70, and possibly Capt. Gerald Reed, the other sector FAC, I believe call sign Walt 71. I am sure that some of our army "Bird Dog" pilots were committed throughout the day, but my principal point of contact was the USAF FACs. We also had a number of very high-flying aircraft at one point that must have heard all the transmissions and actually came over to do a little sightseeing. Also, a major assigned to Advisory Team 38, who was inbound to Dilinh in a chopper, started reading off a supply list, including how many pounds of butter, etc., he was delivering. Since we didn't have an alternate "push" (radio frequency), he was on the same one as we were, but I rapidly used appropriate words to tell him to get the hell off the net. By this time, it was obvious that if we couldn't be somehow extracted by air, we were doomed.

There was no way that Lai and I could drag six wounded men through a cordon of one thousand enemy soldiers, but an extraction seemed impossible. Westby told me that he had a "slick" (troop-carrying helicopter) that had volunteered to try it. I thought it was extremely risky, but he could try it. I later found out that the pilot was an individual who usually was our "sector" ship, [who moved] . . . supplies and people around in the 4,200 square miles of Lam Dong province. I believe his name was Capt. Don Hosey.

Westby had a flight of Australian B57 Canberras inbound, and the plan we worked out was to involve them. We would crawl back to the edge of the road, and the Canberras would fly west to east virtually wing tip to wing tip, guiding on the plantation house and making a 20mm run on both sides of us. Meanwhile, I would crawl out to the middle of the road and lay in an "X." I told Westby that

I would be the only body so symmetrically arranged and would be easy to spot. The slick would come in skimming the tea from the south up the road to arrive right after the Canberras made their gun run. He would then land as close as possible to me, and Lai and I would toss everyone in the chopper and jump in and leave. Everything worked out, and the slick slammed in next to me. Lai and I jumped up and started loading. I could see an enemy soldier standing about fifty feet in front of the helicopter, shooting out the Plexiglas with an RPD machine gun. Three of the five wounded Vietnamese soldiers were killed as we tossed them in. Henry was untouched. One door gunner had his arm broken by a bullet, and the pilot was shot in the leg. Everyone was in but me. For some reason, I looked to the rear of the tail boom and was amazed to see a Vietnamese soldier laying by the edge of the road, raising his arm. I had previously thought he was dead! I ran back there only to find that there was no way he could be picked up. His entire intestinal tract was lying beside him, and I could literally see his spine from the inside. I knew that if I lifted him up, he would break in half. By the time I realized that it was impossible to save him, the pilot couldn't hold it anymore and took off.

I was now alone with 1,000 enemy soldiers. Actually, several days later, when I got back to Dilinh, I found out that Sergeant Lai, with the life-giving radio on his back, saw that I wasn't on the chopper, and as it bounced along the tea before gaining altitude, jumped back off to try to rejoin me! He wasn't successful in doing so and had his own harrowing experience in escaping and evading, in some cases by throwing hand grenades over his head as he ran. He even managed to find two other Vietnamese soldiers who had escaped earlier and were hiding in the bushes. Meanwhile, seeing the chopper depart was my signal to get out of the immediate area and attempt to go to ground like a rabbit escaping from a hound.

I dove into the tea and crawled down the rows, all the time hearing shouting of Vietnamese voices. I kept switching rows to move down and shortly came out to where I could see the plantation house. It was abandoned and unscathed. I remembered telling Captain Westby earlier to avoid hitting the area around the house because of the presence of the French plantation owner, who in the past had provided intelligence information to us.

After an indeterminate time, I came out in view of Highway 20 and a water tank by the roadside. At first, I considered working my way up to it and hiding inside it but rejected the idea because there would be no possibility of escape if I was discovered. I eventually worked my way up to a gulley, which paralleled the north fence line of Bobla hamlet, which now seemed quiet and abandoned. Apparently, the people had fled somewhere to the west when the air strikes started going inbetween them and Hill 955.

I crawled up to the fence, which was made of saplings bound together. Bobla was not a strategic hamlet and therefore was not a fortified defensive position surrounded by barbed wire obstacles. It did not have a Popular Force platoon, which provided a security force. As I moved along the fence, I heard movement on the other side of the fence. I looked through the openings between the stick fence and saw an enemy soldier crouched down over a radio. As I watched from less than five feet away, he gave the customary Vietnamese commo check on the radio: "Mot, hai, ba, bon, challoi," which means "one, two, three, four, answer."

Looking west along the fence line to the forward slopes of the hill overlooking the hamlet highland rice fields, I could see a screening force of well-camouflaged positions, which could observe any movement of ARVN forces coming from the direction of Bao Loc. I then backed up along the fence line to the east and discovered that there was a VC 60mm mortar position in some low brush about 50 meters from the east side of Bobla hamlet. The crew seemed relaxed and [they] were sitting with their backs against some small trees surrounding the clearing where the mortar was set up.

I realized that the time had come for audacity and stood up and walked to the south on a line between them and the village. I held my M16 flat against my right side and hoped that with my dark hair and short stature, I would be mistaken for one of their own. I noticed in my peripheral vision that one of the soldiers stood up to get a better look, but then sat down again. As soon as I disappeared over the crest of the hill leading down to Highway 20, I broke into a run and crossed the road into some scrub jungle. I then cautiously worked my way west, until I saw vehicles and soldiers in ARVN camouflage uniforms and helmets standing around. The vehicles were obviously stopped because of the combat action to the east, but I carefully checked the soldiers out through my riflescope, because on more than one occasion, I had encountered VC units that used ARVN uniforms as a ruse. However, I could recognize a lieutenant that I knew from the 23rd Ranger Battalion, which was also the most likely unit to be reacting to the earlier combat actions.

To avoid being shot by accident, I hooted and waved my arms before emerging and walking slowly towards the elements of the Ranger battalion, hatless, and with tattered jungle fatigues. I encountered Capt. R. J. Wooten, senior advisor to the battalion, who smiled as I approached and said into the handset of his PRC 25 radio that "34" (my call sign) had just returned to friendly control.

R. J. was an Academy graduate and one of the best advisors the 23rd Battalion ever had. It was only after I stopped in front of him that I realized how badly my knees were shaking. As we stood there talking, a toothless old lady, who was squatting down by a blackened tea pot over a fire, tugged on my trouser leg and put a cup of hot green tea in my trembling hand. That cup of tea tasted better than anything in my lifetime, before or since!

I went over the incidents of the day with R. J., especially the fact that there was a powerful enemy force to the east of Bobla hamlet, and that the main elements seemed to be in the vicinity of Hill 955, which Highway 20 crossed. Also in question was the whereabouts of the Dilinh district command group, including the two advisors. R. J. already had been made aware of the bogus radio transmissions. ARVN ranger battalions are lightly armed, but at least they had the additional firepower of M16 rifles and M60 machine guns, plus much better communication equipment than RF companies.

For the second time that day, I moved into the area. We moved past Bobla hamlet and the plantation house without making any contact, and found the dead RF troops in the area where I had been surrounded. We also found what happened to the command group and advisors, near the copse of trees that had been the steering point for the 407th Scout Company. Captain Hoi was lying dead in an old bomb crater, partially submerged in stagnant water. The exposed parts of his body were charred by one of many napalm strikes. Major Graney and Captain Van Hoose were lying close together. It appeared as if Van Hoose had been shot in the legs innumerable times as he lay there. Don Graney had a major head wound. The bodies of the troops that had accompanied them were scattered around them. As per usual, their boots were missing, as were any weapons or radios. Possibly their own radio had been used to transmit the bogus messages. We also counted over sixty-five unrecovered enemy bodies in the vicinity of my earlier contact to the north, which was encouraging because VC and NVA forces made every effort to remove their own dead from the battlefield, so they must have suffered many more casualties. At least we knew that they had been badly hurt, but probably not enough to render them ineffective.

We made a surprising discovery in the vicinity of the plantation house, when we heard someone calling for help from a well. The Dilinh district intelligence lieutenant had survived by climbing down into the well. We moved towards Hill 955 with two ranger companies abreast and made no contact until we crested the hill. The VC had developed a reverse slope defense with well dug-in positions and claymore mines awaiting a reaction force. These were the main positions of the enemy. I was moving forward with Sgt. Clifton Tanksley, from the battalion advisory team, and a ranger M60 machine-gun team, when the concentrated enemy firepower drove the lead elements to the ground. Sergeant Tanksley would be killed while serving with the battalion less than ten months later. As I no longer had a radio, I could only monitor the transmissions of the ranger advisors. Captain Wooten was talking to an FAC with the call sign of Walt 72.

The FAC had a heavy team of four 155th Aviation Huey gunships under his control. They immediately responded to the enemy fire, but shortly after they started to work over the VC positions, one of their choppers was badly damaged by small-arms fire. They broke to the rear to escort the damaged gunship out of the contact area. It was always my experience that the Huey model gunships were very vulnerable when attacking anything more than a company, especially if they were dug in.

I recently found out that one of the gunships had sixty-two bullet holes in it after this action. The less vulnerable Cobra gunships were not widely available to nondivisional aviation units at that time. Earlier, some gunships had prepped the area and called Bao Loc for rearmament. The bogus radio station encountered earlier imitated Bao Loc tower and told them that they would have to return to BMT (Ban Me Thuot), their base station, to rearm, as Bao Loc had no ammo or rockets available. Fortunately, this information was corrected by the real tower station. When the heavy team departed station, there was a break in available air support. When queried by the ranger advisors about available air strikes, they were told by the FAC that he had a flight of F-4s about six minutes out. At this time, and possibly as a result of monitoring the information about available air strikes, the VC force came out of their foxholes and bunkers and assaulted the two forward ranger companies with fixed bayonets. With what was probably at least a five to one advantage for the enemy, the situation looked dire. The last message transmitted to the FAC, concerning the flight of F-4s, was, "It looks like that's going to be about five minutes too late!" After monitoring this last message, the FAC aircraft banked over and fired his remaining white phosphorus marking rockets into the attacking VC.

A hail of small-arms fire tracked the route of the Bird Dog aircraft, shifting much of the fire from the now-retreating rangers. The plane came around again, but this time, since it was now unarmed, the pilot delivered bursts of M16 fire from the right window as he flew less than 150 feet over and parallel to the attacking troops. Amazingly, he came around a third time to repeat this small-arms attack, after replacing his twenty-round magazine in the rifle. In the way of actual damage, the pilot's rifle fire probably caused an insignificant number of casualties, but the presence of this low fly-ing and vulnerable target brought the forward movement of the VC to a halt and caused them to redirect all of their small-arms fire at the aircraft.

Pieces of the "Bird Dog" could be seen flying off as bullets impacted on its unarmored body. It was common knowledge that the act of shooting down an airplane was considered one of the highest levels of achievement for a VC/NVA soldier, and was one of the only acts that rewarded an individual with a home leave, even if it meant returning to North Vietnam. It should be noted that by 1967 there were many North Vietnamese soldiers who were fed into main-force VC units as replacements. Redirecting the fire skyward permitted the rangers to break contact and come under the protective supporting fires of the battalion reserve and heavy weapons, causing the whole attack to falter.

At the end of the third pass, the airplane climbed abruptly, and after gaining a few hundred feet, the engine began to sputter as if it was running out of fuel. It banked over and silently glided over us and crashed with what looked like relatively little damage in the tea fields at the base of Hill 955. Sergeant Tanksley and I started running towards the aircraft, which was about 150 meters behind us. I believe that Capt. Gary Vote, assistant battalion advisor, also accompanied us. As we approached it, the VC started bracketing the downed plane with 60mm mortar rounds. When we neared the plane, we kicked a hornet nest, and swarms of angry hornets started to sting us. I said, "For Christ's sake, Tanksley, what else can go wrong today!"

The plane was riddled with bullets but relatively upright, and we pulled the door open and lifted the pilot out and lowered him to the ground. The first thing I noticed was his nametag, which read "Wilbanks." Captain Hilliard Wilbanks, known to all of us as "Willy," had been a Lam Dong Sector FAC until a few months before but had then been reassigned to Tuyen Duc Province. At that time, Tuyen Duc was considered a quiet province, and Willy had two months left on his tour and a set of twins he had never seen at home. Apparently, he had been loaned to us to assist in covering the daylong battle that had begun early that morning.

The aircraft was riddled with bullets, but it appeared that only one round had hit Willy; a single bullet that hit his cheek and ranged upward into his brain. He still was breathing, but was unconscious. We immediately called for a "dust off," but when the medevac came, it was turned back by intense ground fire. Shortly after, a 155th Aviation Company slick [helicopter] boldly came in and picked him up. We received a radio message that he died shortly after arriving at Bao Loc. There was no question in my mind that Willy had sacrificed his life to save us, as he above all knew how vulnerable an O-1 aircraft would be when flying 150 feet above and parallel to a line of attacking troops with automatic weapons.

Captain Wilbanks, a former fighter pilot, would be the recipient of the second USAF Medal of Honor in the Vietnam War. The battalion streamed back, carrying dead and wounded, and assembled in the vicinity of AN765802. The decision was made that the entire area of Hill 955 would be prepped with artillery and air strikes, after which the rangers would conduct a night assault. By then a U.S. infantry battalion was moving into the area of Dilinh, about five kilometers east of us, and artillery had also been displaced to deliver massed fires on the objective. Two Vietnamese Commando armored cars had also arrived, and they parked adjacent to the road with their twin .30-caliber machine guns pointing towards Hill 955.

All afternoon and into the early evening, artillery and pre-planned air strikes were delivered on the target. Bombs as large as one thousand-pounders were dropped, and as darkness fell, AC-130 gunships and flare ships continued to illuminate the objective and direct a stream of bullets from their Vulcan cannons on any potential routes of withdrawal. During one air strike with a one thousand-pounder, a three-foot-long piece of bomb fragment clanged off the front of the armored car I was standing next to. I told R. J. that I wanted to accompany the attacking troops onto the objective, but in the darkness I passed out in the bed of a 2 1/2–ton truck and was awakened when the troops returned without a shot being fired. They retrieved the bodies of more ranger dead, and also recovered some wounded who had played dead in front of the VC fortifications and miraculously survived the bombardment.

They told of watching hundreds of VC file by in the darkness despite the air strikes and artillery, carrying their wounded with them. They also mentioned that they saw, in the light of the flares, a Caucasian individual who was moving with the VC and assumed that he was a prisoner. Later information revealed that this was not so. The only enemy casualty remaining was an individual who was burned by napalm over most of his body, and who died as they covered him with a poncho.

Once again, the VC demonstrated their amazing ability to exfiltrate a position even under fire and live to fight another day. The next morning, a helicopter called in to say that they were inbound to pick up the bodies of Major Graney and Captain Van Hoose. Unfortunately, Capain Wooten and I discovered that the bodies of the two advisors had been loaded first in the bed of a 2 1/2–ton truck and covered with the bodies of thirty-five to forty

Vietnamese soldiers. The Vietnamese soldiers who were present refused to unload the truck, so R. J. and I had to do it ourselves.

When we lifted Don Graney's body out of the truck, the back of his head came off. We placed it in the body bag; so much for the glory of war. Finally, a few Vietnamese assisted us in this grisly task, and the bodies of the Vietnamese soldiers were put back in the truck. That afternoon a U.S. infantry battalion started operations along the probable withdrawal routes of the enemy units, but their operations made no contacts whatsoever.

The VC and NVA plan their withdrawals as carefully as their attacks and normally break into smaller groups and move on multiple routes to predesignated, concealed assembly areas. There have been cases in which whole battalions have disappeared into spider holes, prepared prior to the operation, which are undetectable unless you actually step on one of the positions. Local guides are normally provided to facilitate getting withdrawing units to the right locations expeditiously. Therefore, I was not surprised that the enemy had disappeared without a trace, especially considering the ponderous way in which most U.S. units announce their intentions by displacing and registering their artillery and then conducting obvious reconnaissance overflights.

In the afternoon, I arrived at Dilinh and got the opportunity to remove my shredded jungle fatigues and wash off the mud and blood from my body. I took one of Captain Van Hoose's T-shirts to replace the one I had torn up for field dressings. I also discovered the fate of some of the other participants in the previous day's actions. Lai had made it in with his two RF soldiers. I found out that the helicopter pilot who extracted Sergeant Henry and the Vietnamese soldiers tried to kick off his crew and return to the area to find me after he had unloaded the casualties, despite a leg wound and a bullet-riddled helicopter. Supposedly, he had to be wrestled out of his helicopter.

I also heard that our advisory team security squad, which consisted of six young U.S. infantrymen and was accompanied by Staff Sgt. Giles Hamby, my usual "second" on combat operations, had somehow talked another "slick" into inserting them somewhere north of the operational area to look for me, but were extracted after meeting with no success and being engaged by an unknown-size enemy force. This was after a nine-hundred-man U.S. Army Airmobile infantry battalion declined assaulting into the area! I have never been able to confirm this, nor will any of the participants own up to it, but if it happened, it is further evidence of the incredible loyalty and courage within the human spirit, even if any sane person would consider it almost suicidal.

On the evening of February 25, I walked from the district advisor's compound to the top of the hill and climbed the water tower that overlooked Dilinh, to be alone with my thoughts. Shortly after I settled on the platform of the fifty-foot tower, I saw a ghost-like image climbing up the metal ladder in the moonlight. It was Captain Hoi's son, dressed in white robes, the color of mourning clothing in Vietnam. He said he wanted to thank me for my efforts to try to rescue his father. We sat there silently for several minutes while he held my hand, and then he climbed back down and disappeared into the darkness.

On getting back to Bao Loc on the next day, I had the U.S. Navy MILPHAP team check my back. I believe that Doc Dick Dolbec checked me out and took an x-ray. It looked like a small fragment had penetrated and then ricocheted off my shoulder blade. I told him not to submit a casualty report. I then talked to Sam Phillips, who worked as an intelligence specialist for an organization called the

Central Registry Detachment, about the imitative radio transmissions that were monitored during the combat actions of February 24 and the sightings by the wounded rangers of a Caucasian filing away with the Viet Cong as they withdrew.

One of Sam's principal missions was tracking of captured U.S. personnel, and it seemed possible that the individual in question might be someone who was a turncoat, like the well-known Bobby Garwood. Sam received additional information from several Montagnard residents of Bobla hamlet who reported a Caucasian individual who was seen in the presence of the VC on the morning of the 24th. Several days later, an officer from Sam's headquarters flew up to our location and briefed Sam and I about an individual who had been identified by innumerable reports as a former POW who had become a collaborator.

Sam Phillips, by the way, was one of the individuals I trusted to "second" me on combat operations, even though it wasn't his job. In fact, he accompanied me on several two-person night ambushes with my silenced Sten Gun about one or two kilometers from the advisor compound. Not the kind of thing you would expect an individual who normally worked in civilian clothes to participate in!

Sam was killed in October 1967. Some of the information provided by Sam's organization was based on reports from former ARVN POWs who had been released or who had escaped. The individual in question is still listed in an MIA status. We encountered who we believe to be the same individual transmitting bogus radio messages in operations in early March 1967.

To me the most astonishing thing about the actions of February 24, 1967, was not the intensity of the combat, because I had several other experiences that equaled or exceeded it in the forty-five months that I spent in Lam Dong Province. It was the exceptional heroism and sacrifice demonstrated by many of the participants, both U.S. and Vietnamese, in order to come to the aid of their comrades, even if it meant sacrificing their own lives. If you asked any of these men why they did it, they would probably shrug their shoulders and say, "It was my job," but common sense says otherwise; in the midst of extreme violence can be found extraordinary acts of love.

5 | GRENADA AND PANAMA

(1983–1989)

Capt. Patrick M. Higgins, U.S. Army

The late October 1983 invasion of Grenada was the first major operation conducted by the American military since the end of the Vietnam War, eight years earlier. Captain Higgins, an operations officer with the 82nd Airborne Division, learned that the "fog of war" can start to cause confusion even before the battle starts. And even when you have overwhelming force, the other side won't necessarily give up without a fight.

ONE OF THE PRIMARY CONSIDERATIONS in planning Operation Urgent Fury [1983] (the code word for the rescue mission) was secrecy. As a result, the extremely limited number of individuals involved in planning restricted the range of experience that could be drawn upon to orchestrate the resources of an airborne division. It was not long before more key personnel, especially logistical experts, were called in to assist in the troop leading procedures. Our METT-T [mission, enemy, terrain and weather, troops and support available–time available] analysis yielded the following information.

The 82nd Airborne Division's mission, as it finally evolved, was, on order, to conduct a parachute assault on Grenada, attack to destroy resisting enemy forces there, restore order, and secure and evacuate the U.S. nationals on the island. Several mission-essential tasks were stated or implied by this.

Just how much resistance we could expect on Grenada was not known. It was generally believed that we would be facing a light infantry threat of up to five hundred Cuban troops backed by as many as one thousand soldiers of the Grenadian People's Revolutionary Army (PRA), armed with an assortment of arms from the Soviet Union or other communist countries. Several BTR-60 armored personnel carriers were known to be on the island, but no tanks were expected to be found there. Of particular interest, though, was the half-dozen or so ZSU 23-2s [antiaircraft guns] centered chiefly on the high ground around Saint George's and on the hills overlooking the Point Salines Airstrip. With a rate of fire of two thousand rounds per minute, these 23mm towed antiaircraft guns would figure prominently in the air deployment plan.

The state of training of the average PRA soldier was not believed to be very good, a fact that would later be borne out during the fighting. Of the Cuban force, however, over one hundred were thought to be first-class troops and probably veterans of Cuba's "advisory activities" in Angola. The rest of the Cubans were thought to be engineers sent in specifically to assist in the construction of the Point Salines Airstrip and of unknown fighting ability. The ability of the enemy to employ chemicals was considered extremely doubtful, and as far as was known, Grenada had no air force at all, assuring total United States air superiority over the island to support ground operations.

An analysis of the terrain and weather on Grenada was also a major factor in planning the operation. The mountainous regions of the island would inhibit the use of motorized vehicles. This difficult terrain, combined with the effects of the hot tropical sun, would make dismounted movement punishing to bearers of a military pack. Grenada's narrow roads were known to be largely unimproved, which was a factor to consider if any armored units were to be employed. Our logistical planners allowed for large quantities of potable water and medical supplies for the treatment of heat injuries.

Immediately available to the operation planners were seven airborne infantry battalions, an airborne armor battalion with M551 Sheridan armored reconnaissance vehicles mounted with 152mm main guns, the division's air cavalry squadron, a combat aviation battalion, and the complete array of the 82nd Airborne Division's combat support and combat service support assets. Other rapid-deployment force units that could be incorporated into the air deployment package if needed were considered. These included a battery of 155mm howitzers from the XVIII Airborne Corps Artillery and a medium-lift helicopter company with CH-47 Chinooks.

The amount of time needed to prepare and conduct operations on Grenada was also a key factor. The division's alert, marshalling, and deployment standards were based on an eighteen-hour sequence that was heavily rehearsed through the exercise of numerous readiness alerts. The "on order" nature of our mission would necessitate a condensed version of this sequence.

Also important was the consideration of space. Point Salines, bordered on three sides by the Caribbean Sea, was a tight fit for anything larger than one battalion in a tactical configuration. Protection of the force while bottled up there, and a rapid push to Saint George's, would be imperative.

As planning continued, several courses of action were considered, but always the options available centered around the need for the Point Salines Airstrip. Finally, it was decided that a two-battalion force from the division's ready brigade (DRB) would be used to make the initial assault. Key leaders from the Division Ready Force One battalion (DRF1), the 2nd Battalion (Airborne) 325th Infantry (2-325), and the DRF2 Battalion, the 3-325, were brought in on the planning.

My job at this time was the orchestration of a marshalling and an air deployment plan for these initial assault units. As the plan refined, I finalized the priority vehicle list (PVH) of the initial assault echelon. Squeezing every available inch of space left us room for the sixty vehicles and pieces of equipment selected for the deployment, based on the division and brigade commander's guidance. These included the division, brigade, and the battalion's command and control vehicles, reconnaissance and mortar vehicles, field medical ambulances, and field artillery assets. Also included were elements of the brigade's forward area support team (FAST), essential to set up an arrival airfield control group complete with materials handling equipiment and to provide for our immediate logistical needs. Particularly useful during this time was the load planning computer programs of our automated data system, which could load plan in seconds what would normally have taken us hours manually.

We continued to refine our plans and make preparations under the utmost secrecy until our notification orders came. At 2100 hours on Monday, October 24, the alert marshalling order was received, and the procedures to recall all division personnel for Operation Urgent Fury were immediately initiated.

The first few hours of the 82nd's alert sequence proceeded according to plan. From Fort Bragg's loading area control center (LACC) adjacent to Pope Air Force Base, we received a constant flow of intelligence updates. The 1st and 2nd Battalions of the 75th Infantry (Ranger), we learned, were in on the operation too and would conduct a low-level airborne assault to seize Point Salines and immediately pinpoint and collect the American medical students located at True Blue Campus. Meanwhile, marines from the 22nd Marine Amphibious Unit (MAU), recently diverted en route to Lebanon, where they were to rotate with the 24th MAU in Beirut, would land on the eastern side of the island to seize Pearls Airport. Once the rangers were in control, we would then air-land instead of jump (apparently, the airstrip was not in as bad a shape as we originally thought). We would then receive the battle handover and drive to link up with the marines pushing inland.

As more and more participants now realized that this alert was no mere recall muster, marshalling procedures began moving at breakneck speed. The basic load of ammunition and C-ration meals were issued, as were two-quart canteens, mosquito netting, and other tropical combat necessities from the post's contingency stocks. There was no time for hand receipts, much to the mortification of corps and division support personnel, and by dawn our troops began moving towards "Green Ramp," the aircraft loading area at Pope Air Force Base.

En route we received some alarming news. The rangers had parachuted into stiff resistance, and a full-scale battle for control of the airstrip was in progress. Faced with the need to provide immediate reinforcements, our delivery means changed again, back to a parachute assault. Our support personnel reacted with speed and efficiency, and by 1000 hours, the first C-141, with the division commander and his assault command post aboard, lifted off. Within thirty minutes, all twelve aircraft had departed, loaded with pallets of T-10–type parachutes and reserves for an in-flight parachute rig.

The initial loads of parachutes and equipment were lined up in chalk order, having weighed in on the departure airfield control group scales, ready for loading as soon as aircraft became available. I coordinated with the army ground liaison officer at the command center and was told to expect to load at any moment. The original plan to bring the vehicles to Barbados and then transfer them to C-130s had not changed. Upon my return to the loading area, I received a rude shock. Apparently, some overzealous individual, acting on erroneous instructions that our field artillery assets must receive first priority in deployment to the objective area, had directed the removal of all our support battery's howitzers and prime movers out of the initial chalks and began reloading them on separate "artillery only" chalks. After a highly emotional display, this issue was rectified and the vehicles returned, but it demonstrated a problem that was becoming more and more apparent at Green Ramp, namely, a lack of control. During the first three critical days of Urgent Fury, priorities on just what and who were to be out-loaded were directed by numerous individuals who assumed control by virtue of their rank, position, or authority. Many personnel, with their vehicles and equipment, managed to simply "prioritize" themselves into the out-load completely unsupervised.

Because of this, the follow-on vehicles and equipment of the initial assault brigade, badly wanted for added combat power, logistical support, and command and control on the ground, never reached Grenada. Whether or not they would have made any difference in the course of the battle is a matter of debate. Nonetheless, their presence on the island would undoubtedly have been considered more important than the pallet loads of cots for Corps Headquarters personnel that began arriving on D+3.

In spite of these issues, our aircraft were ready to load by 1330 on D-day, and we were on board and en route to Barbados in short order. While flying south, we received new instructions. The rangers had managed to clear the runway of both the Cubans and their obstacles. It was decided to cancel the parachute drop and air-land the division's lead element directly on Salines Airstrip. Once all twelve personnel aircraft were down, my plane would land at Salines, too, followed by the rest of the air-land vehicle loads. Unfortunately, the Salines airstrip could only support one C-141B at a time, and consequently the delay involved in unloading each aircraft left each subsequent flight circling the airfield, awaiting clearance to land. For my plane, this meant a five-hour flight followed by six hours of circling the island in a holding pattern. During this time, the battle to control the airfield was still in progress. All sorts of rumors ran among the men onboard my plane as to just what was happening below, and we all began to wonder if we would live to see the sun rise that morning. Fortunately, we did not have long to wait. At 0330 on Wednesday, October 26, our plane touched down on Grenada and taxied to a halt before depositing us on the eastern end of Salines airstrip.

As we disembarked from our C-141B, we were surprised to find absolutely no activity around Point Salines, as if the war had been suspended until sunrise. After linking up the assault echelon vehicles with the battalions on the ground (which were only seven hundred meters off the airfield proper), I set out to find the 2nd Brigade assault command post to begin performing my secondary duties as a tactical operations center (TOC) officer. Fortunately, the TOC, located on a small peninsula south of the strip, was easy to find, and I was soon given a complete rundown of the previous afternoon's activities.

Our first two battalions had made it in without casualties, fanned out at the east end of the airstrip, and formed a tight defensive semicircle. Battalion 2-325 was in the north (left), oriented northeast, and 3-325 occupied the southern side, oriented east and southeast in front of the True Blue Campus. Link-up had been made with the rangers, and with the handoff of the battle completed, the rangers had pulled behind our forces and taken up new positions north and south of the airstrip to provide local security and to await further missions.

The Cubans, I learned, had bungled badly. Arrayed in defensive positions on the beaches north of the airfield as far east as Grand Anse, they had expected an invasion by sea and were taken completely by surprise when the rangers parachuted onto the airstrip itself. The ranger battalions had quickly fanned out to secure Point Salines and to get the True Blue Campus under control. They had also cleared obstructions from the runway using captured Cuban construction equipment. (Two 82nd Airborne Division engineers had accompanied the Rangers on their combat jump to aid them in that task.)

These missions were accomplished in good form, but not without stiff resistance and several casualties. The Cubans at Point Salines had made quite a fight of it with everything in their arsenal, including three BTR-60 armored personnel carriers, which had tried to push their way onto the airstrip in the late afternoon. Spectre gunship fire, the 20mm cannons of A-7 fighters from the carrier USS *Independence*, and 90mm recoilless rifle, Dragon, and LAW antitank fires from the rangers and paratroopers on the ground destroyed these. Had the BTR-60s made it over just one more rise onto the hills overlooking the airstrip itself, they could have wrought havoc on the unloading C-141Bs with their 14.5mm machine guns.

In spite of this resistance, we had taken several hundred prisoners. Many other Cubans simply threw off their uniforms and tried to blend in with the civilian population. The prisoners were quickly handed over to a three-hundred-man force of troops from the Organization of Eastern Caribbean States (OECS) countries: Antigua, Saint Lucia, Saint Vincent, Dominica, Jamaica, and Barbados. These were brought in by C-130s from our forward operating base on Barbados.

Meanwhile to the north, elements of the 22nd MAU, striking by helicopter from the USS *Guam*, had seized Pearls Airport after a short skirmish. Finding only token resistance there, they then sailed around the island and conducted an amphibious landing north of Saint George's at the "Queen's Racetrack," a soccer field on the ocean's side. A sharp fight was ensuing here for control of Richmond Hill Prison and Fort Frederick, the nerve center of the RPA. Numerous air strikes had to be called in to reduce the fortifications there.

Hasty plans for the morning's attack were made, and at dawn on Wednesday, October 26, 2-325 and 3-325 crossed the line of departure for movements to contact northeast towards Saint George's for a link-up with the marines. Contact was not long in developing. Outside the small town of Frequente, the Cubans put up a desperate fight for control of a major arms and equipment storage depot. The battle raged all day before Frequente fell, and then only after concentrated attacks supported by A-7 aircraft strikes with bombs and 20mm cannon fire. My old company, B Company, 2-325, bore the brunt of it, and as I listened in over the radio, I would have given anything to have been there with them. Two good men were lost here, among them my friend Capt. Mike Ritz, the company commander, who was shot while doing a leader's reconnaissance before the battle.

Meanwhile, 3-325 in the south was moving apace with the 2-325 over difficult terrain that was contested by individual and team-sized Cuban elements every foot of the way. By the end of the day, the forward edge of the battle area (FEBA) had been pushed out only 1,500 meters, and we had not yet overrun the Grand Anse Campus. With darkness coming fast, the task force commander, Admiral Metcalf, anxious over the dispositions of the American students at Grand Anse, ordered the rangers to conduct a raid to retrieve them to the Salines Airstrip where their safety could be assured. This was accomplished after precision air strikes to soften up the Cubans around the campus. One of the helicopters, after taking several hits, had to force land and transfer its precious cargo to the remaining aircraft. The squad of rangers on board had to be left behind, however, and escaped and evaded from Grand Anse towards our lines, where they linked up with 2-325 the following morning.

Thursday, October 27, promised a repeat performance of the type of operations we had seen on the first two days of Urgent Fury. Operating from caves, dugouts, and houses, the Cubans and PRA continued to fight desperately. We were forced to search every "nook and cranny" in the Salines area, but by the morning of D+2, we were not alone. Elements of the division's Third Brigade were now arriving and moving up on our right flank, using the main east-to-west paved road as a brigade boundary. With these additional forces, we continued our clearing operations.

The marines were now in control of much of Saint George's after several short, sharp firefights that had been settled in their favor. No doubt, the appearance of their M60 tanks, which were now ashore, helped to persuade numerous PRA soldiers to give up the fight. Our bag of POWs had grown also, and the terminal buildings north of the Salines Airstrip now housed over five hundred prisoners. A factor slowing our advance was the almost unbelievable amount of weapons and ammunition that we found on the way towards Saint George's. Processing the sheer number of these weapons to the rear, many of which were still packed in creosote, delayed our movement. It was apparent that the entire Salines area had been turned into a major military staging base for the Cubans and the PRA. Important in easing our clearance efforts was the assistance of the Grenadian people, who clearly regarded us as an army of liberation. Their help was instrumental in helping us to quickly find many key Cuban and PRA personnel who had disguised themselves as civilians, and large caches of weapons and material hidden in cellars, caves, and ditches.

Back at the airstrip, a large buildup was underway. With the students evacuated to safety off the island, reinforcements and logistical support was flowing in at a rapid rate, and during the afternoon, our brigade TOC displaced to the hills west of Frequente to get out of the way. Six infantry battalions and numerous service support elements were now packed into an area only eight to ten kilometers in size, and more personnel and equipment was arriving by the hour.

Our new TOC, set on commanding terrain, seemed like a good place to be. Late in the afternoon, however, we learned it was not. A four-man Cuban element, bypassed by the advance on the other side of the Frequente Valley, began taking us and the compound under fire. The thirty-man detachment guarding the captured compound was more than sufficient to handle this threat. Unfortunately, someone decided that a timely A-7 aircraft strike was needed as well. Screaming down on the Cuban positions, the A-7s bombed and strafed our brigade TOC location by accident. This mistake cost us seventeen casualties and an intense distrust of all U.S. Navy pilots. It also enlightened me as to the reason why the Cubans, who have been subjected to similar treatment over the past three days, were becoming more and more eager to surrender. The four Cubans, held up in a small house, soon became eager too, and they told us that they had been left behind to attempt to hold the Frequente area at all costs until a counterattack could be launched to crush the "invading yanquis."

In spite of this, by Thursday's end, our forces were in control of the Grand Anse area, while 3rd Brigade units were pushing northeast past Ruth Howard towards the Mount Hartman Estate. The rangers also had been called up for one final mission, this time to raid a suspected Cuban command and control center at Calvigny, southeast of Saint George's. The stronghold was defended by a squad-sized Cuban element, which was soon routed, but not before costing four men killed in action and three helicopters shot down. Following this mission, the rangers were deployed back off the island.

In and around Saint George's, the marines were now in undisputed control, and by Friday, October 28, a link-up had been established between elements of the 22nd MAU and 2-325 near Ross Point. With this accomplished, all Cuban and PRA resistance on Grenada soon crumbled, and the small number of resistors left not killed or taken prisoner faded into the island's steep hilled interior, presumably to organize some sort of guerrilla activity. For all practical purposes, the battle for Grenada was now over.

With things pretty much in hand on the island by Saturday, October 29, the elements of the joint task force assigned to Operation Urgent Fury had achieved two of their three intended goals: the rescue of American nationals and the destruction of resisting enemy forces. All that remained was to pacify the island and to restore order and democratic process to Grenada. The leaders of our task force now set themselves to just how that challenge could best be met.

Capt. Jonathan E. Tugman, U.S. Army

Taking down Rio Hato airfield was a major objective of the opening stage of Operation Just Cause, the invasion of Panama. The Panamanian Defense Force (PDF) soldiers based at the airfield were among strongman Manuel Noriega's best-trained and most loyal soldiers. The rangers of 2nd and 3rd Battalions, 75th Rangers, accompanied by forward observer Jonathan Tugman, would have to hit hard after parachuting out of the night sky into the Rio Hato drop zone.

ON DECEMBER 20, 1989, as a ranger rifle platoon forward observer in Company B, 3rd Battalion, 75th Ranger Regiment, I participated in Operation Just Cause. The invasion was the United States' effort to remove from power and bring to justice the military dictator General Manuel Noriega and restore democracy to the Republic of Panama. The 3rd Ranger Battalion conducted several missions during invasion, the largest of which was the airborne/air-land assault at Rio Hato Airfield during the invasion.

The rangers had been training for the invasion of Panama for years. Twice every year we conducted joint special operations readiness training exercises (JRTs). We knew during the training that our missions were for "real world" contingencies somewhere in Central America, but we did not know specific locations and names.

All of the missions went into what was called "The Prayer Book," a name given to a bunch of different war plans and possible contingency missions. The mission templates had been rehearsed and validated during the JRTs and other special operations training missions. In the event of a crisis in a specific area, The Prayer Book was pulled out and dusted off, and the units involved would conduct a rehearsal, then deploy. The plans were already developed.

We thought that we were going to deploy for sure in May, after the Panamanian election problems. However, the national command authority determined that that was not to be the case.

During the end of November and early December, the rangers were conducting the first-ever regimental-sized JRT. All three battalions were involved, as well as the other special operations units in the army, navy, and air force. We knew it was something big. By this time, we felt sure that we were going to Panama.

On December 15, we had just finished the JRT. Everyone thought that we were going for sure this time. Then, on the 16th, 1st Ranger Battalion went back to Hunter Army Airfield (HAAF), and 2nd Ranger Battalion went back to Fort Lewis. Expectations and hopes sank again, and everyone started thinking about Christmas leave.

At 1600 on Sunday, December 17, 1989, the ranger regiment was alerted and recalled. The 2nd Ranger Battalion redeployed to Fort Benning. Charlie Company, 3rd Ranger Battalion, deployed to HAAF to link up with 1st Ranger Battalion. "Operation Blue Spoon," as it was originally called, then changed to Operation Just Cause, was about to commence.

The Mission of Task Force Red (Rio Hato) was to conduct an airborne/air-land assault onto Rio Hato Airfield. The rangers would then neutralize the 6th and 7th Panama Defense Force (PDF) companies, isolate and secure the airfield, establish a lodgment site for the launch of other follow-on operations, and receive elements of the 7th ID for a relief in place. The 2nd Ranger Battalion would clear the built-up areas to the south of the airfield, to include Noriega's summer home and the military institute barracks. The

3rd Ranger Battalion would isolate the airfield; clear and secure the camp headquarters, the camp communications center, the motor pool, and the air operations complex; and sever the Pan American Highway.

The estimated enemy strength that was on the airfield was 220 men in the 6th PDF; 200 men in the 7th PDF, Noriega's elite "Macho de Montes"; and approximately 200 students in the military institute located in Rio Hato at the time. The enemy was believed to be armed with a total of over 150 automatic rifles, 42 machine guns, 9 bazookas, 4 recoilless rifles, 23 mortar systems, 19 armor vehicles, and six ZPUs [antiaircraft guns]. The PDF troops concentrated at Rio Hato were part of Noriega's best-trained and most loyal forces.

The 837 rangers of 2nd and 3rd Battalions, two AC-130 Spectre gunships, two AH-64 Apache attack helicopters, and two F-117 Stealth fighters, would accomplish the task of "taking down" Rio Hato Airfield.

Between the alert on the 17th and the deployment on the 19th, all rangers prepared themselves and their equipment. Detailed information was briefed all the way down to the individual ranger. Ranger leaders conducted thorough back-briefs to the chain of command. We were as ready as we could be.

Overnight, on the night of the 18th, fifteen C-130 transports landed at Lawson Army Airfield (LAAF). On the morning of the 19th, we moved to LAAF to receive ammo and finish packing. We were all freezing while waiting outside. The weather that day was very cold and rainy. No one wore cold weather gear, because we were going to rig our chutes before loading the aircraft, and there would be no chance to remove it after we took off. The next stop would be the ninety-degree humidity of Panama. Fortunately for us, someone went to CIF and cleared them out of wool blankets and brought them to us at LAAF.

Colonel Kernan gathered all the rangers around him to give a speech. His demeanor and inspiration gave even more confidence to all the rangers assembled. After the speech, there were small religious services held all around the site for those who wanted to attend. Small groups of friends were getting together to shake hands, hug, and say farewell before splitting to go to their different sites. It was a stomach-churning event that I will never forget.

Everyone moved to their rigging sites and started getting on their gear. As people finished rigging, they were shuttled on airport luggage trailers out to their respective chalks, scattered around the airfield. It was too far to walk to most aircraft with the weight of the parachutes, rucksacks, and logistics combat elements (LCEs). Each ranger had about an additional two hundred pounds strapped to him.

At 1530, the last of the rangers were aboard. At 1600, the first aircraft lifted off for a nine-hour flight to Panama.

The flight to Panama was long, and it provided all rangers with plenty of time to reflect on everything: the mission, on the lives that they had led, on family and friends, and on death. The aircraft I was on, Chalk 1, was quiet most of the time, except for the dull drone of the engines. Sitting across from me was Staff Sergeant Kelly, a very colorful platoon sergeant from A Company. He was a Grenada vet, and he kept those of us within hearing distance entertained with stories from Operation Urgent Fury. This would be his second jump into combat.

After spending several long hours in the harness, many people started to get restless. The combination of the anxiety, coupled with the nagging pain associated with being rigged for so long, was starting to become unbearable. If a ranger had to urinate during the flight, he would have to readjust his harness and relieve himself into a large plastic jug that would be passed around and then passed down to the loadmaster to empty into a proper receptacle. It was miserable. We had eighty jumpers on my aircraft. Under normal circumstances, there would only be a maximum of sixty-four jumpers on any given aircraft, but these were not normal circumstances. Additionally, in training, the jumpmasters send everyone out the door, then follow the stick out, with the safety remaining on board the plane. In combat, the jumpmaster leads the stick out, and the safeties control the stick.

As time on target (TOT) approached, the aircraft became alive inside. At two hours out from hit time, we received word that the mission had been compromised and that the enemy knew we were coming. This only heightened the anxiety, because we all knew there were potentially a lot of enemy forces on the ground that would now be waiting for us. At forty-five minutes out, the jumpmasters started with their commands. We got everyone up, hooked up, and lifted seats to make movement to the doors easier. The loads everyone was carrying made it impossible to stand for very long, so everyone went to his knees after hooking up. At around ten minutes out from the drop, one of the jumpmasters came over the intercom and led the Rangers in reciting the Ranger Creed. The words of the creed take on a whole new meaning when you are just minutes out from parachuting into a war zone. I will never forget the emotions that rushed through me at that time. Immediately following the creed, the loadmaster announced, "Blackout time is now," and the inside of the aircraft became as black as pitch. The only illumination inside came from the small red jump lights at the doors and the small window hatches along the sides of the plane. At around three minutes out, I saw two quick flashes of light from the window, and we received word over the intercom that the prep fires on the objective had begun. There was no turning back.

At 0100, two F-117 Stealth fighters flew in at four thousand feet and dropped two two thousand-pound bombs near the 6th and 7th PDF barracks. This was designed to shake up and disorient the PDF soldiers. The decision was made at a much higher level not to drop the bombs directly on the barracks to reduce the collateral damage. Immediately following the fighters, two AH-64s [attack helicopters] commenced an attack run on ZPU-4 antiaircraft guns that had been identified by the AC-130s [C-130 cargo planes converted into gunships] flying in orbits ten thousand feet above. At 0102, the AC-130s opened fire on the remaining antiaircraft positions and any targets of opportunity. It was essential to destroy all antiaircraft guns prior to the slow-moving transport aircraft flying over. The terrible fear of any paratrooper, even more than being shot while descending or while entangled in his chute, is to have his aircraft hit before he jumps. At the low altitude needed for a quick descent, five hundred feet, there is little chance if an aircraft gets shot down.

We had been flying just above sea level, as we approached from the ocean. As we approached, I felt the aircraft slow to jump speed and quickly rise up to the jump altitude of five hundred feet above ground level. The light turned green, and we started exiting as fast as we could. Once I got out into the night sky, the sights and sounds of war interrupted the usual quiet peace of a parachute descent. There were sounds of explosions, fire on the drop zone, the sounds of machine guns firing, and bullets cracking as they passed by. The sky was lit up with tracers coming up from the ground to meet us.

I had decided earlier to not lower my rucksack during landing as our standard operating procedure (SOP) states. I had decided to keep it close in the hopes that it might catch and stop a bullet that was destined for some other location on me. The tracers in the sky convinced me that this was the correct decision.

I know that the descent to the ground didn't take very long, but at the time, it seemed to take an eternity. I came down on the northeast side of the airfield, near what would become known as the Bullring. I came crashing through the roof of a thatched-roof building, probably somebody's residence. I was entangled in my gear, and I had to quickly cut my way out of my harness as necessary and put my weapon into operation. The small, one-room construction was uninhabited at this time, and I wasn't going to wait around to see if anyone returned. I quickly gathered up my LCE and rucksack and moved to some nearby five-foot Kuna grass about forty to fifty feet away.

I was low in the grass, putting my radio into operation, when I looked up and saw one of the C-130s, carrying one of our heavy drops, fly over, and the large bundle that it carried dropped out of its rear. I saw the enemy .50-caliber machine gun that had been raking the drop zone transition its fires up to the descending bundle, covered in blue chem-lights. I wondered if my friend, Staff Sergeant Bouma, was okay. He was the squad leader of the stick that was chasing the bundle out.

The early warning that the PDF received ensured that they were not in their barracks asleep as the planners had originally hoped. They were alert, dispersed over the airfield, and they were firing in all directions. This made things very challenging and dangerous for all of the rangers.

All the time I was on the ground, I kept hearing little sounds I had never heard before in the tall grass above my head. They sounded like small cracks of a whip. I then realized that those were bullets passing just over my head and that someone was shooting at me. I was just finishing up with my radio and was preparing to move when I caught something out of the corner of my eye. I saw a small, dark-skinned man rushing at me from about thirty feet away. He was wearing brown pants and a white T-shirt and was carrying something that turned out to be a machete. He may not have been coming directly at me; I thought I was pretty well hidden in the grass. Regardless, I picked up my CAR 15 and shot him with a quick burst of fire.

I then figured it was time to get the hell out of there. I started to move in the direction that I believed my platoon assembly area was located when I made a link-up with my first friendly face. It was Staff Sergeant Stangel. He was the Air Force E-TAC attached to A Company. We continued to move together, linking up with other individual rangers and teams along the way.

When I reached my platoon assembly area, I learned that about half of my platoon had already assembled and was finishing up the first of the tasks that the platoon had to accomplish that night. The fence that was located near the Pan American Highway where it crosses perpendicular to the middle of the Rio Hato Airfield was not as tough of an obstacle as it was initially believed to be. Instead of a double chainlink fence, the obstacle was just a three-strand barbed wire fence. The platoon was able to reduce the obstacle very quickly. This was the only major obstacle that was located on the airfield to prevent the aircraft from conducting the air-land offload of additional gun jeeps and bikes.

After the fence obstacle was reduced, the platoon's next mission was to establish a dismounted blocking position in the vicinity of the intersection of the airfield and the Pan American Highway.

The platoon leader (PL) placed the squads in position, and some rangers put some hasty obstacles on the road to slow vehicles. Our mission was to prevent anything from entering or exiting the airfield along the route that we were covering. Since the highway was a major thoroughfare, there was a lot of traffic on the road. We stopped several vehicles at the position, pushed the vehicles off the road, and detained the personnel in a collection point, not only for their protection but for ours as well.

Meanwhile, the rangers in 2nd Ranger Battalion were fighting through, clearing, and securing all the buildings in the south. The resistance they faced in some areas was tough, so progress was slow. Alpha Company, 3rd Ranger Battalion, was also facing some tough areas in the clearance of its objectives on the west side of the airfield.

Not long after we established the blocking position, we saw a white Toyota Corolla come speeding down the road. It appeared to be trying to bypass the obstacles placed in the road. We fired a few well-placed tracers over it in an attempt to get it to stop on its own. The warnings were not heeded, and the platoon opened up with a hail of fire on the vehicle that lasted for several seconds. The car was literally knocked off the road. A fire team was sent to clear the car. All of the occupants of the car were dead. There were two dead men that looked to be in their mid- to late twenties; a young woman that turned out to be eighteen, based on the age on an ID that was found; and a young child who we guessed to be between four to six years of age. There was this feeling of guilt that we had just done something terrible. Was it possible that we just killed an innocent family? Further inspection of the vehicle revealed two RPG-2 rockets in the trunk of the car. We now believe that the men in the car were on their way to the airfield to destroy some of the aircraft that were now starting to land. The young woman and the child were in the car to act as decoys to throw us off. We could not understand how these people could risk an innocent's life like that. It was a very sobering event.

As the aircraft landed, they offloaded the remainder of the battalion's gun jeeps and bikes. The jeep and bike teams then pushed out the perimeter from the airfield in several directions and established blocking positions. By the time the sun started to rise on the morning of the 20th, the airfield was fairly secure, and the rangers were clearing out any small pockets of resistance that remained. The battle for the airstrip was short, never really in doubt, but confusing and pocketed with violent firefights.

The company moved into platoon tactical assembly areas as the sun started to rise. We occupied areas just off the road in the wood line to the north of the highway and east of the runway. Our next task was to clear the village and other remote buildings in the area that I had landed in the night prior.

At around 0800, Bravo Company was postured to start its systematic clearance of the buildings on the northeast side, Objectives Lead and Copper. The 2nd Platoon was arrayed on the left, with 3rd on the right. The 1st was going to remain in position around the highway to be the company reserve.

We started to receive suppressing fire from an enemy sniper located in a block building forty to fifty meters away on our left flank. The squad closest, Staff Sgt. Larry Barnard's squad, was returning fire on the enemy. The fire from the enemy kept us from maneuvering on him. I monitored a call for fire (CFF) from the company fire support officer (FSO) to the AH-6s that were in orbit near our position. I informed my PL that an AH CFF was being sent on the building. He acknowledged and transmitted the word to his squad leaders. I contacted the FSO who was finishing the CFF and informed him that I would take over terminal guidance, since I was closest to the building and had a better view of the target that he did.

I positively identified the building to the pilots, cleared the helo for a "hot" gun run, and then told everyone to get down. The "Little Birds" were coming in hot. The helos came in at treetop level, guns blazing, directly over my position. They fired their mini guns and launched rockets into the face and windows of the building. The sounds were deafening. The expended brass from the mini gun was falling on our heads, and the force of the explosions rattled our insides. As the helos were pulling off, I transmitted the end of mission call. Also, as the helos pulled off, Staff Sergeant Barnard started maneuvering his squad to clear the building. The squad was almost to the building when the helos came in for another run on the building. Due to the noise level of the first gun run, the pilots were unable to hear my end of mission call, and as per their internal SOP, they reengaged the target. The pilots saw the squad near the building and thought that they were the enemy and engaged them with mini gun and rocket fire. When the first helo started to fire, the bullets were landing about fifteen feet from me and made a straight line up to 3rd Squad. The rockets were also deadly accurate. I again transmitted an immediate cease-fire, and fortunately, this time, the second helo heard the call prior to firing another lethal volley.

The effects were devastating. One ranger was killed immediately, and three others were wounded horribly. Private Brown was instantly killed; Private Killgallen received shrapnel wounds in his upper legs and lower back; Private Dunham received gunshot wounds to his lower legs; his left knee was completely gone; and

Staff Sergeant Barnard received shrapnel wounds to his lower extremities and both arms severed at the shoulders. Medical personnel in the platoon and company immediately began treatment on the rangers, as 2nd Squad cleared the building.

After the wounded were evacuated and the company had regained its composure, we moved out to clear the village. We moved from building to building. The clearance of the village was slow and systematic. About halfway through the clearance, 3rd Platoon encountered a most gruesome sight. Unknown at the time, it was the first casualty that the Rangers suffered during the operation, and every paratrooper's worst nightmare. A young ranger from 2-75th, Private Price, had had a malfunction with his parachute during the exit from the aircraft, and he had burned in.

The company continued to clear the village and then established platoon battle positions, in the north and east, along possible dismounted avenues of approach. We began to establish hasty fighting positions and await a relief in place that was scheduled to come from the 7th Infantry Division (ID) after landing the next day. The remainder of that day and night was pretty uneventful, except for an occasional inaccurate mortar attack. Both battalions finished securing their objectives by around 1700 on the 20th.

The next morning, the company learned that Staff Sgt. Barnard had died and that Killgallen and Dunham were both in critical condition. Everyone was in a state of shock. Had I just killed one of my best friends and mutilated two others? I was devastated.

On the evening of the 21st, the first elements of the 7th ID started to air-land. When they got off the aircraft, they were disoriented, and a few did not even know where they were. They didn't have much situational awareness, and their ammunition loads were minimal. When they started relieving our positions, individual rangers traded ammo, grenades, and explosives with soldiers in exchange for tobacco products. By this time, almost six days had passed since the rangers had been alerted. Everyone was pretty much surprised by the alert, so no one had packed extra tobacco. Most rangers who used tobacco were out and really starting to crave the nicotine by this time. The 7th ID soldiers had the tobacco but not much ammo. The rangers had more than enough ammo, so they were more than anxious to make a trade.

Early the morning of the 22nd, 3rd Battalion received an order for a follow-on mission. We were going to the city of Panoname. We flew out on transport helicopters an hour later. We executed the mission and returned to Rio Hato the next afternoon. At this time, over a four-hour period, all rangers boarded C-130 transports and flew to Howard Air Force Base to refit and plan for future operations.

The rangers suffered a total of four killed and forty-four injured. The majority of the injuries were parachute jump–related. The PDF casualties were 34 dead, 362 taken prisoner, and 43 civilian detainees. All others fled after they figured out the fight was not going well for them. All enemy equipment on the airfield was either destroyed or captured. A total of 18 V-150 armored vehicles, 1,800 assault rifles, 55 machine guns, 11 ZPU-4s, 100,000 rounds of ammunition, and 48 RPG-18 rockets were captured. The airfield seizure was considered a huge success. Friendly casualties were at a minimum, and the 6th and 7th PDF companies were no longer a significant threat to U.S. operations in Panama. After sixteen days and three additional follow-on missions, Gen. Manuel Noriega was captured. Two days after that, 3rd Battalion redeployed back to home station to recover, clean equipment, and mend wounds, both physical and emotional.

6 | OPERATION DESERT STORM
(1991)

Capt. James M. Petro, U.S. Army

Lost in the desert, in the dark, and in the rain, no less, with an M1 Abrams tank and two Bradleys was the last place mechanized infantry company executive officer (XO) James Petro expected to find himself. And it was only the second day of the first invasion of Iraq, February 25, 1991.

DURING OPERATION DESERT STORM, I was assigned to Bravo Company, 5th Battalion, 16th Infantry Regiment, 1st Infantry Division (Mechanized), as executive officer and was part of the initial breach for VII Corps, the relief of the 2nd Armored Cavalry Regiment in the Battle of Norfolk, and the subsequent securing of the Safwan Airfield for the peace talks.

On August 2, 1990, Iraqi forces invaded its neighbor to the east, Kuwait, to secure oil reserves, refining capabilities, and Persian Gulf port facilities. A United Nations coalition, led by the United States, rejected Saddam Hussein's annexation of Kuwait and demanded the immediate withdrawal of all forces from Kuwait. Iraq refused, and a buildup of American forces began in South West Asia (SWA) to prevent the invasion of Saudi Arabia and force the withdrawal of Iraqi forces from Kuwait.

The Big Red One [1st Infantry Division] was alerted for deployment to South West Asia on November 8, 1990. The 5th Battalion,

16th Infantry Regiment, painted its one-hundred-plus vehicles with special chemical agent–resistant coating (CARC) paint, using the division paint facility and a hasty paint shop built in a brigade motor pool. Ammunition for the Bradley fighting vehicle's 25mm gun, 7.62mm coaxial machine gun, and TOW missile system was issued and stored aboard the vehicles before movement to the division rail load site. The vehicles were loaded in about six hours aboard flatcars for movement to the port at Galveston, Texas, and shipment to Saudi Arabia.

Troops were issued desert uniforms and desert environment items in addition to receiving needed dental treatment and medical shots. Refresher training in NBC [nuclear, biological, and chemical weapons], air defense, combat life saver, and desert operations filled the few weeks prior to troop departure. An unexpected seven-day leave during this period put a lot of pressure on commanders and individuals to perform even better under already stressful conditions, but saved many marriages and tied up many personal loose ends that would have caused trouble later.

As executive officer of Bravo Company, I was responsible for advance party operations in preparation to receive the company main body. I deployed with about fifteen other Bravo Company infantryman early on December 27, 1990, from Forbes Airfield in Topeka, Kansas, and landed late on the 28th at Bahrain International Airport, Saudi Arabia. The Devil Ranger Battalion drew its Bradley fighting vehicles from the downloading ships and moved out along Tapline Road to TAA Roosevelt to build combat power and prepare for its primary mission: breach the Iraqi defenses and open a lane for VII Corps' units to attack Iraqi Republican Guard units.

TAA Roosevelt was a division assembly area near the Wadi Al-Batin, straddling Tapline Road. As the January 15, 1991, United

Nations deadline approached, tension began to grow among the troops. On the afternoon of January 13, a mission came over the radio: Bravo Company move as part of 5-16 Infantry to the south-west corner of TAA Roosevelt and set up a blocking position to protect the 1st Infantry Division's open flank from a possible Iraqi attack. (We were told that the Iraqis were planning a five–armored division attack down the Wadi Al-Batin to disrupt VII Corp's building of combat power and to embarrass the United States, thereby swaying media support away from the United States.)

The company commander and platoon leaders were doing a reconnaissance of other company assembly areas when the order came from battalion and did not answer radio calls. I took charge and had the platoon sergeants break down our three-day-old camp and upload for combat. The soldiers worked at a feverish pace packing, loading, and preparing for a completely unexpected mission. Within sixty minutes, the vehicles were lined up and beginning to move south as the commander returned with the platoon leaders. Each linked up with their element, and we continued without a pause. I was impressed with the company's speed, competence, and ability to perform without their primary leaders, a good omen for a unit with a trench-clearing mission.

The Iraqi attack never came, but the American air attack did. At 0220 on January 17, 1991, we became aware of the air war with the order to don protective masks in anticipation of an Iraqi chemical retaliation. Men move quickly from a deep sleep when the word "gas" is yelled. They understand what can save them from a death they cannot see. The "all clear" was received about forty-five minutes later, and the masks always stayed close afterwards.

The battalion task organized with the 2nd Battalion, 34th Armor Regiment, swapping two infantry companies for two

M1A1- [Abrams] equipped tank companies. Bravo Company task organized with Alpha Company, exchanging its 2nd Platoon for Alpha's 1st Platoon. With the addition of a fire support team [FST], a medic team, and a maintenance team, Bravo Team now began to train for its primary mission: open two lanes through the Iraqi obstacle and secure Objective 2KB to allow the remainder of the brigade and corps to pass through.

The engineer battalion attached to the brigade built replicas of the battalion objectives based on intelligence from the S-2. It included concertina wire, training mines, and the trench system we were to attack. The task force leaders assembled to war-game the initial plan. The task force would attack with Teams Delta and Bravo abreast, company columns, to open two lanes in the obstacles. Team Charlie would deploy in a support-by-fire (SBF) position to the right of Team Bravo, providing suppressive fire from left to right on the objective. Alpha Team would follow Delta and Bravo through the lanes and set up a blocking position north of the trenches to prevent counterattack from a tank company.

To open the lanes, current U.S. Army technique was drastically modified. Although the task force planned for support, breach, and secure missions, the breach method was completely different from training. Traditionally, a lane is blown in the minefield with MICLIC [mine clearing line charge] or cleared by hand with engineers, then engineers or infantryman open the wire obstacle with grappling hooks or wire cutters. Instead, the task force used M1A1 tanks fitted with mine plows and mine rollers to quickly cut lanes.

Practicing on the engineer mockup showed this technique to work very well. Instead of thirty minutes to several hours to open the obstacle, from plows down to plows up took only two and a half to three minutes for a four hundred-meter deep obstacle. No one was exposed to enemy small-arms fire or artillery, since it was done completely buttoned up.

Once the lane was open, the next task was to clear three five hundred-meter trenches. Team A, with one infantry platoon, would take the northern five hundred-meter trench. Team Bravo, with two infantry platoons, would clear the two southern trenches. Three-man teams practiced trench clearing, while ammunition was assembled to cover the requirement. The idea of putting men into the trenches did not sit well with the battalion commander, Lt. Col. Sidney F. Baker Jr., so war-gaming continued in the TOC [tactical operations center] and at the obstacle mockup.

During one session at the mockup, M9 ACEs [armored combat earthmovers] followed the lead company through the lanes to push sand into the trenches, but troops still had to get into the trench and go toe-to-toe with other infantrymen. I was standing with Lieutenant Colonel Baker, the S-3, Maj. Brian Zahn, Team B Commander, Echo company commander, and several lieutenants when it was suggested to use the tank plows to fill in the trenches. By driving a tank on either side of the trench with the inboard blade down, a four-foot trench-line would turn into a small mound of sand.

After a test proved the plows would work, a Bradley was added to the outer side of each tank to suppress down the trench while two followed the tanks to destroy anything missed by the lead Bradleys and the plows. Having stood in the trench during a rehearsal, I know how terrifying 120 tons of tank with steel teeth bearing down on you at 8 miles per hour feels.

Word of the trench-filling plan was passed up to division, and it became the method for the division to clear the trenchline and minimize the exposure to troops (Initial estimates of casualties for Task Force 5-16 for the mission was 750 soldiers!).

The plan was solidified and rehearsals continued. Squads worked on trench clearing in three-man teams (just in case), and larger-size elements were added until the brigade did a full-up rehearsal the first week of February 1991.

The task force moved up to the twenty-foot-high berm that designates the Saudi-Iraqi border on February 16, 1991, in a division formation, three brigades on line, and made final preparations to attack. While there, company teams rotated pulling watch from the berm to provide security from enemy reconnaissance and incursion (like Ra's al Khafji). "Berm Guard" provided not only a live ammunition practice, but occasional comic relief. Team Alpha spent four hours "chasing" a cargo truck and dismount squad with mortars, 7.62mm coax, 25mm HE, and 120mm main gun rounds. No debris nor bodies were found the next morning. Team Bravo spotted a BMP [Soviet-built infantry fighting vehicle] at about three thousand meters, but a grounded-out TOW missile at seven hundred meters influenced the platoon leader not to shoot again and chance being the lieutenant who shot the ground twice! Ground surveillance radar attached to Delta Company kept mistaking wild dogs for dismount troops, so the commander eliminated the confusion with .50-caliber machin-gun fire.

The initiation of ground warfare was scheduled for 0530 on February 21, 1991 (G-Day), but the Moscow peace initiative slid that back three days. On February 24, 1991, at 0538, Task Force 5-16 crossed through the berm and moved north to its assault position. For reasons unknown to me, the brigade held up in the assault formation for almost five hours. Sitting on a piece of high ground offered me once-in-a-lifetime view of armored vehicles from horizon to horizon. I almost pitied the Iraqi commanders, who could undoubtedly see this massive armor formation but had no assets to stop it. It must have been a few long hours for them.

Companies transitioned into attack formation, an eleven thousand-round artillery prep was fired, and the lead tank dropped plows at 1535 hours.

The breach went according to rehearsal through the six hundred or so meters of obstacles (there was no concertina wire), but not [during] the clearing of the trenchline. As in two of the four rehearsals, the lead two tanks continued past the first trench and started on the northern trench (Alpha Team's objective). The lead tank/Bradley group worked its way down the trench, firing two 120mm main gun rounds down the trench to get the Iraqis' attention. My APC [armored personnel carrier] came out of the lane, and I saw the first trench had been missed. I decided the first trench still had to be cleared before the Iraqis began firing north into the flanks and rear of the rest of Bravo Team. (The tank platoon sergeant's tank was fitted with the mine roller and was at the beginning of the northern trench uncoupling the roller.) I called him over to the southern trench and told him to parallel my APC down the trench using .50-caliber machine guns to destroy anyone in the trenches. To my chagrin, he opened the hatch and began to load his machine gun. My gunner fired down the trench until the tank was ready, and we proceeded down the trench using .50-caliber machine-gun fire to clear it until we caught up with the remainder of Bravo Team. The team had completed clearing all three trenches, while Delta Company screened north and Team Charlie suppressed the trench, occasionally shooting at us. Enemy prisoners were moved (by foot) back to the entrance of the lanes where an engineer unit staged a temporary brigade holding area. Around 0200 hours, the task force consolidated just north of the initial objective.

At 0100 hours (February 25), a FRAGO [fragmentary order] was issued to continue the attack along Axis Jupiter to destroy enemy on OBJ [objective] 12KB, the battalion command post. Team Charlie was the main effort, with Alpha following Charlie and Bravo following Alpha. At 0500, the attack to expand the breach continued.

Team Charlie commander decided to accomplish his mission using a technique he described as "secure by fire." He instructed his men to shoot at every suspected position and anything that moved. In a completely hostile environment, this is acceptable, but to get to OBJ 12K, the task force had to cross back in front of the lanes opened twelve hours earlier, which were already being used to pass the 1st U.K. [United Kingdom] Division and support elements north. After the first few shots, the battalion commander quickly regained control of Team Charlie and guided the task force through the congested area and on to Axis Jupiter. Once clear of the lanes, Team Charlie resumed the attack.

Little resistance was found on OBJ 12KB, which can be attributed to the intense artillery prep. Burning vehicles littered the area, along with several DPICM [dual-purpose improved conventional munitions] fields. My M113 ran over a bomblet, cracking a track shoe, which broke at the next turn. Throwing track in a minefield is not fun; fixing it there was even less fun.

Initial casualty estimates had the division combat ineffective at this point, thus the corps reserve mission. But Task Force 5-16's three casualties were indicative of the success of the division, and late on February 25, it went from corps reserve to being ordered to move one hundred miles north-northeast to assume a blocking position against withdrawing Iraqi units.

To set the stage for the division move, the task forces were positioned at the northern portion of PL New Jersey. It was a fifteen-kilometer movement north for Team Bravo, and my commander decided to send out a quartering party to secure the area prior to the rest of the team arriving (this is normally only done when setting up a defense, not on the attack). As the executive officer, this was my responsibility, and I departed at 1700 hours with a tank and two Bradleys.

By this time, the sun had set, the cloud cover lowered, and a light rain began to fall. About five kilometers into the movement, we encountered a unit's trains element who were not supposed to be there, and we had to bypass them. As we moved east, the satellite coverage for the GPS [global positioning system] went into a "down" window, turning my $2,900 Magellan into a paperweight. It was dark, rainy, with visibility at two hundred meters, so I jumped off my APC to use a compass to get us back on course.

I continued what I thought was another five hundred meters (it was really about 1,500 meters) and headed north. We trudged along what seemed a crawl, looking in mist to avoid Iraqi forces. At one point, we passed a berm that revealed a tank shape I think was a T-62. He had us dead to rights, and we moved past him hoping he was abandoned. About nine kilometers from the new staging area, the GPS regained satellite coverage, and I discovered how lost I really had been.

We continued north for what seemed an eternity. The tank in my group ran over a bomblet. The already anxious gunner yelled over the radio, "They're shooting at us, they're shooting at us," and swung the turret to the right. What he saw was many tanks swinging their turrets towards us. I prayed it was TF 2-34 moving into position (and not retreating Iraqis) and yelled over the radio, "Don't shoot! Don't shoot!" I don't know what kept him from firing, but I knew if he let a round fly, many tanks would return fire. That few seconds was the loneliest, scariest time in the entire one-hundred-hour war. I thought I was going to die in the desert, in the middle of nowhere, without the enemy in sight.

We pulled into the new staging area at 2135 hours to find the rest of team Bravo already there. The only redeeming factor happened when we pulled up to the lead vehicle in Bravo's column, removing some doubt from the soldiers, eyes that this lieutenant was lost!

At 2330, we refueled the tank platoon (the support platoon had positioned the LRP [load and roll pallet] adjacent to a minefield, which made for another exciting trip in the rain), and at 0530, we moved north. We encountered rain and two sandstorms in the next one hundred miles of Iraq, but no Iraqis. We had penetrated the first defensive belt, and were now in unoccupied territory. We stopped around 1600 hours and set up a blocking position to the northeast to stop retreating Republican Guard units.

At 1715, while in the midst of refueling, a net call came over the radio: relieve the 2nd Armored Cavalry Regiment (ACR), who were in a heated battle with a retreating Republican Guard Division. At 1800, the battalion moved out, five Bradleys abreast, to link up with the 2nd ACR. As the forty kilometers shortened between the 2nd ACR and the Devil Ranger Battalion, word came down to pick up the pace: the 2nd ACR was running out of fuel, but not targets. On a dark, overcast night, it sped faster and faster across enemy territory, doubling the normal daylight movement speed for a mechanized task force. When it reached the battle handoff point, the column was moving thirty-eight kilometers per hour. The tank-heavy and tank-pure battalions of the brigade led the attack, while Task Force 5-16 followed behind to clean up any bypassed elements and dismounts. Vehicles exploded in all directions as the brigade pressed onward through the cornered guard division. Throughout the night, Iraqi tanks, BMPs, and trucks were picked off by an enemy they could not see, nor kill when found. An American Bradley was hit when TF 1-34 and 2-34 drifted apart, but the scout screen did not. The 1-34 Armor scout platoon leader's vehicle was initially hit by a RPG, then an M1 main gun round. When the sun rose, the task force had reached OBJ Norfolk, and "Fright Night" was history.

We continued northeast on the 27th, heading for Basra. At 0732 on the 28th of February 1991, word came down: At 0800 hours, a cease-fire was in effect. We had won.

A new mission came down for the 5th Battalion, 16th Infantry Regiment. It was OPCON [operational control] to 2nd Brigade and would move north to a little town called Safwan and secure the area for the peace talks. It was very tense for a few hours, because a Republican Guard Division commander did not want to give up the area, but Colonel Moreno gave him an ultimatum: be out in ninety minutes or be decimated like the rest of the Iraqi Army. They complied, and it became our piece of land without a shot fired.

The 4th Battalion, 37th Armor, cleared the airfield to be used for the peace talks, while platoons from Bravo and Charlie companies cleared the large hill overlooking the site. I was in charge of this operation and, except for a few hiding, hungry troops, found the electronic collection station on top of the hill to have been visited by the United States Air Force. There were a lot of large holes and debris.

The battalion spent eight to ten days in Safwan, then moved back to the Iraqi-Kuwait border for ten days. It moved due west back into Iraq to take up XVIII Airborne Corps positions, so it could return to the states. In late March, the division moved back into Saudi Arabia and began redeployment on May 1, 1991. I landed at Forbes Field in Topeka, Kansas, on May 2, 1991.

Capt. Rembert A. Edwards, U.S. Army

Scout platoons usually lead the way, seeking out the enemy in front of and on the flanks of the battalion as the eyes of the commander. Scout platoon leader for the 2nd Battalion, 18th Infantry, Rembert Edwards experienced plenty during the short ground war of Operation Desert Storm, including finding himself in the middle of a flock of sheep!

As THE SCOUT PLATOON LEADER for the 2nd Battalion, 18th Infantry, 197th Infantry BDE [brigade] (M)(S), my unit arrived in Saudi Arabia on September 1, 1990. Although the 197th was a separate brigade, it was not deployed as such, but as the 3rd BDE on the 24th Infantry Division out of Fort Stewart, Georgia. For five and a half months, we trained. By the time we were called into action, we were at a high proficiency level on everything from individual tasks to task-force maneuvering.

When Operation Desert Storm was launched on February 24, 1991, 2-18 Infantry was on the west flank of the 24th ID (M) and the last U.S. mechanized force on the west flank. The only U.S. forces farther west were the 101st Air Assault and 82nd Airborne Divisions. Our mission, as part of the 24th ID, was to seize objectives located on the six-lane highway that ran along the Euphrates River Valley down into Kuwait. Once we had seized our objectives, we were to establish blocking positions on the highway to cut off the resupply of Iraqi forces in Kuwait.

At 1500 hours, on February 24, 1992, we crossed the Iraqi border en route to defeat the Iraqi Army. After moving continuously for about nine hours, at approximately 0200 hours, our task force reached PL Lion, which was just short of OBJ [Objective] Brown 1, our intermediate objective. Immediately following a USAF close-air-support attack by A-10s, the scout platoon was sent forward to "get eyes" on OBJ Brown 1. With near zero illumination from the moon, and a sudden change in terrain from a totally flat desert to a series of steep wadis, movement nearly halted. After two hours of much confusion and difficult maneuvering, the scouts arrived on OBJ Brown 1, just as dawn began to break. We reported no activity on the OBJ, as no enemy personnel or vehicles were found. Our immediate task was to establish screening positions to the east and west to ensure there were no forces coming on the OBJ as we cleared it. We cleared the surrounding area mounted, but we did not clear the buildings that were on the OBJ. The task force, moving much faster now that it was light, began to arrive around 0630 hours. My platoons moved out to conduct our next mission, which entailed moving to our west flank and linking up with the 101st Air Assault Division. As the task force rolled onto the OBJ, eleven Iraqi soldiers came out of a building and surrendered. By 0700 hours, the objective was secure, and by 0845 hours, link-up with the 101st was complete.

For the next nine hours, four of my platoon's vehicles were in an assembly area with crews, resting, while two vehicles, including my own, were awaiting new transmissions at the combat trains location. With only one transmission on hand, work began on my vehicle, while the track belonging to Staff Sergeant Jones, my junior squad leader, was towed to the field trains location. While my track was being worked on, I was able to get a couple of hours of sleep, but my driver and track commander worked diligently to fix our vehicle.

At approximately 1800 hours, on February 25, our task force began to move again. The task force was already under way as the last bolts were being tightened on my track. By the time I had caught up with the rest of the scouts and gotten out in front of the task force, darkness had fallen, and this night was the same as the previous one. There was no moon! Our mission at hand was to follow along a route marked by our brigade's tank battalion to attack position Kelly, our launching point for our assault onto OBJ Guard. OBJ Guard was our final objective before establishing BP 101, which was our brigade's blocking position of the six-lane highway to the north.

Although the route was marked with yellow flashing lights, the darkness of the night and the number of vehicles traveling this route made the task force movement difficult. Finally, at 1000 hours on February 26, we reached attack position Kelly. The task force quickly moved into a small assembly area and conducted maintenance as Lieutenant Colonel Olson met with the brigade commander, Colonel Reid, to coordinate the final plans prior to the brigade attacking.

At 1300 hours on February 26, the scout platoon moved out ahead of the task force. As we moved out of the attack position en route to the line of departure (LD), the scout platoon encountered very soft, mushy ground. Thinking we were just crossing a creek bed, we traveled deep into this terrain before realizing it was not suitable for the battalion task force to pass. My platoon was ordered to return to the attack position, as the task force was going to take a different route to the LD. It was at this point that we learned just how bad the terrain was. As my platoon attempted to turn around, two of my vehicles became stuck in the mud. These two vehicles, as it would turn out, would not return to my control again until the cease-fire was announced, because recovery vehicles were unable to get to their location. The recovery of these vehicles was done by the individual crews digging themselves out with shovels. In addition, a third vehicle of the scout platoon was located in the battalion field trains, because it was awaiting a new transmission. The remainder of this operation was conducted with only three scout platoon vehicles.

We arrived at the line of departure just as dusk approached. This was the point where we were to deploy into our battle formation and assault our final objective. There were a few small problems, however, in our task force proceeding as planned. The terrain had turned very wet and soft, similar to that which my platoon had encountered earlier, and traffic was limited to the roads across the desert. Attempts at traveling cross-country were halted after several tanks and other vehicles became stuck immediately upon leaving the trails.

A second problem was the direction the roads were leading across the desert. Our map reconnaissance showed that the roads only headed north, but our objective was to the northeast. It was at this point [that] Lieutenant Colonel Olson, the task force commander, sent the remainder of my platoon forward to find a route that would take us to our objective. As we proceeded forward, our attempts to find a direct route were failing, and the distance between us and the task force was increasing. Realizing we had no support, Lieutenant Colonel Olson sent forward the advance guard company (TM Dawg) to assist us in the event that we made contact with enemy forces.

As our element moved farther and farther north, trafficability became worse. Lieutenant Colonel Olson, who had followed behind TM Dawg, decided that the road had become impassable for any more vehicles and ordered the rest of the task force back south, with instructions to travel farther to the east before heading north again.

Meanwhile, my platoon had reached what appeared on the map as a hard-surface (blacktop) road that would lead us to our objective. At first, I thought we had come to a dirt road with a berm on either side, and the map was incorrect about the road. I did not realize exactly what we had discovered until we dismounted and reconned across the second berm. It was only then that I discovered the paved road and that the two berms were actually speed bumps emplaced by the enemy's engineers. After a few more minutes, TM Dawg was at our location.

With TM Dawg's arrival came the word from Lieutenant Colonel Olson for my platoon to move across the berms and a couple of kilometers to the north to make sure the area was clear of enemy personnel. As we moved forward, all we could see were vehicles traveling along the six-lane highway about four kilometers to our north. As far as enemy personnel in the area, there appeared to be none. With our report, Lieutenant Colonel Olson withdrew us back south of the berm, and we began to move our small force to the southeast toward our original objective. As we crept along, I began to receive reports from one of my squad leaders, Staff Sergeant Little, that he and his crew could see flares and white flashes of light. At this point, I was cautious as to what I would report to higher for a couple of reasons. My men had heard over the BN [battalion] radio net only about fifteen minutes prior that the marines had taken Kuwait City, so I knew they were eager to see some action themselves. Also, the last time our adrenaline had been this high (when we were allowed to conduct operations along the Iraqi border prior to the ground war), the platoon sent in spot reports that did not accurately depict the real situation. As

Staff Sergeant Little continued to send these reports, I thought about the source that was sending them. I had been the scout platoon leader for sixteen months now, and during that time, I had learned that Staff Sergeant Little was a particularly professional NCO [noncommissioned officer], and his credibility throughout the battalion was high. Had I not had so much confidence in Staff Sergeant Little, I may not have taken to heart the reports I was hearing, because I was only a couple of hundred meters from his vehicle, and I had not seen any of what he reported. I reported Staff Sergeant Little's reports to the . . . [battalion commander], and his reaction was much like my initial reaction. He told us to continue moving toward our objective and to keep our eyes open.

The next report dismissed my thoughts that we were making things up, because just as Staff Sergeant Little reported it, I too saw it. A truck full of people was driving without any lights along the road that we had been following. The truck was coming toward us on the paved road. When I sent this report higher, I was told to disregard it, because it was probably just Bedouins. The truck drove right past (a couple hundred meters) and continued traveling west. No sooner had I received the word to disregard the vehicle, when we found ourselves in the middle of a flock of sheep. This made me believe that the truck was full of Bedouins. We turned our formation to the south to bypass the sheep and then north again to the berms before getting back on course. As soon as we returned our formation to the berm, we spotted six stationery vehicles on the horizon to our left front. By this time, Lieutenant Colonel Olson had received word from the BDE commander to treat all vehicles operating without their lights as enemy. With this information, Lieutenant Colonel Olson had our formation conduct a left flank to orient our force toward the vehicles. This put us with approximately sixteen vehicles on line. My three vehicles were on the east flank of Delta Company. Once in position, we were given permission to fire warning shots at the nearest vehicle to our location. We fired, but there was no indication of a response. The TC (track commander) for my vehicle brought my attention to what appeared to be white flashes through our night vision devices. Moments later, we realized these white flashes were actually the muzzle flashes from the enemy's small-arms weapons.

To solicit a response from the vehicles, Lieutenant Colonel Olson ordered the lone tank in our formation to engage one of the enemy vehicles. The response was not exactly what we had expected; multiple explosions began occurring, but none that were directed at us. The vehicle was a truck full of ammo that was now on fire and igniting the munitions. As I continued to look through my thermal night site, I began to pick out a few personnel moving around on the objective.

Our next course of action was to suppress the objective with Mk 19 [40mm grenade launcher] fires. As I continued to observe through my night site, I reported that we were still only receiving a minimal response. The battalion FSO [fire support officer], Captain Eisminger, had been working on getting us fire support. We had sent our mortars and the battery of field artillery that was trailing our element along the new route with the rest of our task force, so our support was limited. After about twenty minutes, artillery began falling on the objective from the battery in support of our sister infantry battalion located five to six kilometers to our east. It was at this time that I observed through my thermal night site two to three hundred personnel running across the objective toward the northwest where Tallil Airfeld was located. My request to the battalion FSO was to shift artillery fires "left one thousand" to cut off their withdrawal. However, this adjustment of fires was too great because of the positioning of the artillery. The maximum adjustment the artillery could provide us was "left five hundred." With several communication exchanges over the radio and the time it took to deliver the fires, the artillery had a minimal effect on our objective.

Once the fires were complete, Lieutenant Colonel Olson gave the order for TM Dawg to assault across and clear the objective, with my platoon screening to protect its right flank. We moved forward on line and crossed the berms. Once across the berms, we discovered enemy dug-in positions in a linear defense along the paved road. For the next few hours, Delta Company cleared bunkers to its front, while my platoon began discovering position after position extending to our east. We began to work on our own, clearing bunker after bunker. All crews dismounted their tracks except for drivers and track commanders. The tracks were used to over-watch the bunkers as the dismounted teams went in to clear them. For approximately four hours, we searched. All enemy personnel appeared to have departed the area but had left numerous weapons and supplies.

At about 0300 hours, Lieutenant Colonel Olson told me to bring my men into TM Dawg's assembly area to allow us a couple hours of sleep, because he anticipated having to send us out later in the morning for follow-on operations. As we pulled back to TM Dawg's area, we ignited some demo we had rigged to a bunker full of mortars. A fire caused by the explosion could still be seen burning as I put my men to rest. Three hours later, we were up and at it again, only our job was easier as dawn had already begun to break.

As we were provided the light of day, the speed in which we were able to clear the objective area increased tenfold. With great initiative and aggressiveness, the soldiers in my platoon acted upon the skills that they had been taught and trained. Before we had received word to move on to our next mission, the scout platoon had taken twenty-three enemy prisoners of war, cleared one hundred plus bunkers, and captured and destroyed numerous enemy weapons and equipment.

7 | SOMALIA
(1993)

Capt. Thomas Di Tomasso, U.S. Army

*Second platoon leader of B Company, 3rd Ranger Battalion, Thomas Di Tomasso and his fellow rangers had front-row seats for the first Battle of Mogadishu (*Black Hawk Down*), as they fought through the night to save the downed pilot of Super 61 . . . and themselves.*

ON AUGUST 26, 1993, Bravo Company (B Co.), 3-75th RGR [Ranger], special mission units, and aviation assets from Task Force 1-160th AVN RGT were deployed to Mogadishu, Somalia, in support of the United Nations in Somalia II (UNOSOM II). Major General Garrison was the task force commander. Lieutenant Colonel Danny McKnight, battalion commander of 3-75th, was the senior commander from the ranger regiment in Somalia. Captain Mike Steele was the Bravo Company commander. Lieutenant Colonel Tom Matthews was the commander of Task Force 1-160. There were also some Special Forces officers (names classified) that deserve more credit than they have received for the leadership they provided and the decisions they made. These commanders and their soldiers comprised Task Force Ranger.

At the time B Company was alerted, it was participating in a joint readiness training exercise at Fort Bliss, Texas. I was the second platoon leader, and Sergeant First Class Hardy was my platoon sergeant. Around the 10th of August, Captain Steele called all the platoon leaders and platoon sergeants into the company planning tent. We were told that we were deploying to Fort Bragg to rehearse with special mission units in preparation for a real-world mission. The mission was classified, and the cover story would be an emergency deployment readiness exercise (EDRE). We were not to discuss anything about the exercise until we reached Fort Bragg.

Once established at Fort Bragg, we immediately started rehearsals. The mission of Task Force Ranger was to increase the security in Mogadishu by dismantling the high infrastructure of the Somali National Alliance. The special mission units had already developed a plan on how they would take down the targets. The rangers were to insert with, or just prior to, the assault elements, and isolate the objective. The objective was defined as the building complex or vehicle that a specific target (person) was in. Specifically, we would isolate it by preventing the crowds from influencing the assault, the targets from escaping the objective area, and any militia or armed civilians from reinforcing the objective area.

Rehearsals were long and tiring, but we were all excited about the chance of executing a real mission. This excitement was a new feeling, mixed with both adrenaline and fear. As a platoon leader, I often wondered what it would be like to take my platoon into combat, to do something real. Later, I would learn to be more careful of what I wished for.

The rules of engagement were published and studied by every ranger. Yet, there was still confusion as to who would be regarded as a noncombatant. Some Somalis were allowed to carry weapons as part of their job. The Red Cross and other humanitarian agencies hired locals to provide security against looting gangs and militia.

Task Force Ranger rehearsed several different techniques prior to deployment and eventually developed two "templates" for actions on the objective. These two templates, the strongpoint and the convoy, would be applied to any situation on the ground.

The strongpoint technique would be applied to any structure or building where there were targets. Four elements (chalks) from first and second platoons, consisting of fifteen men each, would isolate the objective block. Assault teams would clear the buildings within the block, searching specifically for certain people. Third platoon, prepositioned on vehicles, would be prepared to come forward to exfiltrate the POWs and the U.S. forces.

Primarily, the force would insert by helicopter, either landing or fast-roping. If a suitable landing zone (LZ) was found close to the objective, we would also exfiltrate by helicopter. If no LZs were found, we would plan for a ground extraction with the vehicles. Not wanting to set a pattern by primarily using helicopters, the task force also planned for vehicular ground insertions. At times, the helicopters would launch as a deception just prior to the force inserting by vehicle.

The convoy technique used the same load plan as the strongpoint. It was designed to track, stop, and capture personnel moving by foot or vehicle. Attack helicopters would stop the vehicle by deterrence or fire. Instantly, assault forces would fast-rope directly in front of and behind the target vehicle. Blocking positions would insert one hundred to two hundred meters ahead and behind the target to isolate it. This technique usually started out as a strongpoint and then developed into a convoy if the target fled the objective prior to the assault.

On August 24, 1993, the first elements of Task Force Ranger departed Fort Bragg for Mogadishu. We had been deployed from home since August 2 and regretted not having the chance to say goodbye to our families. Telephones and mail were offlimits, and when the rest of the battalion redeployed to Fort Benning from Fort Bliss, rumors had already started as to the mission of Bravo Company. "The first time I heard about rangers being sent to Somalia was on TV," stated one wife. Babies were being born, and their fathers wondered if they would ever see them. The men in the platoon were concerned about back home, but they were focused on what they had to do and why. They were rangers and knew operational security was critical to the mission's success.

Prior to loading the aircraft at Fort Bragg, I gathered the platoon together. I told the men that they would be tested and that all the training they have ever done needed to come together now. I told them that not everyone may come home alive, but they all would come home. I stressed the importance of each soldier keeping track of his ranger buddy, to prevent capture, and to always stay alert. I told them that their families would be taken care of; the only thing that mattered when they hit the ground was mission accomplishment and each other. One ranger said a prayer.

At Fort Bragg, we studied the culture and environment of Mogadishu, Somalia, as much as possible. The enemy was a combination of trained militia (urban guerrillas) and local civilians who fought for food, water, money, power, and their homes. According to the United Nations, the Somali National Alliance (SNA) militia was estimated at one thousand "regulars." The SNA officials claimed they had twelve thousand. The SNA divided Mogadishu into eighteen military sectors linked by radio, each with a duty officer on alert at all times. They had no doctrine; however, during our missions, we discovered Chinese and Vietnamese manuals on guerilla war fighting.

For the next three months, the home of Task Force Ranger would be an old aircraft hanger on the western edge of the Mogadishu Airfield. The rats inside the hangar were as big as some small dogs, and the hawks, nesting up in the rafters, provided interesting nightly entertainment as they consumed their daily meal.

The rangers quickly began fortifying the hanger by emplacing sniper positions, guard towers, and fighting positions around the immediate area. The joint operations center (JOC) was erected in a nearby building and resembled a porcupine, because of all the antennas protruding from it. Shower points and a makeshift mess hall were opened within days of our arrival.

Seven missions were conducted in the city of Mogadishu. This was the enemy's backyard. Task Force Ranger trained extensively on military operations in urban terrain, and this is what it was made for. Although we learned a lot about this type of warfare in Somalia, techniques and theories we had been using in training were validated.

The first night we were in Mogadishu, we were welcomed with three mortar rounds that wounded a few helicopter crew chiefs. There was not a thing that we could do against the indirect fire, except turn the hanger lights off. The next night we sent patrols into the city to discourage anyone from firing at the hanger. While the patrols were out, no fire came into the hanger. Second Platoon was the first unit to conduct these patrols in the city. This was our first look at the city up close. I felt safer there than in the hangar. Normally, the streets were vacant from 2200 hours to 0430 hours. However, once the local Somalis realized we were patrolling at night, they took more interest and stayed up to greet us. Most of them were happy to see us. The elders wore long beards, which they dyed red along with the rest of their hair. Among the villagers, these men were honored as the tribal chiefs, and they were the ones who talked with us.

We continued to rehearse our tasks and hone our marksmanship skills. Daily we would fly down the coast, away from the city, where it was a barren desert. We set up targets and shooting houses to practice in. We tried to train on every possible contingency. We were also able to train with actual demolition charges that we would carry on the missions. This training proved its worth during the Battle of the Black Sea, just days later.

The templates worked well after being tested under fire on seven actual missions. Between thirty-five and forty missions were planned, reaching various degrees of planning before being aborted due to unconfirmed intelligence. Major General Garrison established a strict launch criteria, which he followed for every mission.

Six missions were executed prior to October 3, three during the day and three at night. Two were convoy hits that turned into strongpoint missions. During one mission, we infiltrated by vehicle rather than helicopter. Another mission involved exfiltrating by foot, trying not to establish a pattern. Both sides took some casualties, but no one from Task Force Ranger had been killed, yet. Several militia and key leaders of the SNA were captured. The most significant was Osman Ato, captured on September 21. Mohamed Farah Aideed was quoted as saying, "Those people [Task Force Rangers] are horrible and dangerous."

On October 3, 1993, we received intelligence that two primary leaders of the clan's infrastructure were going to meet in a building near the Olympic Hotel, a known SNA headquarters. The gathering would include two tier-one targets: Osmar Salad Elmi and Mohammed Hassan Awale. Further study of the area determined that the target was right in the middle of "bad guy" country. The

Bakara Market, one mile west of the target, a known militia gathering area, provided a concealed area for distribution of weapons and munitions that were smuggled into the country. The Sheke Adere Compound, another known militia area, was one mile to the east. Intelligence reports, days prior, indicated that two hundred new militia from a foreign country had just arrived in Mogadishu, adding to the existing enemy force.

The chalk leaders were called into the JOC, and plans were discussed on how we would attack this strongpoint. As intelligence reports came in to the JOC confirming the targets, the task force, as a whole, was brought to a higher state of alert. At approximately 1523, the commander gave the order to execute the mission. The chalk leaders quickly briefed their team leaders as they loaded the helicopters. Everyone was very sharp by this time and knew exactly what he had to do on the ground. As I passed around my diagram of the objective for the rangers to study, I discussed with the pilots exactly where we needed to be inserted.

At 1533, we launched. We approached the objective from the north. As we got closer, I was again amazed at how the pilots could navigate and avoid obstacles as they "flared hard" to stop on a dime. They put us exactly where they said they would. I could hear explosions that sounded rather close, and I fought to swallow my heart again. Small-arms fire cracked overhead as the helicopter, Super 65, pulled away.

Thankfully, the blocking position was established quickly, as crowds massed to its north and east. In addition to the militia, scores of Somalis sprinted through the streets in a confused melee. Every Somali in South Mogadishu who could put his hands on a weapon seemed to press toward the battle. Staff Sergeant Yurek's team was oriented east, and Staff Sergeant Lycopolus's oriented north with

Specialist Nelson and his M60 [machine gun] crew. Both elements of Chalk 2 emplaced their chase teams, consisting of two rifleman, on the inside corners of the intersection facing the objective.

Specialist Coleman reported to me that he heard Chalk 4, Staff Sergeant Eversmann, report an urgent litter casualty. At the same time, I noticed that I could not see Staff Sergeant Eversmann's team from my position. This was a standard visual link-up that all the chalk leaders conducted to ensure that we had mutually supporting blocking positions. Staff Sergeant Eversmann reported that due to obstacles, he inserted one hundred meters short of his planned position. I immediately moved my northern team further north to attempt visual recognition with Chalk 4 and possibly assist in casualty evacuation. Here was where we got our first look at the crowd that was forming to the north. We could also see Sergeant Eversmann's team moving the casualty and manning its blocking position.

Abandoned vehicles in the street provided good cover for my men. This was critical, as several grenades came over a wall on the eastern side of the street. Some exploded; some did not. Specialist Nelson, who was looking back in my direction when the grenades came over the wall, screamed to me and pointed to the wall. Both primary teams were in contact. The only men that were available to take action were Specialist Coleman, Specialist Struzik, Staff Sergeant Lycopolus, and me. We moved across the street and stacked near the half-open gate. It all happened very fast. I took out a fragmentation grenade; pulled the pin; let the spoon go; counted one thousand, two thousand; and threw it through the gate. As soon as it exploded, we moved through the gate and scanned our sectors. We cleared the lot and captured four POWs. During this action, the code word for "targets secure" was sent over the radio.

The assault force had captured Awale, Salad Elmi, and others. All we had to do now was move to the extraction site. We had planned to move by foot and link up with the vehicles approximately two hundred meters away.

At this point, the whole operation changed. Specialist Thomas, my forward observer, was calling Super 61 to help disperse the large crowd to our north. Super 61 was a MH-60 (Black Hawk) that provided a sniper platform to aid in aerial security and surveillance. The Black Hawk was coming in from our northeast when a rocket-propelled grenade (RPG) hit it. The aircraft spiraled down and crashed approximately four hundred meters away. Specialist Thomas, seeing the whole thing, yelled to Specialist Coleman, who, in turn, told me that a "bird had gone down."

By this time, Staff Sergeant Yurek had come over to my position. I told him to keep his team at the blocking position. I took Specialist Nelson's M60 team and Staff Sergeant Lycopolus's team, a total of eight men, and started moving towards the crash site. As we started running, I noticed that the crowd to our north had also seen the crash. They were paralleling our movement with the same intent: to get to the crash site first. Specialist Coleman called the company commander during the movement and told him what we were doing.

It seemed like every window and door had a weapon firing from it. As we made the last turn, I was shocked to see that an AH-6, a Little Bird, had landed in the street just behind the downed helicopter. Bullets were popping off the walls and ground from every direction. As I stumbled over two dead bodies, I could see one pilot firing his weapon from inside the cockpit, while steadying the aircraft with one hand on the joystick. He looked right at me as I tapped the top of my head, questioning the headcount. He shook his head no. I then knew there were more casualties. Simultaneously, the other pilot was trying to load two friendly casualties into the rear compartment of the AH-6 helicopter. As I ran around the tail, the Little Bird strained to lift off in a hail of gunfire and RPG explosions. One of those casualties died en route to the hospital.

Through the concealment of the rotor-wash, I moved across the street to the downed helicopter. Specialist Nelson immediately positioned his team facing north to keep the crowd that had rounded the corner from overwhelming the crash site. I told Staff Sergeant Lycopolus to secure the northeastern side, at the same time directing Staff Sergeant Yurek to come to the crash site. There was constant firing going on. I could not hear myself scream. There were several Somalis already climbing on the helicopter. Once they saw us, they decided to leave. Kneeling beside me, Specialist Coleman was struck in the left earflap of his helmet with an AK-47 round. It knocked him flat on his back. I thought he was dead. Luckily, he jumped back up after a few seconds and assured me that he was okay. Specialist Coleman continued to demonstrate exceptional physical stamina and mental courage, never removing the twenty-seven-pound radio from his back.

A crew chief was stumbling around with his hands over his face. Specialist Coleman tackled him and tried to keep him out of the line of fire. I moved to a corner to position Staff Sergeant Yurek's team as it came around the corner. All of a sudden, I could not breathe or see anything due to intense rotor-wash and brown-out. The combat search and rescue (CSAR) helicopter, Super 68, hovered just overhead, inserting its teams, consisting of Special Forces medics and ranger security elements. This CSAR team was developed for such a contingency, and I was very happy to see them. However, as the teams fast-roped to the ground, an RPG hit the tail of the helicopter. The pilot naturally lurched the bird up and away but instantly remembered that there were men still on the rope. He miraculously settled the aircraft down to hover again until the last soldier was off the rope. The crew chiefs cut the ropes, and the chopper limped back to the airfield. Machine-gun fire strafed Super 68 constantly until it left the area.

As the CSAR teams started treating the casualties from the crash, I linked up and positioned Staff Sergeant Yurek's team on the southwestern side of the crash. I also sent Specialist Gould's M60 crew, that traveled with Staff Sergeant Yurek, to the northeast with Staff Sergeant Lycopolus.

For the ninety U.S. soldiers consolidating near the helicopter, Freedom Road and the adjoining alley had become a killing zone. AK-47 bullets flew overhead with a loud pop, punctuated by the shriek of RPGs. As the teams fought to keep the crowds back, target identification was becoming a problem. There were combatants mixed in the crowds of noncombatants. Women and children were screaming and running at us from all directions. Some of them had weapons, and some did not. The weapons ranged from machine guns to small knives and machetes. Some men were standing near the corners of the buildings; they looked like they were noncombatants, just observing the action. Unknown to us, another man, hiding around the corner, would reload a weapon and hand it to the man that was in sight. The man at the corner would fire the weapons as fast as he could, hand it back to the loader, and just smile and wave his hands at us.

Women would walk in front of the men, acting as human shields. The man would fire his weapon from behind and under the armpits of the woman as they both walked towards us. The soldiers did not know what to do at first. Some soldiers yelled across the streets at me, asking what to do. Small children had weapons. Sometimes, they were more of a threat because they had no fear.

The CSAR team was trying to stabilize the casualties and protect them from further injury by the gunfire. Sergeant John Bellman was using the Kevlar floorboards from inside the helicopters as makeshift walls to protect the medics and casualties; however the 7.62 bullets were passing right through them. The CSAR team commander informed me that one of the pilots, killed during the crash, was trapped inside the helicopter.

When the helicopter crashed, it made a large hole in the side of the building directly southeast of where it landed. The decision was made to try to move the casualties inside the building for better protection. Both Specialist Coleman and the radio man from the CSAR element were trying to get vehicles from the ground force up to the crash site for evacuation, but the vehicles never made it. Some were ambushed en route, and others just could not make their way through the maze of the streets. The lightly armored HMMWV [high-mobility multipurpose wheeled vehicle, or Humvee] was not that well protected against several volleys of RPG hits.

Every time someone tried to pick up a litter, he drew fire. It was as if the enemy could see our every move. One soldier and I tried to pick up one end of a litter when a bullet pierced through the soldier's right rear hip, knocking him over. The decision was made that we would wait until dark to move the casualties inside the building.

It felt like hours just lying there, waiting for the darkness. The teams had settled into good positions and were successfully keeping the crowds away from us. It was during this time that Specialist Coleman told me Super 64, CWO3 Durant's helicopter, had gone down. I wondered to myself if the rest of the task force could get to Super 64. All of us knew exactly who Super 64 was. I realized we would be here for a while.

Directly northwest of the downed helicopter, on the other side of the wall, people were throwing hand grenades onto the helicopter. Some exploded; some did not. The RPG shots never seemed to slow down: the enemy knew that we were around the craft, and if they shot at the craft, they would hit us. They were right; all of us around the immediate area of the crash received shrapnel wounds.

When darkness fell, we immediately started moving the casualties into the building. The litter patients went first, then the walking wounded, and then the dead. Once we were inside the building, the next problem was finding a way out that would not expose us to fire. Specialist Lamb and some of my team members cleared the rest of the building in reconnaissance of a safe evacuation route. The compound we were in was actually two different homesteads separated by a wall within the compound. With the recommendation of Specialist Lamb, I directed Staff Sergeant Yurek's team to blow a hole through the wall to create our own route. We believed if we could get into this next building, there would be an exit on the other side. We were right. The demolition charges made a perfect hole to carry the casualties through, and there was a gate on the far side of the building where we could pull up vehicles. All we had to do now was wait for the vehicles.

We still had to provide security for the aircraft, while two-man teams continued to saw through the fuselage to free the pilot. The squadron commander and the other officers, virtually without debate and with universal acquiescence, decided that this comrade would not fall into enemy hands. At the crash site, that decision had already been made, to the very last man.

The attack helicopters (AH-6) executed continuous fire missions to provide aerial security around the crash site. They were our eyes and ears. Throughout the night, the pilots would call my forward observer with reports of "ten or fifteen gunman, running toward your position from the north, stand by." These brave pilots logged a record of eighteen hours of flight. In teams of two, they would rotate to the airfield, rearm/refuel, and return to continue the mission. As they flew overhead, firing, the hot brass would burn our necks as it rained down from above. While the AH-6s worked, a Black Hawk dropped medical supplies, ammunition, and cans of water to the men below. Most of the one hundred task force soldiers had been wounded.

As my RTO tried to keep track of 3rd Platoon, the vehicle convoy, the medics continued to sustain the wounded. We ran out of morphine and decided to save our last intravenous solution bag (IV) for the first casualty that slipped into shock. We had given all our water to the casualties or had consumed it, and the men were showing signs of severe dehydration.

Specialist Lamb found a water spigot in the courtyard. We used our purification tablets and passed around the canteen. I was unsure about drinking it, fearing the risk of disease, but we all critically needed water.

The firing had calmed down to just sporadic skirmishes. Once in a while, a few gunmen would attempt to run down the street at us, but we were ready and had the AH-6s on call. I could hear in the distance the sound of .50-caliber machine-gun fire. This was the rest of the ground force trying to break through the roadblocks to get to us. I wondered how long it would take them.

The casualties were very brave, refraining from crying out in pain or making too much noise. It was very dark inside the rooms. If any of us used any type of light, he would be shot at. After the first couple of times, we learned that we were still being observed by gunmen. Total nonmission capable casualties at the site were thirteen: two KIA, three litter urgent, and eight walking wounded. Between the CSAR element and Chalk 2, we did not have enough men to carry the casualties and secure the crash site at the same time. We were not going to leave the crash site without the trapped pilot.

At around 0400, October 4, two Malaysian APCs [armored personal carriers] drove by the intersection that we were observing. I ran out after the vehicles with Sergeant John Bellman and backed them up as close to the gate as we could get them. I had never seen these vehicles up close before and had to search for the door. Once we found the door, it would not open; it was locked from the inside to prevent unwanted passengers from entering the vehicle. The Malaysian driver and track commander were the only soldiers aboard, and they were not about to leave their stations to open the hatch. After some yelling and banging on the windshield with my rifle butt, they understood that we could not get the doors open.

The vehicles were a welcome sight; however, they also attracted gunfire. The worst part was that the seats were still in place, and there was no room for three litters. We could only fit one litter casualty in the APC at a time. The walking wounded had to stand around the litter, hanging onto whatever they could on the inside. We also put one of the KIA up on top of the APC.

The second APC carried the next-most-critical litter casualty and the rest of the walking wounded. We still had one litter casualty and the one trapped KIA pilot. I looked out across the intersection and saw a Humvee pulling security to the west. I ran over and told the crew that we had a litter casualty that needed to be evacuated. They drove the Humvee over to the gate and jettisoned everything that they had in the back to fit the casualty. They also gave us some life-saving water.

With all of the casualties evacuated, we could now concentrate on the trapped pilot. At one point, a 10th Mountain Division Humvee was used to try to pull the aircraft away from the body. At around 0405, the sun started to come up, and it was time to make a decision to how much longer we could stay in position and survive.

Finally, the medics freed the pilot, and he was put on a Humvee to be brought back to the airfield. It was now time to exfiltrate. We placed demolition charges and incendiary grenades on the helicopter to destroy any remaining equipment that we could not take with us. As we moved across the street to link up with the rest of the company, I could hear the explosions and see the black smoke rising above the helicopter where friends had died.

It was good to see familiar faces. Larry Perino, 1st Platoon Leader, was a close friend, and I had listened on the radio as he reported the status of one of his team leaders who was mortally wounded. Captain Steele briefed us that we would have to move by foot to National Street, approximately two miles away. From there we would link up with Malaysian and Pakistani armored vehicles, Humvees from the 10th Mountain Division, and our ground force, Third Platoon.

Everyone was exhausted. Lieutenant Perino's platoon, Chalks 1 and 3, would lead the run out; my Chalk 2 would pull rear security. Chalk 4, the other element of my platoon, had exfiltrated back to the airfield on a Humvee, after numerous attempts to link up with me at the crash site.

Chalks 1 and 3 (First Platoon) split their forces on either side of the road. I did not have enough men, so we all stayed close together and on the same side. I can remember how tired everyone looked and how I felt. As we came to major intersections, I watched rangers summon all their energy to sprint across the intersection. Bullets strafed the streets, kicking dirt around their feet. When it was my turn to cross, I backed up two or three paces to get a running start. The man in front of me, Specialist Strous, our company medic, had just been hit in the ammo pouch of his pistol belt. The bullet ignited a smoke grenade, ultimately burning his leg. He was able to recover the bullet that lodged in his pistol belt and now wears it around his neck for good luck. Another bullet passed through the empty canteen and canteen cup of another ranger.

Luckily, my rangers and I made the run relatively uninjured and now awaited our turn to load a Malaysian APC or U.S. Humvee at the link-up point on National Street. After a seemingly endless cramped ride in the back of a Humvee, we arrived at the Pakistani stadium. The Pakistanis had converted an old athletic stadium into their headquarters. When I looked around, I could see bodies lying everywhere—wounded comrades from Pakistan and Malaysia, but mostly American friends. It was here that I learned of the death of one of my team leaders, Sgt. Casey Joyce. He was killed moving with Chalk 4, trying to get to the crash site after the team had evacuated Private Blackburn. Blackburn had been severely injured during the insertion. All my emotions and fatigue came together in a slap of reality.

As I continued to walk around the stadium, visiting with the other wounded, I saw several foreign soldiers filming the dead and wounded with a home video camera. I can remember getting very angry and trying to take the cameras away. I thought it very unprofessional and indecent to film what was going on. They eventually stopped filming.

I eventually returned to the airfield, where another medical team was working on lots of casualties. It was a MASH unit. It seemed to be doing a great job prepping the wounded for the flight to a German hospital. Second Platoon sustained eight wounded in action that were evacuated to hospitals in Germany and one killed in action. All returned home to the United States.

There have been many after-action reports and "armchair quarterbacking" about the mission. Task Force Ranger had accomplished what it had set out to do, snaring two-dozen key members of Aideed's staff. We learned many lessons about urban warfare, and leaders are already incorporating them into future training. I learned more than I can express about the human dimension of warfare. The training that we are conducting today in our army works. As an army officer, I am fortunate to have witnessed the essence of infantry training: shoot, move, and communicate. I am also one of the most unfortunate army officers, having felt the weight of a dead American warrior in my arms.

Eighteen U.S. soldiers were killed and eighty-four wounded. Somali leaders say they had 312 killed and 814 wounded.

When the president or Congress tells a soldier to go and do a mission, the soldier accepts it and will do everything in his power to accomplish that mission.

The hours of fighting contained the most intense combat by U.S. infantrymen since Vietnam, with consequences that immediately altered U.S. policy toward Somalia and are likely to shape American involvement in future foreign entanglements.

On January 18, 1994, the last eight Somali prisoners in U.N. custody were released. These included three of Aideed's lieutenants,

Osmar Salad Elmi, and Mohamed Hassan Awale, captured by Task Force Ranger on October 3, 1993, and Osman Ato, captured in mid-September. On January 20, these men gathered with hundreds of other Somalis at the parade grounds on Via Lenin in a boisterous rally to celebrate their newfound freedom.

Capt. Charles P. Ferry, U.S. Army

Task Force Ranger wasn't the only American unit involved in the first Battle of Mogadishu. On the night of October 3, 1993, infantry company executive officer (XO) Charles Perry of the 10th Mountain Division found himself in the unexpected position of riding into battle with his soldiers—as light infantry, they're used to walking— inside Malaysian armored personnel carriers to rescue the rangers trapped inside the city.

WHEN THE UNITED STATES first entered Somalia in December 1992 to facilitate the delivery of humanitarian aid, combat incidents were rare and, when they did happen, were on a small scale. After turning this mission over to the United Nations force in Somalia (UNOSOM II), the United States left approximately six thousand of its soldiers to ensure that the U.N. operations could continue without interruption.

The only U.S. combat force in the country was the quick reaction force (QRF), made up of one light infantry battalion, one attack and assault helicopter battalion, and a brigade headquarters. The first to assume the QRF infantry battalion's duties was the 2nd Battalion, 87th Infantry, 10th Mountain Division (Light), followed by a sister battalion, the 1st Battalion, 22nd Infantry.

In June and July 1993, UNOSOM II became more aggressive and, after a Pakistani unit was badly ambushed, decided to try to disarm the opposing clan factions in Somalia. In July, the 1st

241

Battalion, 22nd Infantry, conducted several cordon and search operations in Mogadishu and a raid on the Abdi House, which received a lot of news media attention.

On August 1 my unit, 2nd Battalion, 14th Infantry, also of the 10th Division, assumed the QRF mission. I was XO of Company A.

On the first night in our university compound, we were attacked by 60mm mortar fire, and two soldiers from a nearby logistical unit were wounded. This was just a taste of things to come. During August and September, the battalion conducted numerous operations, raids, attacks to clear, cordon and search, convoy security, rescue of downed helicopters, and it reinforced other units engaged with Somali guerrillas under the control of Gen. Farah Aideed.

By the end of September, every company had been involved in several sustained firefights with the enemy and had also taken casualties. Our compound continued to be attacked by mortars, rocket-propelled grenades (RPGs), and small-arms fire at least every four or five days. Although the battalion never sustained any casualties from these attacks on the compound, neighboring units did.

When the U.N. intensified the hunt for General Aideed in late August, the United States sent a unit of special operations forces specifically equipped to conduct fast raids and prisoner recoveries. The task force, called TF Ranger, consisted of a company of rangers, a contingent of assault and attack helicopters, and other elements. Our battalion was assigned a liaison from the task force, and our company conducted rehearsals with the rangers to prepare for contingencies in which our assistance might be needed. The least expected of these contingencies called for us to reinforce TF Ranger in the event it was in danger of being overwhelmed, but that is the one the battalion was called upon to execute on October 3–4, 1993.

For my company, this was a nine-hour battle in which we fought our way in to the surrounded rangers, evacuated all the casualties, and fought back out the following morning under continuous enemy fire.

During the battle, eigtheen U.S. soldiers were killed and more than seventy-seven were wounded. Two companies (plus) from our battalion and one company-sized element from TF Ranger more than held their own against incredible odds. We were literally surrounded, engaged in a pitched battle at night, in the heart of Aideed's guerrilla stronghold. According to intelligence reports received several days later, more than three hundred Somalis were killed that night, and another seven hundred or more were wounded.

From September 30 through October 2, Company A conducted close-quarters battle live fires at an old Soviet military base on the outskirts of Mogadishu. The company's morale was high as a result of an operation a few days earlier in which we conducted a successful predawn raid on a confirmed mortar launching site. During our exfiltration, we became engaged in a fifteen-minute firefight and successfully withdrew under pressure to a nearby U.N. compound. Several detainees from that raid provided a wealth of information for future operations. This was one of several combat operations in which the company proved itself under fire. We were confident in our abilities and had no doubt that we would soon see combat action again.

On October 2 we received word to be prepared to move by helicopter from our training site to the Mogadishu airport. A coordinated U.N. operation was planned in which units from Pakistan, Malaysia, and other nations were to conduct simultaneous missions to retake several previously abandoned checkpoints throughout the city. The battalion expected to be called upon to assist and had made contingency plans to enable it to react quickly. The U.N. mission was cancelled, however, and we continued our training, returning to the university compound around 1000 on October 3.

As soon as we arrived at the compound, the company began recovery procedures. It was standing operating procedure (SOP) to conduct maintenance and redistribute ammunition, so we could react quickly if alerted, even when we were not currently the QRC for the battalion. (The QRC normally had up to thirty minutes to roll out of the compound on a quick-reaction mission, although it was often faster than that. The other two rifle companies had an hour to be prepared to move, but were often able to do it in fifteen minutes).

I supervised recovery operations and by 1500 was able to lie down for a short nap. Around 1630 I was awakened by one of the company radio-telephone operators (RTOs) and was told that Company C had just gone to alert status and was preparing to move out. When my company commander and I went over to the battalion tactical operations center (TOC) to see what was going on, we were told that TF Ranger was in the middle of an operation and might need assistance. It was obvious by the concerned look on the face of our ranger liaison, listening intently to his radio with a set of headphones, that something was not right.

I suggested to the commander that we grab some chow now, because I had a feeling Company A would also be alerted soon. We had just sat down in the mess hall when a runner from the battalion TOC told everyone that the company was to go to RedCon-1; that is, bring the company to full alert and be prepared to roll out the gate as soon as possible. We left the mess hall and headed back to the company area.

While the company commander went back to the TOC, I supervised the issue of additional ammunition and special equipment in accordance with our rehearsed SOP. (All soldiers in the company normally kept their personal basic loads of ammunition and grenades and received AT4s, LAWs, demolitions, and the like upon going to RedCon-1.) This took ten or fifteen minutes. The first sergeant assembled the platoons and ensured that precombat inspections were made, while I went to the TOC to be briefed and to get guidance on how to configure the company for movement and learn what attachments it might receive. Depending on the mission, sometimes we would either walk to an objective or ride on trucks. We would normally receive an engineer squad, a forward medical treatment team (FMTT), a psychological operations (PSYOPs) team, and a military police platoon, if we were the QRF company. Since we were the second company in line this time, I wasn't sure what attachments the battalion had in mind.

As I walked over to the TOC, Company C and the battalion tactical command post (TAC) moved out on HMMWVs (high-mobility, multipurpose wheeled vehicles, or Humvees) and five-ton trucks. When I linked up with my commander in the TOC, he could tell me only that a helicopter had been shot down and the rangers might be in trouble. A week earlier, a 10th Mountain Division UH-60 Black Hawk helicopter had been shot down, and Company C had engaged in a two- or three- hour firefight to recover the crew and equipment, taking several casualties. The commander just told me to get the company lined up and ready to move.

I assembled the first sergeant and the platoon leaders and passed the information. Then I directed the platoons to take some time to make a more thorough precombat inspection and to request more ammunition or special equipment if they wanted it. I also told them that I thought it looked like we would be going out.

The first sergeant and I reviewed what other tasks we needed to accomplish before the commander returned. We agreed to plus-up our contingency load of ammunition (usually at least one-half extra basic load for the company), which was normally carried on my Humvee. We then made a company communication check, and I told my communications chief to monitor the battalion command net to find out what was going on. The first sergeant and I then began getting the company Humvees and five-ton trucks lined up in the SOP order of movement. By now, we had received as attachments our usual engineer squad and medical treatment team, which included the battalion surgeon.

The commander soon joined me where I had the orders group gathered. He briefed essentially the same thing he had told me earlier and said we were going to move the company near the gate entrance to the compound and be prepared to reinforce Company C if needed. By 1700 the company was lined up, and we waited. Like many of our previous QRF missions, we had little information and, once we moved out on a mission, could only recheck our equipment and rely on rehearsed SOPs and battle drills.

It was late afternoon, the sun was beginning to fade, and we could hear heavy small-arms and rocket fire in the distance. On the battalion command net, it soon became apparent that Company C was engaged in a stiff firefight and had sustained several casualties. The battalion TAC, consisting of two Humvees, was with Company C, and—judging by what we were hearing on the radio and the tracer rounds and explosions we were seeing in the city—it was obvious that something big was happening. The company commander, listening intently on the radio, tracked the battle on the map, expecting at any moment to be ordered to reinforce Company C.

Company B was also ready to move and standing by in its company area. The battalion scout platoon, the combat trains, and the PSYOPs element were lined up behind our company, also preparing to move. It was almost dark. I was concerned about sitting at the gate in the open—the compound had been shelled several times over the previous month by 60mm mortar fire, and I hoped we wouldn't be hit now.

The situation was becoming clearer: Company C had been tasked to link up with the ranger ground reaction force (GRF) platoon that was attempting to break through to a downed helicopter. The ranger platoon had been unable to break through after being badly ambushed, losing one or two vehicles and suffering several casualties. Company C had managed to effect a link-up but was now also in heavy contact and taking casualties of its own. Company C was ordered to withdraw to the Mogadishu airport, which was near the engagement. It was apparent that neither the ranger GRF platoon nor Company C was going to be able to fight through to the crash site.

We still did not know the full situation of the rangers on the ground. (By now, in fact, two helicopters had been shot down in the Bakara Market area in the heart of General Aideed's guerrilla enclave. A third helicopter had been hit but had limped back to the airport. A company-size element of TF Ranger was surrounded and fighting for their lives, taking heavy casualties.) When the engaged elements were ordered to withdraw to the airfield, my company commander called for instructions. We were told to stand by, and a minute later to stand down, but to be able to be recalled to move in five minutes. Five minutes later, we heard the battalion commander order his XO to move the rest of the battalion to the airfield as soon as possible and be prepared to conduct further combat operations.

The battalion XO radioed instructions to both remaining rifle companies and support elements, breaking us up by convoy serials ten minutes apart. Our convoy of about fifteen Humvees and five-ton trucks moved first, with the battalion scout platoon following. We moved along the main supply route, which was a roundabout way to get to the airfield, but a secure one. It took the company about forty-five minutes to get there, driving blacked out with night vision goggles.

When we arrived at the airfield at 2030 hours, the company commander reported to the battalion commander to receive instructions. Company A was lined up behind numerous vehicles from Company C and TF Ranger in what was almost a traffic jam. The company commander returned a minute later and told me a company-sized element of TF Ranger was surrounded in the Bakara Market area, had taken a lot of casualties, and was in danger of being overrun. We were to move behind Company C and the rangers to the New Port and prepare to mount another attack to break through. Company A would lead the battalion attack.

Knowing the rangers' situation, it seemed to take forever to move the two kilometers from the airfield to the New Port. After thirty minutes, the task force had moved and was now staged on a large parking lot next to the loading docks. About two dozen white, Malaysian Condor armored personnel carriers (APCs) were lined up waiting for us.

The company commander returned from the attack order and told me to hand out every bit of extra ammunition I had on my truck, essentially doubling everyone's basic load. After about ten minutes, the orders group gathered around the commander's map, and he briefed the plan in about five minutes under a flashlight.

The company was task organized as follows: 1st Platoon had the mortar and fire support squad, a medic, and three APCs; 2nd Platoon had the engineer squad, a medic, and three APCs; 3rd Platoon had a medic and two APCs. Under company control were the FMTT, with the frontline ambulance (FLA) and surgeon, a Pakistani tank platoon (four T-55s), and one company Humvee.

The Somali guerrillas completely controlled all areas outside the U.N. compounds during the hours of darkness. In the Bakara Market area, Aideed had as many as two thousand guerrilla fighters and a sympathetic populace as well. They were armed with a mix of Soviet bloc and NATO assault rifles, machine guns, RPG-7s, mines, and demolitions. In past firefights we had been in, the Somali guerrillas had proved to be aggressive and bold, even in the face of tremendous firepower. They were capable of operating in fire team– and squad-size elements and of coordinating the movement and actions of larger elements. They always seemed to know when we were coming, and on which routes, and built hasty obstacles to try to slow our mounted movement. They were fighting in their own backyard and knew it well.

The enemy on the northern helicopter crash site (crash site #1) surrounded a company-sized element of TF Ranger. They had taken twenty to twenty-five casualties and were in danger of being overcome. The situation at a southern helicopter crash site (crash site #2) was unknown, and there had been no communications with that site for several hours.

A task force had been put together at the New Port to make the rescue attempt under the command of our battalion commander. It consisted of Companies A and C with Company B in reserve; the battalion antiarmor platoon, the scout platoon, and an attached antiarmor platoon from the 1st Battalion, 87th Infantry, of TF 2-14 Infantry; the TF Ranger GRF platoon (six armored Humvees); fourteen to sixteen Malaysian APCs (with drivers and track commanders only); and four Pakistani T-55 tanks. Supporting the task force were 10th Mountain Division Cobras and other attack helicopters.

Company A was to attack to break through and link up with the besieged rangers at the northern crash site to recover all American casualties. The concept of the operation was simple. The company would ride on the Malaysian APCs, attack mounted as far as possible, and break through to TF Ranger. Once on the crash site, we would load the casualties onto the APCs and fight back out to a secure U.N. compound. The order of movement to the objective would be tanks, commander, [and] 1st and 3rd Platoons, followed by the Humvee FLA [frontline ambulance] and the rest of the battalion.

The company commander made sure we all understood that we would not come back without all American dead and wounded. As was usual for combat missions, I back-briefed him on the complete plan, order of movement, and contingencies, to make sure I knew what to do if he should become a casualty. He decided to take his Humvee with its two powerful radios for command and control, despite the fact that he and his RTOs would be more susceptible to enemy fire in it. (This later proved to be a good decision.) I was to move at the rear of the last platoon, in one of the Humvees of the attached platoon, so that I could better see to navigate along the attack route.

While the company commander went to make final coordination with the Pakistani tank platoon leader and the Malaysian company commander, I supervised getting the platoons loaded on the APCs. The Malaysian soldiers did not speak English but showed us how the APC weapons and doors worked. Being light infantrymen, none of us were accustomed to riding inside an armored vehicle, but it seemed like the way to go, considering the enemy situation and the importance of moving quickly.

The company was ready to move by 2145. I found the company commander, who seemed to be negotiating with the Pakistani tank commander about the route. Both the Malaysians and the Pakistanis had U.S. liaison officers with them, but neither officer seemed to be able to influence what their units would do. It seemed that the tank commander had been ordered to go only about half-way to the objective, and that did not support the plan. The issue finally seemed to be resolved, however, and we prepared to move out.

It took a few more minutes to get the lead tank platoon to move. A sharp exchange over the radio between the company commander, the battalion commander, and the Pakistani liaison officer eventually did the trick. About 2200, the rescue column began to move north along the designated route toward National Street.

The city was very dark, and the street we were on ran west and then turned north again. For a while it was as quiet as our vehicles moved toward National Street. The battalion command net was heavy with traffic, and my RTO kept me informed. The anticipation of enemy contact was agonizing. Every alley and building was a potential Somali ambush position. The lead element of the company made the turn onto National Street and headed west. I made the turn and reported to the company commander.

Suddenly, near the head of the column, red streams of enemy fire erupted from both sides of the street, and the familiar sound of incoming small arms and RPG fire broke the silence. Almost simultaneously, return fire was concentrated on several buildings and alleys. After about two minutes or so, the firing died down, and we continued to move. After moving several more blocks, the entire company came under fire. Small-arms fire whizzed over my Humvee, and an RPG round exploded near the vehicle in front of me. Everyone in the column was firing into every building and alley that could be used as an enemy firing point.

I had stepped out of the Humvee, crouching for cover, trying to monitor the company and battalion nets. The sound of small-arms fire mixed with enemy RPG, friendly Mk 19 automatic grenade launchers, and M203 round explosions was deafening. My RTO yelled that he saw some Somalis and started firing down an alley. I turned, spotting the running men, and also engaged them. They disappeared into the darkness. Not knowing whether we hit them, I returned to the company net and called the company commander to try and get guidance on what he wanted. I recommended that the company dismount and fight forward on foot, since I felt that the APCs were attracting the heavy RPG fire and was concerned that entire squads might be destroyed inside them. But the company commander said the battalion commander's orders were to fight mounted as far as we could. (He was absolutely right, because the APCs were crucial to our task of evacuating the wounded once we had linked up with TF Ranger.)

The columns started moving again under steady enemy fire. I called all the platoon leaders to remind them to exercise fire discipline, because we did not want to run out of ammunition. Communications with the platoons were not very good, because they were inside the APCs and their radios were not transmitting well, but all three acknowledged.

The column kept moving and stopping. Along with the commander and First Sergeant, 2nd Platoon had dismounted to clear several obstacles. I again asked the commander if we could dismount, and his RTO said, "Negative." The Pakistani tank platoon was now nowhere in sight, and I didn't see them again until the next morning (apparently, they had been ordered to go only so far on National Street and not to advance any farther.)

The column again stopped five or six blocks short of the turn toward the Olympic Hotel. The two lead APCs, with the 2nd Platoon leader, one of his squads, and an engineer team, were separated from the company. The platoon leader had been unable to get his Malaysian driver either to make the correct turn or to stop. The two lead APCs continued down National Street past the intersection where the company was supposed to turn north and continued out of sight of the company commander. The commander repeatedly tried to contact him by radio without success. This element was now separated from the company and out of communications, and we would not hear from them again until early on the morning of the 4th.

After being separated and taking a wrong turn to the south, their vehicles were stopped and ambushed. Both vehicles were hit by multiple RPG rounds. The lead APC was set on fire, killing one Malaysian and wounding two soldiers of 2nd Platoon. Just after they dismounted the APC, it was destroyed by coordinated RPG fire. The platoon leader ordered his surrounded element into a nearby building—after blowing a breach point into it with a large satchel charge from the engineers. For the next several hours, they fought for their lives until Company C finally linked up with them.

The company commander now decided he must continue the mission instead of trying to recover the two lead squads. When the new lead APC halted at another obstacle and enemy fire intensified, the commander decided to dismount. The rest of 2nd Platoon, under the leadership of the platoon sergeant, was already clearing the obstacle by hand while one squad with its M60 machine gunner laid down suppressive fire. I got off my Humvee and moved up the company column, pounding on the APCs to get 1st and 3rd Platoons to dismount, and then directed them up toward the lead element of the company. Enemy fire was still flying everywhere, but the soldiers moved quickly along both sides of the street. Squads moved across alleys and streets by having one fire team lay down suppressive fire while the other bounded across.

We were now by the main intersection of National Street and the street Olympic Hotel was on. The company was stretched out about three city blocks on both sides, with the APCs in the middle. I made my way to the commander to get an idea of what he wanted. He said we would continue to fight into the northern crash site, but that he was having a hard time getting the Malaysian APCs to move under fire. I moved back to tell the leaders of 1st and 3rd Platoons what we were going to do and to push the rest of the company forward.

The company again started to advance, attacking toward the Olympic Hotel (the original objective of TF Ranger several hours earlier). We had no direct communication with the APCs; so I had to move into the street several times to pound on them and motion them forward. They were buttoned up, making it difficult to get their attention or to direct the fires of their heavy machine guns, which they were not firing. I ran back to the attached antitank platoon, which was still firing to the south and north along National Street, and told the platoon leader that my company had started to make the right turn up to the north and they needed to watch their fires, especially the Mk 19 that was pounding some nearby buildings from which they had taken fire. After cautioning him to maintain control of his fires and watch his ammunition, I moved back toward the front of the company, by now three or four city blocks up the street.

Laboring heavily under the weight of the AN/PRC-77 with his ear to the hand mike, my radio operator kept me updated on what battalion was saying and constantly reminded me to stay out of the street.

When I made the turn back north, the company was stopped, with a lot of incoming and outgoing fire. So I wouldn't be mistaken for a Somali, I yelled, "XO coming through," and moved up past 3rd Platoon, which was hunkered down on both sides of the street. A destroyed U.S. five-ton truck was still smoldering in the middle of the street. Both 1st and 2nd Platoons were taking and returning a large amount of small-arms fire from the Olympic Hotel and nearby buildings and alleys. One APC was up next to the lead platoon. The M60 gunner was mortally wounded, and two other soldiers were hit and yelling for a medic. The battalion surgeon, the first sergeant, and two soldiers from 1st Platoon moved into the intersection under fire to give them aid. Nearby, soldiers laid down heavy suppressive fire until the casualties could be pulled into the relative safety of a depression next to a building.

The commander was pinned down with 1st Platoon. There was bad crossfire from the hotel and several buildings. Despite the efforts of the liaison officer, the lead Malaysian APC refused to move, effectively stopping the company's progress. The company was only five or six blocks from TF Ranger and having a hard time pinpointing which street we should take to make a link-up. (Our maps often did not match up with the ground, and it was difficult to find intersections, especially at night.) The commander moved into the street to make the lead APC move and wanted me to call battalion to get a better fix on where the rangers were.

I moved back to where the casualties were being cared for under cover and called the battalion commander on the radio. I gave him a brief situation report and our casualty status, and told him we were having difficulty getting a fix on the rangers' position. He said to continue to push to link up, and he would get the ranger liaison, who was with him, to notify the surrounded element that we were nearby and have them ensure that their infrared strobe lights were on (the link-up signal). The company commander then came on the radio to give the battalion commander a more detailed report.

The company was still pinned down, and the commander told me to get a Humvee with a Mk 19 up to the front of the company. I left my RTO with the casualties and moved back along the column, carrying an AN/PRC-126 squad radio on the company net anyway.

Three or four blocks back through the company, on National Street, I found a Mk 19 Humvee near the front of the column, the squad leader coolly directing the fires of his Mk 19 gunner. I told him we needed his firepower and to inform his platoon leader I was taking him. Enemy fire was still intense, and there was still heavy friendly fire all along National Street where the battalion TAC, the antiarmor platoon, and the scouts were. We worked our way back through the company, the Mk 19 Humvee following me. It was having a hard time getting by the APCs, and I had to ground-guide it up on the sidewalk several times.

We finally reached the front of the company where the lead APC was stopped and learned that the fire was coming from the large hotel on the left side of the street, about fifty meters to the front of the lead platoon. I guided the Mk 19 Humvee up onto a steep sidewalk so the gunner could get an effective shot and told him to watch my M16 tracer rounds and to work the building from top to bottom. I fired several tracers into the hotel; he fired a spotting round into one of the top-story windows and then fired the grenade launcher on automatic, hitting every single window in the building. The effects were devastating. Concrete fragments flew everywhere, and one or two Somalis fell out of the building.

When the gunner ceased fire, I asked the lead man again where the fire was coming from now. He said it was from the right side of the road. I made sure I could see our lead man on the right side and directed Mk 19 fires onto a building about forty meters in front of him. I felt that if we could start attacking forward again, the APCs would follow.

I crossed to the left side of the road where the lead man was and told him we were going to continue the attack. I moved to the front of the platoon and forward about a block. The platoon then stopped and directed fires onto the opposite side of the street to cover the lead squad, which now bounded forward. Both squads had fired and maneuvered forward about a block, and I moved back to the casualty collection point.

The battalion surgeon had stabilized the two wounded soldiers at the CCP [casualty collection point], behind 1st Platoon in a small depression next to a building. I had my RTO turn his radio to the battalion administration/logistics net, so I could make a casualty report and coordinate a medevac. The battalion XO wanted to send a ground medevac forward from the New Port, but I asked him to stand by. I knew an aerial medevac would be destroyed and a ground medevac would almost certainly be ambushed. I also felt there might be more urgent casualties soon and didn't want to waste the asset yet; the surgeon said he could keep the casualties stable for at least several hours. I called the battalion XO and told him I wanted to keep the casualties with us.

As the company was advancing toward the embattled rangers, 3rd Platoon had moved up next to the CCP. 1st Platoon had taken the lead of the company and was eliminating sniper positions as it neared the rangers' position. The company's senior medic brought the Humvee FLA forward, and we loaded the wounded soldiers onto it while 3rd Platoon poured suppressive fire down the alleys to cover us. By the time we had finished, the entire company had passed us.

I told the FLA driver and the commander's Humvee driver to stay with the antiarmor platoon near National Street and then led the FMTT and my RTO to catch up with the company several blocks in front of us. We moved at double time past several alleys, from which we received sporadic small-arms fire, and in a short time linked up with the company again.

The lead elements of 1st Platoon made contact with the rangers around 0030 hours. The company commander linked up with the TF Ranger commander to coordinate the recovery of casualties. The first sergeant, the platoon leaders, and I met with the commander to get instructions on how he wanted the company deployed. Our company commander continued to direct the operation, while the ranger commander concentrated his efforts on his casualties.

The situation on the objective was well under control. The TF Ranger soldiers were consolidated in two or three buildings with security, while more than twenty wounded and three or four dead soldiers were being kept inside. The Black Hawk helicopter was just outside the perimeter on the east side, crushed inbetween two buildings, with the dead pilot trapped inside. We were still receiving small-arms and RPG fire, but as long as we stayed out of the intersections, we were fine. The special operations soldiers were understandably tired and short of water and ammunition. They seemed happy to see us, and we were happy to see them as well.

The company commander and the platoon leaders quickly deployed the company into a perimeter around TF Ranger. I went to one of the buildings to coordinate with the medics for the loading of their casualties onto the APCs. Inaccurate small-arms fire was still coming in, with an occasional RPG round landing near the APCs; the APCs were attracting most of the enemy fire now. I had to go into the street numerous times to bang on the driver's periscope to get his attention and then guide him forward. Eventually, we got two APCs into the perimeter and next to one of the buildings, where the medics began to load the casualties. I talked with several soldiers to find out how many wounded they had and where they were, so I could move other APCs into position.

Out in the street, another of our soldiers was wounded by RPG rounds fired from a nearby building, and a minute later, without warning, an attack helicopter hit the building with 20mm cannon and 2.75-inch rocket fire. I thought the helicopter was firing on our position until I saw the tracers hitting the building only fifty meters north of our position. The expended shell casings dropped into the perimeter. I told the officer who was controlling the air strike to warn us next time. I had never been so close to an air strike, and all of us were plenty scared. For the next several hours, aircraft continued to fire all around our position, thirty-five to sixty meters from us.

I continued guiding the APCs around. As one was filled, another one moved up to receive casualties. While the casualties were being loaded, several TF Ranger soldiers and one of our squads moved to the helicopter crash site to try to extricate the body of the pilot. One of the soldiers had a power saw for just such a purpose. Meanwhile, four or five other APCs were filled with dead and wounded. By 0330 all casualties were loaded, about twenty wounded and three or four dead.

During this time, small-arms and RPG fire continued to come into the company position. At one point the Somalis fired hand-held illumination flares, and shortly afterward, we received several mortar rounds in the perimeter, wounding one soldier. Enemy fire would build, two or three RPG rounds would be launched into our position, followed by heavy outgoing suppressive fire and attack helicopter strikes; then things would quiet down for a few minutes. This cycle continued until morning. Three more men from the company were wounded, stabilized, and loaded with the other wounded.

On the south side of the perimeter, we began receiving heavy machine-gun fire, most of it two or three feet over our heads. The commander, the first sergeant, and I had been running from position to position through the night, checking the perimeter and reassuring the soldiers. The incoming fire was from the south, mostly machine-gun and sporadic RPG fire that was landing about a block away. No one was firing back because the fire was ineffective, and we knew we had friendly units (Company C and the battalion TAC) to our south. At first I thought it was friendly fire, but battalion assured us that no friendly fire unit was firing to the north. The commander repeated his previous instructions to engage only well-identified targets to the south. The 2nd Platoon showed tremendous fire discipline, engaging only a few targets, and about half an hour later, the fire died down a bit.

Meanwhile, the team trying to extricate the dead pilot from the Black Hawk was not making much progress. The power saw was taking too long, and one of the Delta operators asked if we had a cable. We did not, but I remembered that armored vehicles usually have tow cables. I found one mounted on the driver's side of an APC, pulled it off with the help of my RTO, and gave it to the recovery team. They took the Mk 19 Humvee and the cable and pulled the aircraft apart one piece at a time, while the rest of the team provided covering fire (the Black Hawk was still attracting Somali gunfire). The rest of the company and the rangers stayed in the perimeter, awaiting word to move out.

At 0500 the recovery team was still trying to recover the pilot. We all knew that once the sun came up, it would be difficult to fight our way back out, but we knew we couldn't leave without the dead pilot. By now, the company commander and the ranger commander were war-gaming how we would fight back out. The APCs we had ridden on earlier were now full of wounded, the sun would negate our night-vision advantage, and it was more than three kilometers through the city to the nearest U.N. compound.

The battalion commander put an end to the discussion by ordering us to exfiltrate back to National Street by the same route we had come in on. The street was secured by the TAC, the scout and antiarmor platoons, the ranger GRF platoon, and some Malaysian APCs and Pakistani tanks. It was the only road that would really allow the movement of the APCs and tanks; many of the side streets were too narrow.

By 0600 the pilot's body had been recovered and placed on the Mk 19 Humvee. The order of march back to National Street would be 3rd Platoon, 1st platoon, 2nd Platoon, and then TF Ranger. The APCs would travel in the middle of the formation.

The sun was now up, and 3rd Platoon began to move out quickly. The commander moved behind them, and the first sergeant and I picked up the trail of the company, with the rangers behind us. Although I was not told so, I felt it was my responsibility as company XO to ensure that not only my own company was cleared off the objective but also the sixty or so of TF Ranger who were still effective.

As soon as the company began to move, heavy small-arms and RPG fire erupted on all sides. Squads and platoons bounded by fire and movement, laying down heavy suppressive fire, while elements sprinted across alleys. Several Somali gunmen were shot and killed at almost point-blank range by the lead element. The Somalis seemed to know we were making a break for it and were giving us all they could.

The company was now spread out along a distance of four or five city blocks, firing and maneuvering at a fast pace. In the tight confines of the streets and alleys, the incoming and outgoing fire was deafening. The commander directed Cobra gunship strikes along both sides of the road to cover our movement and to suppress heavy fire from the Olympic Hotel. Several more soldiers hit by small-arms fire were quickly treated and put on a nearby APC. The Malaysian APC machine gunners were now spraying the second and third floors of surrounding buildings. The lead platoon of the company was now moving so fast that 2nd Platoon and the ranger soldiers were falling behind. Several times, other leaders and I had to run into the street to get the Malaysian APCs moving again.

As my RTO and I neared the hotel, an RPG round exploded several feet behind me. A few moments later, my RTO was hit by a bullet through the arm; its force spun him around and knocked him down. Although bleeding, he picked up his M16, and the first sergeant applied an ace bandage on the move.

I returned my attention to the TF Ranger element that was beginning to break contact with us. They were visibly tired, having to double-time and fight, and many of them were walking wounded. I moved back to encourage them to keep up and continued to bang on the APCs to keep them moving. Now intermingled with the TF Ranger element, I maneuvered with them, trying to make sure everyone stayed together.

The rest of Company A had now reached National Street, and the commander told everyone to get on a vehicle any way they could. When the ranger element and I reached the intersection that turned onto National Street, it was receiving heavy automatic fire from two directions. Several rangers and I laid heavy suppressive fire down both streets while the rest of the element rushed past onto National. We then ran to catch up with the company.

We linked up with the rest of the battalion, and there was still a lot of fire, both incoming and outgoing, especially near the rear of the column at the intersection we had just passed. I grabbed an antiarmor platoon machine gunner and told him where to direct his fires to cover us while we loaded onto vehicles. While the TF Ranger soldiers loaded, I double-timed forward to let the commander know we were clear of the objective. I ran past several alleys and had to be careful as many solders were firing off the vehicles; I had to run up behind a vehicle to get their attention before running past.

I eventually came upon the TAC, with the battalion commander, the sergeant major, and the battalion S-3. I told the battalion commander we were cleared of the objective and asked if he would relay that information to the company commander. (I had failed to retrieve my battalion net radio when the RTO was hit, and my small squad radio on company net was not reaching the commander.)

I jumped onto a vehicle loaded with the scout platoon, whose leader had one radio on the battalion net. Then I heard the division commander, in a command-and-control helicopter overhead, tell the battalion commander that several special operations soldiers were still making their way to National Street. I couldn't believe it; I thought we had everyone. I jumped off the vehicle and ran to the rear of the formation, where I could see two Pakistani T-55 tanks and two M113 APCs moving fast to catch up to the column. Behind them, six or seven soldiers were running as fast as they could under fire to catch the vehicles. But the APCs didn't stop.

I ran up to two armored TF Ranger Humvees and sent them back to retrieve the soldiers. I jumped in back with the rangers, and the Humvees moved backwards four hundred to five hundred meters toward the intersection that was receiving heavy fire. Over our heads in the back, the .50-caliber machine guns fired, suppressing both sides of the road for the running soldiers (and nearly blowing out our eardrums). Once we were near the intersection, the Humvees stopped, and I jumped out to help the soldiers get onto the vehicles. Small-arms fire buzzed all around us, and for a few moments, we were badly exposed. Both Humvees were so full that there was no room for me, so I jumped onto the hood of the front vehicle and hung on for my life as we sped to catch up to the column. Soldiers in the back fired at every alley, taking no chances of being hit.

Soon we were with the column, and I jumped off and ran forward through the convoy to find a safer ride and a vehicle with a battalion net radio, so I could tell the company and battalion commanders that the last element was out. I found the S-2's vehicle and jumped on. My message was relayed, and we finally began moving east along National Street toward the Pakistani compound (in an athletic stadium). Sporadic fire was still coming in, and everyone in the vehicles suppressed alleys and intersections as they passed.

Finally, the firing began to die down as we neared the stadium. When the convoy pulled into the safety of the compound, I breathed a sign of relief. I dismounted the vehicle I was on and moved back to make sure the casualties were being unloaded. Then I moved inside the stadium to find my company. I was physically and mentally exhausted, dripping with sweat, and my cargo pockets bulged with empty M16 magazines. I had fired more than eight magazines and had three left that I had reloaded from the first sergeant's extra bandolier.

Inside the stadium, dozens of wounded soldiers were spread out, going through triage with medics and doctors. Medevac helicopters continued to fly in and out with wounded. I found the company commander and the first sergeant, who looked as tired as I did. Then I found my RTO on a stretcher, awaiting his turn for medevac. He was going to be fine.

Several hours later, the company was airlifted back to the university compound, and per SOP, we began recovery and prepared to go out again if we were called.

The mission to relieve the rangers and recover all the dead and wounded was a complete success for the company. In all, Company A's casualties were one killed in action, one died of wounds, and fifteen wounded in action. Numerous other soldiers had minor injuries.

Despite these casualties, the company as a whole felt proud of accomplishing the mission under very tough combat conditions.

We had fought our way in, retrieved all American soldiers, and fought back out again, essentially according to plan. In about four days, after a full recovery and a memorial service for our dead, the company was prepared for, and expected, further combat operations. A cease-fire had been declared, however, and we had only minor enemy contact until we left Somalia in December.

8 | OPERATION IRAQI FREEDOM
(2003–2004)

Maj. Robert "Todd" Sloan Brown, U.S. Army

With the ten-year-old lessons of Mogadishu still fresh in the minds of young mechanized infantry company commanders like Todd Brown, he and his soldiers are able to tackle the dangerous streets of Samarra and learn a few new lessons of urban combat to pass down to soldiers of tomorrow.

THE RUINS OF SAMARRA [IRAQ 2003] date to the twelfth century. The minaret, coliseum, and mosque were built during the reigns of the tenth and eleventh caliphs, whose remains are in the mosque. This makes the city a huge tourist (terrorist) site for Shiite Muslims. Although they represent 5 percent of the population, their buildings represent 100 percent of anything worth saving culturally. With twenty-one large tribes, the locals are fighting one another as much as they are fighting you. Legend has it that Saddam Hussein did not attempt to subdue Samarra, rather to just buy it off. This makes sense when you note the parity in relative wealth of the city, the Wild West attitude, and general anti-Western and anti-Semitic ideals. While 5 percent of the city actively opposes you, 90 percent of the city dislikes you, and 5 percent of the city sees an opportunity to get Western dollars, power, and support.

The youth look very militaristic and fit. The Arnold Schwarzenegger gym speaks volumes to their tough-guy bravado and fighting spirit. Their general desire to fistfight with you when you attempt to detain them perplexed me initially, and we were forced to play "hacky sack" (get in a fistfight) with more than one of the guys we simply wanted to question. The physical aspects of the city demonstrate the classic urban sprawl discussed in army field manuals. The old part of the city has a very European flavor to it with regard to alleyways, shops, random turns, and a general lack of traffic organization, as it came into being prior to the automobile. As you move out of the downtown sections of Market Street and Zone 7, you find a street pattern developing that supports vehicular movement and the street movement techniques we found useful.

Our company's urban movement evolved throughout our Iraqi experience, but the classic Mogadishu lessons learned never rang more true for me than in the streets of Samarra. The alleyways, rooftops, crowds, and multitude of different buildings and shops create a nightmare of keyhole shots and in-your-face engagements that tanks and Brads [Bradley infantry fighting vehicles] just aren't designed for. We knew and understood this going in. You have to walk the streets, and the infantry must get out front. Brads scan deep and look at rooftops, while the infantry covers doors, windows, and alleyways. When in contact, the Brads move forward to suppress and provide cover for the infantry to move across the streets and down the alleys. The infantry moves out front, continually working its sectors and soft-clearing everything. The guys must know: gun in every door and every window; rooftops, long security; right side cover; left side high and deep (and vice versa); Rolling T; high-low clearance of alleys; travel off the walls to avoid bullet corridors; clear cars; and always know exactly where the next piece of cover will come from. Everything you see in the street can also see you and subsequently engage you. Moving down the streets is an exhausting exercise in paranoia, and the men figure it out real quick with the rocket-propelled grenade (RPG) and small-arms attacks as a teaching mechanism. We never had issues with clearing rooms: we trained at our shoot house quite extensively, and everyone knew their role in clearing a room inside and out. However, you fight and die in the streets—all the leaders knew and understood that. The safest place in Samarra is entering a building and clearing a room on a planned raid late at night.

Our first night in Samarra, my 2nd Platoon came back to me from being attached to A/1-66 AR. We still had responsibility for manning the southern OP [observation post] to protect FOB [forward operating base] Stoddard. They would travel down with a tank section going to another blocking position while the rest of the company got settled into the foot-deep moon dust of FOB Daniels. They traveled on Route Rattler and took RPG fire on the south side of Zone 9. A quick map check will show you that the enemy uses interior lines on that route. They spot you coming around the north side, drive to the south side, and set up their RPG ambushes.

It took us getting ambushed on the north side with the enemy using their TTP [tactics, techniques, and procedures] in reverse to figure this out. I didn't claim to be smart, just trainable; stupid does hurt. The initial volley had two RPGs. The unit attempted to regain contact with the infantry and tanks. The Brads pushed out a little ways when the platoon leader (First Lieutenant Jiminez) and his gunner (Hansen) identified an RPG firer aiming and firing. They engaged with 25mm HE (high explosive) in a classic shootout. The RPG missed. The platoon leader did not. We had a terrorist split in half with a smoking RPG launcher in his hand. I sent a platoon down there with a tank section, since we didn't know the city and it was night. My Blue Platoon detained seven bad guys who had all suffered injuries in the shootout. The Alpha tank company commander, Captain Deponai, was with the tanks and directed the fight; we were just guns for hire. This proved our only multiple RPG shootout, although they had a plethora of multiple RPG contacts prior to our arrival. While we did engage victoriously, I think we were a bit hesitant to start shooting without a known target.

Observer-controllers and commanders will beat you up on live-fire ranges for the "noise-ex" and collateral damage. However, it's necessary to start shooting here to save Americans—even at inanimate objects if you don't have definitive targets. It throws the enemy off balance, so they flee the scene after a single shot, or they do something incredibly suicidal. The reason for returning fire immediately is twofold. The "donk" of the RPG terrifies and freezes trained professional soldiers from the company commander down to the new private, and you must get them moving again with confidence in their weapons. Second, our firepower against bush-league terrorists terrorizes them much more than their donk does us. I continually give my gunner inanimate objects, mitigating collateral damage, to shoot if we take contact in a given area. One can argue the hearts-and-minds campaign all day on this point; but they will lose, especially among those of us who have been donked. Firepower breeds fear in the enemy and local populace. Samarra will never like you, so they must fear you. Fear coupled with our general target discrimination and efforts to limit collateral damage, associated with just being American soldiers, will breed respect, and that's the best you can hope for here. Bottom line: return fire immediately, even if it's out into an open trash field. It will throw the enemy off and continually remind the populace that we will fight. I know it works, because human intelligence reporting skyrocketed after our most violent contacts. I am not trying to justify my TTP or violent responses. It is war—get used to it.

Our early-day presence patrols proved uneventful. We always rolled ten Brads deep with the associated infantry on the ground clearing forward. I figured mass coupled with seeing the infantry on the ground would deter any attack. It did for a while. We went on the offensive with an operation called Industry Clean Up, in which the company seized fourteen caches and filled up five five-ton trucks–worth of improvised explosive devices (IEDs), RPGs, mortars, small arms, ammunition, etc. I thought we had them on the run and scared of us. We got out into the town and walked, talking to the locals and passing out candy to the kids. No worries.

The next night we were coming back on Route Rattler south-to-north when my internal commo went out. I had created an eight-hundred-meter break in contact by the time I got the XO briefed on my troubles and my wingman came forward to guide us back. The enemy, thinking the vehicle in front of me was the last vehicle, engaged it. This quickly turned into a real bad Reserve Officer Training Corps/Ranger School leadership lane: you can't talk to anyone, your new platoon leader is getting shot at, and you have a giant gap in your formation. Take action, cadet! We really didn't have a good fix on what happened, and I got to the scene after the fighting took place. Fortunately, the platoon leader knew to dismount and assault. The infantry engaged a vehicle, but it escaped.

That night we discovered the ephemeral nature of contact in the city and the necessity for immediate application of controlled violence. I also learned that rolling ten deep didn't make us immune, maybe if we had infantry on the ground. We'll start working a section of the city each night en route back from the OP gun run. We were all very frustrated at the nature of the elusive enemy and our inability to regain contact, especially the commander, whose sole situational awareness due to commo problems was the donk. We must have infantry on the ground in the places we are most likely to make contact, but it's a commander's call where that is going to happen. You can't walk the entire city every night.

The day patrols proved uneventful. It's Dr. Jekyll and Mr. Hyde, seemingly. This OP in the south is really starting to aggravate me because of the numerous mine strikes in areas we return to, but we have to keep Stoddard safe from the mortars. Unfortunately, there are only so many places you can go down by the river. I decide to walk Market Street on the way back from the gun-run OP insertion. This is my first night not rolling a tank section with the Brads. We dismount the infantry and start walking the street. The Brads are targets when they move this slowly, but we rely on the infantry to protect them down here. My 2nd Platoon leader points out the building where he received eight RPGs one morning. It's a bad neighborhood. My wingman and I are the lead Brads, which isn't a good spot for the commander, so I start moving a platoon to assume the lead.

As they move forward . . . Donk! Crack! Crack! Crack! The RPG flies by just like a hot roman candle—you instinctively stare at it while it cruises by your head with the rush of heat—and the AK-47s crack down the street. The sound and "pretty" light paralyze you. My first instinct is to jump off the track and assault dismounted, since I treat the Bradley like a big Humvee; however, I fight that urge and start yelling for everyone to open up on where they think the contact came from. My gunner starts shooting an abandoned shed in the completely wrong direction, so I take control of the gun and point him in the right direction, and we lay down a huge base of fire with the infantry and Brads on the area where the enemy fired. We hit a transformer with one of the ricochets, causing a huge light show. The lead squad calls it up as an IED, so we have a little confusion. We move to cordon off the area and get the infantry moving down the right alley. Bingo, we nab their getaway car with seven RPGs and launchers in it. The Brads cordon off the alley, and we start clearing houses. The locals tell me about the incident . . . vast improvement in cooperation since we started shooting. Of course, they will report to the Civil-Military Operations Center (CMOC) tomorrow and file an outrageous claim, but I am willing to trade money for information. I was certain we had casualties, with the amount of contact we had and seeing the infantrymen knocked off their feet from the blast. However, we were all knocked around, shaken, but complete. What a command and control nightmare.

That night the RPG roared down the street, everyone had the opportunity to see it go by and learn the initial terror and paralysis that we all experience with contact. It seems like forever before you regain your wits and react. In reality, we were firing before the secondary explosion of the RPG. Our efforts proved fruitful, as we got the opportunity to "disable" a terrorist car and police up seven RPGs and a bad guy's sandal. Launch Operation Cinderella! Our reaction must be a battle drill. Return fire and seek cover. Know that close urban contact is straight-up terrifying and confusing, so junior leaders must move rapidly and break the seal on the live fire. Otherwise, you just have a company commander's Bradley shooting at an abandoned "enemy" shed because he's pissed off. We also learned that the bad guys are scared and make their own JV mistakes under fire, so shoot.

I realized that you don't have to roll Market Street, Elm Street, or 60th Street to make contact. Those are the most populated, densely packed areas in the city. We continue to roll en masse but along the more open urban areas like 50th Street and Rattler. I have come to the conclusion [that] they will come to you, so make contact on your terms. Build your engagement area. I know rolling the same routes makes you susceptible to IEDs, but there isn't an area in the city from which we haven't taken IEDs or RPGs. That's a known risk and one you mitigate by driving name-tape defilade or lower (keeping the Bradley commanders low in the turret to avoid their taking shrapnel; it limits your situational awareness but prevents you from getting killed). I want to force them out of the alleyways and engage them on the periphery of the city. We start working 50th Street extensively, with the infantry clearing while the Brads move with the field to their backs. It works well, and we load the infantry in the Brads for the easy trip up through Zone 2.

Donk. Contact south. Boom. Trail tank is hit and smoking. "Shit!" We start moving south to secure the tank and gain contact with the enemy. No one saw the contact except for the trail tank. Fortunately, the smoke we see is a combination of Halon bottles and RPG remnants. They return fire with the coax out into the open field, and we get everyone on line and just mow it. Cease fire! Scan for heat signatures. I finally get the report from the tankers, and they come up on company net: superficial damage, and they shot hot spots out in the field. I don't have time to look for bodies tonight. We've been downtown too long, so I call off the chase. The nice thing about 7.62mm is that they have to check into the hospital, and we can find them that way. Tonight confirmed that they hunt us, too. You get ambushed . . . where you are, . . . so always build your engagement area and choose where you make contact wisely.

I couldn't believe they would shoot at us from the field. Not a good move on their part, and they suffered the consequences. The confusion of having a vehicle hit doubles the chaos with returning fire. That, coupled with the southern OP, made fire control difficult tonight, but we had good crosstalk with our OP, who was actually able to walk us onto the RPG flash while the tankers got their breath back after the halon. The key to fighting these guys is to be everywhere at once with standoff and redundant, interlocking fields of fire. I should have had infantry with the trail vehicle and more people scanning south into the field. . . . It doesn't always come from the alleys. These contacts are like *Defense of Duffers Drift* (a book in which a commander fights the same engagement over and over again, improving each time), always revamping our tactics. We deal with a tenacious enemy, not a particularly smart one.

The daylight patrols enable us to see the city and press the flesh while working our street movement. To succeed, everyone can't just know exactly what they must do—they must know exactly what they must do, exactly what their buddies must do, and exactly what everyone else is doing. We start spreading out during the day with multiple clearance axes that can rapidly move to mutually support infantry out front. We clear some alleys and start moving south on Elm Street. Crack! Crack! Crack! We are shooting. I am fifty feet back and see my lead squad shooting up the street at a target I can't see. It looks like they are playing around, shooting at coke cans or something, because they are so calm and moving so smoothly. We got a man in a white man-dress attempting to engage us from the rear with an RPG as we turn on Elm Sweet. We are dictating the contact. Get the Brads out in the road, and let's start moving. I jump down and join in the dismounted hunt. We bounce around some rooftops and do some top-down clearing. You've got to love leading a stack down a stairwell and freezing down the terrified occupants of the house with under-gun lights.

We find a cache of five AK-47s hidden in an abandoned house with lots of ammunition. They hide their stuff in abandoned houses and side stores. Rarely will you find anything in their homes. You must search all stores and abandoned houses. We didn't tag the guy, but the action was on our terms. Classic example of decide, act, and report. Specialist Villegas was pulling north security as the Brads made the turn, saw the enemy, and opened up. His team leader moved to him with the SAW (squad automatic weapon) gunner, and they built a base of fire, while the squad leader bounded his other team. The platoon leader gets the Brads in the hunt, and it's a chase; he reports to the commander, who could have just taken the day off—the platoons are on it.

Shooting from alternate firing positions at ranges greater than 150 meters under that stress is difficult. We work our marksmanship program extensively and shoot daily at our FOB, but sometimes you just miss. The real triumph and lesson learned of the contact was that the army gave you the weapon and the authority to use it, and we are getting that point across. Specialist Villegas saved a Bradley from an ass shot by his aggressive attitude and his flawless application of decide, act, and report, and tanks and Brads are not standing up to the RPGs as briefed. We have plenty of holes in both to tell otherwise. Leaders can't withhold the authority to engage. Privates and specialists must have and feel they have the authority to shoot bad guys immediately.

It's our first daylight engagement. However, we have fixed-site security for the banks tomorrow, which is a definite way to get shot. No Americans in the Sunni Triangle should ever pull fixed-site security now that we have the police and Iraqi Civil Defense Corps (ICDC) standing up. You just become a target. Our fears proved correct, as my platoon guarding the Samarra Bank took a keyhole shot, and we couldn't regain contact. Get out of the fixed-site security. Way too dangerous. That night we worked Route Rattler using a new technique. We split into multiple sectors with the Brads, tanks pushed out to the east covering the movement with a lot more standoff, and we hit the entire route with the platoons moving independently. No one shot at us. Amazing. I definitely advocate using that method of clearance, and sometimes you just avoid routes that limit your ability to fight.

We performed pretty much the exact same maneuver the next morning in daylight along the southern portion of the city. We found a guy burying AK-47s—their national crop—and stopped to detain him with one of the platoons. This caused us to sit on the limit of advance a bit longer than desired, and we knew it would come; but we had good standoff with the infantry in the streets pulling security. The terrorist came out and shot at Staff Sergeant Dewolf, who scanned over and shot the guy on the back of the motorcycle. He fell off, but his buddy threw him across the back prior to running the infantry gauntlet that just riddled them. The velocity of our rounds is such that they go right through the vehicles, causing minimal damage and allowing them to keep rolling unless you punch up HE; but we don't do that with infantry on the ground in the city. They will come to you. Choose your positions wisely. We detained numerous individuals after that action and then moved back to the CMOC.

Donk! A classic keyhole shot on our ride back to the CMOC. All the Brads actioned immediately, and we grabbed a motorcyclist in the alleyway attempting to flee. All bikes within a square kilometer are working together to shoot at you, so you need to detain them all. Our actions couldn't have been faster, but sometimes you don't catch them red-handed; you have to relentlessly pursue and have defined battle drills and good crosstalk. During an alleyway shot, the engaged Brad continues to move out of the alleyway and calls up the contact direction. Then all elements action down different alleyways in the direction of the contact to cut off the enemy and detain anyone suspicious. They shot between the XO's track and mine (at the XO), and we actioned right north of the contact, while the trail platoon moved in the alleyway of the contact and the two alleyways to the south. The tougher the shot they take, the safer you are. However, it makes it easier for them to get away.

Our final day in Samarra would involve daylight presence patrols in Zone 6. We wanted an easy day. We dropped off the infantry, and the men immediately found a huge cache of demolitions, RPGs, rounds, and small arms. We had to call for a five-ton truck to police up all the equipment. We kept the Brads out on the open ground, while the locals uploaded the equipment. I am all about local employment opportunities. The infantry caught all the shop owners as they attempted to flee and physically convinced them to work on uploading all their weapons onto the American five-ton before we took them downtown to the intelligence teams.

We continued to clear all the shops on Albino Street and to work the area for more intelligence. The five-tons arrived and uploaded the gear. Donk! We all dove into the shop and prayed the RPG didn't hit all that demolition—it's a four-foot cube of C4, blasting caps, dynamite, and det cord. We hear coax firing before the next boom, ending the RPG flight of terror. We run out to see Blue Platoon's Bradleys mowing down an alleyway where the cloud of smoke from the RPG lingers. The Civil War charge across the field starts. The XO and I get a little out front running and look back to make sure the infantry is moving. Yes, we have learned to march to the sound of the guns, and quickly. All of Blue's Brads disappear into the alleyway, and our Bradleys catch up to us out in the field. . . . I hated running the 400-meter in track. The breathless crosstalk starts, and the infantry moves to shut down the road while the Brads flush out the prey. [It's a] different dynamic than the Brads cordoning while the infantry flushes, but we adapt our tactics on the fly.

We have a destroyed car, and there are numerous blood trails at the scene. We start following those until we have contact back out on the main road with a black BMW attempting to engage our infantry. Bad choice. The M240 gunner steps into the street and fires a burst from the hip right into the car as it speeds by. The infantry squads unload on the guy, and we maintain the chase, with the Brads following the gas trail. BMW makes a car that can really take a beating. My XO finishes it off with coax as it turns into a back alley. It has dead guys in the vehicle, but the driver got away . . . in real bad shape, [as we could tell] from the blood trail and the bone fragments left in the car. About this time we get the secondary reports on our wounded soldier. Second Lieutenant Tumlinson took shrapnel to the calf. Sergeant First Class Tetu, the platoon sergeant, rolls a section to medevac him down to Stoddard, and I let battalion handle the aircraft while we continue the hunt.

The headquarters guys are all moving down the back alleyways on the blood trail using most of the proper techniques for urban movement. Everyone needs to know street movement. Our little squad has my dismounted radio telephone operator, Cutuca; the XO, Jimmy Bevens; fire support officer, Rick Frank; FSNCO (forward support noncommissioned officer), Staff Sergeant Kerns; Q36 radar chief, Albreche; the commander; and a random infantryman from the back of the track that came with us. We place a barrel in every orifice, soft-clear the cars, Rolling T down the alleys, high-low the corners, scroll to the road on linear danger areas . . . keep moving, look deep, and watch rooftops, windows, and doors—eyes always moving. The blood trail dies. He must have gotten in a car. We clear a couple of buildings, but these guys are like the Viet Cong with policing up their wounded and dead. I know the future donk is coming, so we load up and move back to the FOB. We fought them on our terms today. You always know when they are pissed, because they mortar you when you get back. They were pissed but fired only three rounds. . . . They must have an ammunition shortage. I hope we put a dent in things. That is the lowest incoming mortar count yet.

Maj. Mark Leslie, U.S. Army

An already seasoned soldier with ten years of enlisted service preceding his graduation from officer candidate school (OCS), Mark Leslie also had two company-level commands under his belt when he was selected to be an advisor to the Iraqi National Guard (ING), a challenging and dangerous assignment that this man of action welcomed as saving him from the tedium of a rear echelon staff job.

I entered the army at age seventeen in 1987 and served in a variety of units at Fort Bragg, North Carolina. These included the 2/504th

PIR of the 82nd Airborne Division, E Troop, 1/17th CAV; the 82nd Airborne Division Long Range Surveillance Troop (LRST), XVIII Airborne Corps Long Range Surveillance Company; and [I served] as a Mountain Ranger instructor in Dahlonega, Georgia. I was fortunate enough to be a part of Operation Just Cause (the invasion of Panama, 1989) and Desert Storm (1991). While a ranger instructor, I applied for and was selected to attend officer candidate school and was commissioned in 1997.

Eventually I commanded A Company, 2nd Battalion, 7th Cavalry, 1st Cavalry Division. This company was deployed in support of Operation Enduring Freedom. I was then selected to command headquarters and Company, 2nd Battalion, 7th Cavalry, 1st Cavalry Division. We were deployed to Operation Iraqi Freedom II (OIF II). While commander of this company, I performed many different roles; one of the most important was that of our task force Iraqi National Guard (ING) advisor. Initially this was only a part-time function, but once I changed command, it became a full-time job, which I was happy to have.

Upon change of command, my battalion commander, Lt. Col. James Rainey, informed me that I would not be leaving the battalion. Instead, I was to remain as the full-time ING senior advisor. This was a welcome relief to me, as I did not relish the thought of leaving the field for staff work on the battalion staff. The tradeoff was that I was to live with the Iraqis full time, with a small volunteer detachment, in the Iraqi Patrol Base. We were at Camp Taji, north of Baghdad, and our base, Patrol Base Animal, was about thirteen kilometers north of that along Highway 1 and was a target of constant attacks.

The ING advisors were to be all volunteers. This turned out to be the easy part. My noncommissioned officer in charge (NCOIC), the best noncommissioned officer (NCO) in the battalion, Master Sgt. Steven Vigil, started scouring the task force for volunteers. Although the companies were told to support with a minimum number of soldiers, we wanted volunteers for this duty due to the highly unconventional nature of the mission. We were lucky in that I had commanded two companies, and many of the senior NCOs had worked for me in the past. We were fortunate enough to have a majority of staff sergeants, sergeants first class, sergeants, and a few specialists to fill our small advisory detachment of sixteen men and four Humvees. We asked for and got a medic. Due to the number of contacts that we made and the limited amount of medical support available to the Iraqis, this was eventually increased to two medics. We also had three interpreters, an unusually high number, but absolutely mission essential for our duty.

The Iraqis we were advising were a part of the ING Battalion at Camp Taji, but were significantly larger than a normal company about five hundred on the books. This was due mainly to the tribal relationship of the Iraqi chain of command and the fact that this company maintained a separate permanent patrol base outside of U.S. presence. I think it is conservative to say that about half of the company . . . [were] active insurgents and another quarter passive insurgents. About a quarter of the Iraqi troops we felt we could trust, but very few that would actually protect us if it came down to it. The commander, Lt. Col. Muhammed Waleed, was a staunch if not rather orthodox commander, more warlord in nature than military. He and his small personal security detachment (PSD) were the only ones we felt we could actually trust no matter what. We had developed a very close and personal working relationship with him over the past seven months, and it had paid off in the form of caches discovered and insurgents captured.

On October 19, 2004, we were conducting payday activities for our Iraqi company. This was a very dangerous situation, as we had to have all Iraqis there and had to transport the money to Patrol Base Animal in order to pay them. We rarely had enough troops to conduct combat operations in force, but on paydays they came from everywhere. We did not like to advertise the fact that it would be payday, as this always seemed to draw attacks in the form of either indirect mortar fire or improvised explosive devices (IEDs) and small-arms harassment, but it was an unavoidable situation.

We showed up to Patrol Base Animal early in the morning with the payroll, and once we rolled into the gate, we were greeted with two distinct, separate groups of Iraqis. There was obviously some sort of tribal conflict going on. As we dismounted the vehicles, Lieutenant Colonel Waleed approached me and took me and my security element to a group of Iraqis. The rest of my men proceeded to take up their normal security positions. My Humvee did not move to the position I occupied on previous occasions due to a group of Iraqis occupying that spot.

As we approached the mob of Iraqi soldiers, we could sense the tension in the air and the friction. After several minutes of heated debate, I was still unable to make sense of the situation, and the crowd was becoming more and more frustrated, as was my translator. One of Lieutenant Colonel Waleed's bodyguards then leveled his weapon at the other group and charged it. My men and I were suddenly in the center of a situation of an angry, volatile mob. The other group quickly leveled weapons at the Waleed group, with us in the middle.

One of my NCOs quickly attempted to disarm the Iraqi from the Waleed group to diffuse the situation. We wanted to avoid any direct confrontation, and this particular bodyguard was one that we trusted and assumed he was less likely than the other to engage us with deadly force. While they were disarming him, the other group moved in closer. I and my security, American and Iraqi, told them in Arabic to back away and lower their weapons. They became more aggressive, and suddenly someone fired a round in the air and screamed in Arabic, followed by hundreds of other voices screaming at us in Arabic. I immediately pumped my shotgun and fired three rounds in the air, telling my translator that the next step by anyone would be their last. There was immediate silence, and a sense of order prevailed upon the camp.

Sensing an opening in the mob, I and my security started making our way through the crowd toward our only building. The U.S. and Iraqi NCOs seized the opportunity and immediately started to diffuse the situation by having them line up in formation for payday. As my security and I walked towards the building, a large explosion went off in the middle of a formation that had not been part of the previous madness, immediately killing and wounding the majority of the platoon. This was the exact spot that I had parked my Humvee on many previous occasions.

The Iraqis went crazy running in every direction. There were several bunkers scattered throughout the compound that we had constructed in the event this happened, and they were quickly full. My advisors quickly and professionally moved into their security positions as eleven more rounds continued to rain down on the patrol base. One crew of advisors quickly moved their vehicle to the front gate to prevent a potential attack on the gate, and other advisors moved to the roof of our two-story building to occupy the observation platform. This was all part of our preplanned contingency plan that we had developed for a situation such as this.

The advisors that moved the vehicle to the front gate were quickly met by small-arms fire coming from the northwest across Highway 1, the approximate point of origin of the mortar fire. The small-arms fire was inaccurate and seemed to be from beyond effective range. It was more of an annoyance than a real threat. Once at the front gate, a badly damaged ING truck approached, and one of the officers my soldiers were familiar with dismounted, screaming ambush. He was en route from a location to the north and had two trucks, but had been hit by an IED approximately the same time the mortar attack started. He had several men killed and wounded, and they were in the truck. Once my advisors were sure the truck was clear, they admitted it in the gate.

As the rounds poured in, the concrete "Scud bunkers" that we had scrounged from Camp Taji quickly filled with cowering Iraqis. There were literally dozens of Iraqi soldiers lying throughout the compound, injured or killed. My advisors braved the continued indirect fire of the insurgents and the scattered small-arms fire from terrified Iraqi soldiers firing at nothing to drag them to safety and begin treatment on them as best they could.

My team medic, Sergeant Pico, was attempting to get into the aid station inside our two-story building, as apparently the officer with the key was either absent, cowering, wounded, or dead. He finally managed to kick the door open and set up shop. We had to keep the aid station door locked to keep it from being plundered by our own Iraqi soldiers when we left on missions or went back to get food or fuel. Aid station is a loose term, as it did not mirror in any way what the U.S. soldiers called an aid station: dirty, no running water, and limited medical supplies made it austere at best. But it did have two litter stands that he could [use to] work on patients. Doc Pico immediately began conducting triage, while trying to talk other infantry advisors through the process of treating serious wounds with minimal supplies.

After the first round, I lifted myself up off the ground and sprinted towards my vehicle to get on the radio and request everything we could get as support. Along the way, another mortar round fell about one hundred meters to my left, and I fell and embarrassingly busted my lip. Once I reached the vehicle and got inside, I discovered that my driver, Sergeant Robert Zufall, was already coolly delivering a spot report to our battalion tactical operation center (TOC). Once he saw me, he quickly threw me the mike and gave me a quick run down of what he had reported. He jumped from the vehicle and went to assist the other advisors in moving the wounded Iraqis to safety and treating them. I quickly delivered a spot report to the battalion tactical operation center, requesting immediate air support from whatever was in the air, the main supply route (MSR) patrol from our tank company, [and] C 3-8 Armor, commanded by a great commander, Captain Pete Glass. I also requested medevac and the medical quick reaction force (QRF) from our battalion once the area was secure. The air support showed up before I had dropped the mike and immediately was on our net asking for guidance and how they could help us.

The OH-58 pilots from the 1st CAV at Camp Taji were often the first to respond to our many attacks and became some of our best friends, though we rarely met in person. We respected them due to their willingness to assist us in any way when they were in the air. We always had business for them, and we like to feel they respected us. Once, on one of our days back to refuel and re-arm, we were eating at the mess hall. Our distinct arm bands identified us in Arabic as advisors to our Iraqi soldiers, and the battalion commander came up and asked if we were the Indian (our call sign on the radio was Indian; I was Indian 6) element. Once we responded yes, he immediately went down the line of the table shaking the hands of all my advisors and giving each a coin, stating "It's nice to put a face to the voice on the radio; do you guys ever sleep? Every time I fly, I end up talking to you guys on the radio, and you are always in contact!"

Once the air support showed up, the element from C 3-8, our tanker friends on MSR security, had shown up and blocked the front gate and were scanning with their thermals in the direction we guessed the rounds had come from. The effect of their support was immediate, as the rounds no longer rained in. I dismounted my vehicle to complete chaos. Wounded, moaning Iraqis were everywhere. I got a status from each one of my advisor element leaders and was relieved to learn no Americans had been hurt. That relief was short-lived, as I soon realized that the number of Iraqi wounded was enormous. We were working on getting a count and trying to do triage as much as we could for Doc.

Doc Pico was overwhelmed; the litter-urgent cases had quickly filled his small aid station, and he was in the hallway of the floor of the building, absolutely covered from head to toe in blood, working on casualties. The Iraqis, with a very few exceptions, were useless in assisting us, as they were overcome with grief and shock. They were, after all, at the time, not trained, professional soldiers, but little more than tribal warriors. Two other soldiers, Sgt. John Quinones, the gunner for my vehicle, and Cpl. Jeremy Stafford, the driver for Spc. Robert Haney, my NCOIC at the time, were Doc Pico's main assistants. They were taking the casualties and trying to triage them as best they could. They were also covered head to toe in red blood.

287

Assessing the situation, and realizing that the medical QRF was not going to arrive in time to save many of the Iraqi soldiers, I made the call to move some advisors off of personnel recovery and station my designated marksman with a spotter on the roof. This would make it at least a little more secure; and [I] called in "pickup zone (PZ) secure" to the TOC. Within minutes there were two UH-60 Black Hawk medevacs at our location, and after a final situation report on our net, they descended to start taking casualties.

The bravery and skill of these pilots cannot be overstated. I can't imagine what it looked like from the air, but from the ground it looked like hell on earth: casualties literally everywhere, blood ankle deep in some mortar holes, and body parts randomly strewn, some still smoking, about the small compound. As soon as the medevac bird touched the ground, it was rushed by walking-wounded Iraqis, and it took some not-so-gentle persuasion from the advisors to get them to back off and assist in moving the litter cases on the birds. The medevac medic quickly dismounted and came to me, and I briefed him on what we had; he rushed back to his chopper and grabbed all the litters he had, dropped them on the ground and said: "Here sir, you guys need these; lets start getting them loaded."

Our own litters were in short supply. We carried one on each vehicle and had about four in the aid station, so we were taking them in ponchos, tabletops, anything we had. Once full, we would bring back the litter and continue to load the bird. While this was going on, the second medevac bird started to land adjacent to the first bird. I thought we were going to have a collision, but he made it okay. I guess a medic from the initial medevac had told the pilot that our situation was serious, and in turn, he had told the other pilot he needs to land now, that we had not exaggerated the amount of wounded.

The fact that they got two UH-60 medevac helicopters in such a small space is a testament to their skill as pilots and their humanity and compassion to our plight and that of our Iraqi comrades. Iraqi soldiers were coming up to me while I was treating wounded soldiers and begging to be allowed on the next turn of aircraft. Most of those asking to be evacuated had minor wounds and were turned away. We had gotten an initial count of wounded of about sixty-seven and nine dead. This was not to be the exact count, as many Iraqis left the patrol base by ING vehicle to be treated elsewhere. We quickly exhausted all the CL VIII (medical supplies) we had. We had used every bandage, every piece of gauze, and every tourniquet in every aid bag and combat lifesaver bag (CLS) we had. We had one aid bag and a CLS bag per vehicle. Soon, we were using whatever was at hand to patch holes in profusely bleeding Iraqis. Many of my advisors had ripped the sleeves from their own uniforms to act as ad-hoc bandages, in lieu of anything else.

After the first turn of medevac, Bravo Company 2-162 Infantry from the Oregon National Guard, commanded by Capt. Damien San Miguel, who was attached to the 39th Infantry Brigade, and subsequently assigned to our Task Force 2-7 CAV, 1CD, arrived on the scene to assist. They were meeting with the local Iraqi police when the attack happened and were close by and came to offer assistance. Just in the nick of time, they quickly dismounted and assisted my advisors in prep of the wounded and their treatment. Their medic moved to assist Doc Pico and parcel out his much-needed but limited medical supplies. They professionally assisted in security, treatment, and movement of the wounded to the PZ.

After sixteen rotations of medevacs, the medical QRF arrived, along with our task force commander, Lieutenant Colonel James

Rainey, and his personal security detachment (PSD). I informed the tactical operation center that no further medevacs would be required, as most left were walking wounded and could be treated by the medical QRF. Lieutenant Colonel Rainey looked around at our scene of chaos and coolly replied that it looked like we had it under control and asked for an enemy situation report. I gave him what we had, which wasn't a lot: that we had received about twelve to sixteen rounds of a mix of 60mm and 82mm mortar rounds coming roughly from the northwest direction [and] had one truck hit by an IED, some random small-arms fire from the west, and about sixty-seven wounded and nine dead, no U.S. He asked me what I was doing to bring the fight to the enemy, rather than be here in a defensive posture. I told him that I had the air patrols out looking and that the MSR QRF was on standby by the S-3 to respond if anything was found, along with the Bulldog element if necessary. He then got on the radio and told the MSR patrol to resume their patrol in order to not leave the whole sector unmonitored and potentially become seeded with IEDs.

While this was happening, my NCOIC, Sergeant First Class Haney, was getting a more accurate count. He reported that we had sixty-seven evacuated by air, nine dead that we knew of, nine loaded into the medical QRF tracks, and an unknown number evacuated by the Iraqis to a location unknown. Sergeant First Class Haney was the ultimate warrior; he was cool as ice, smoking a cigarette and spitting off numbers as if he was reporting to the first sergeant back in the states. He was a true professional. During the medevacs, I had seen him stop some Iraqis hauling a litter with a casualty on it to the bird. He bent down, looked close at his head, and then told them to dump that guy because he was dead and we couldn't do him any good. The Iraqis had initially protested because the man in the litter was a relative of theirs, until Sergeant First Class Haney pushed the guy out of the litter, grabbed one of the litter bearers, and told him to take the patient he was working on to the litter, and escorted them to the bird. He was also covered in blood from head to toe.

The situation was now under control, and my counterpart, Lieutenant Colonel Waleed, now emerged with his bodyguards, carrying two M16s [rifles]. At first, I thought they had been hiding out of fear, but I soon discovered that they had been performing security for us. The M16s belonged to Sergeant Zufall and Corporal Stafford; they had laid them directly by their side on the front porch of our main building while they were trying desperately to follow the directions of Doc Pico on how to stop severe bleeding on two Iraqi soldiers. Doc Pico had to talk them through it between bouts of treating his own many gravely wounded patients. While they were trying to save the lives of their fellow Iraqi soldiers, some of the less loyal Iraqis had taken advantage of this chaos to attempt to steal their weapons. Lieutenant Colonel Waleed and his bodyguards had stopped them and recovered the weapons. It is then that I recalled seeing Lieutenant Colonel Waleed and his loyal bodyguards perched on the second story balcony of the main building during the mortar attack, pulling security on his own soldiers for our advisors.

Lieutenant Colonel Waleed knew that some of his own soldiers were responsible for the attack, that the information had come from within, and that one or more of them was responsible. More than one attempt was made that day to harm an advisor by one of our own Iraqi soldiers while the advisor was trying to save the lives of Iraqi soldiers who were wounded. They were all stopped by Lieutenant Colonel Waleed and his bodyguards. This simple act sealed our trust of the man and his desire to help us help him and the people of Taji. We knew we could trust him, and he knew that we would do all we could to help him and his soldiers; he had seen Americans risk their lives for Iraqis.

Once the last of the wounded were loaded into the medical QRF tracks [and] Lieutenant Colonel Rainey and the QRF departed, we went about clean-up of the patrol base. We discovered several body parts and even some bodies in unlikely locations. We had Lieutenant Colonel Waleed and his men contact the families once we had them identified. We conducted a crater analysis of the mortar points of impact and determined that they came from the direction we had guessed to the northwest.

This was truly a team effort, an orchestra if you will, of air support, support from the tankers on MSR patrol, the Bulldog element, the medical QRF, the loyal Lieutenant Colonel Waleed and his bodyguards, and most of all by the ING Advisors (the Indian Element) of Task Force 2nd Battalion, 7th Cavalry, 1st Cavalry Division, the Ghost Battalion. Each man performed like a true professional, pushing and testing beyond comprehension his own medical abilities and maturity. Each was covered from head to toe in blood and was exhausted both mentally and physically, but they performed magnificently. Sergeant "Doc" Pico was awarded the Bronze Star with V device for his actions that day, and all other advisors, minus me, were awarded the Army Commendation Medal with a V device for their actions.

For the next few weeks, we scaled back combat patrols due to a large number of the remaining Iraqi soldiers refusing to work out of fear. In response, we saturated the local area with informants and queries about who was responsible. Eventually, we had several credible sources and informants identify twenty-one suspects. Most of these were names that we knew to be sources of friction and possible terrorism in the area of operations. Also, most of these were identified by multiple informants or sources—that is, by three or more separate sources. Some of these sources were some of our ING soldiers that we had working in the local villages "undercover" or covertly, going about second jobs, to gather intelligence. Lieutenant Colonel Waleed and his S-2 1st Lieutenant Amar had a very good local intelligence network.

Other sources were informants that we had worked with in the past. We waited for the right moment, and about three weeks after the attack, we were ready to conduct our "night of the long knives." I laid out our plan to our Task Force S-3, Major Tim Karcher, and he gained approval from Lieutenant Colonel Rainey. One condition was that this was not to be a revenge mission and to not let the Iraqis get out of control. This was no easy task, but I explained it to Lieutenant Colonel Waleed, and he agreed to ensure his men and officers abided by the rules and our rules of engagement (ROE). We did not inform the Iraqi soldiers of the mission until the time we were to depart, due to operational security (OPSEC) considerations. Lieutenant Colonel Waleed had one of his trusted men round up the informants separately at their homes and blindfold and mask each one, in nondescript uniforms. This was for their safety, so that the ING soldiers, the suspects, and the other informants could not identify them and seek revenge against them or their families at a later date.

Once the informants were gathered at Patrol Base Animal, the order had been issued to the advisors, and Lieutenant Colonel Waleed informed his men. I informed the task force TOC, who informed the MSR patrols and the air assets patrolling our sector of our mission, so that in the event we got into trouble, we had help.

We were heading over to the "west side" of the MSR, a notoriously bad side where attacks often occurred. The time was about 2400 hours. We had patiently waited for a lull in attacks, the right time of night, to ensure most of the suspects would be home, and made sure we had all of the informants so that we could identify the suspects and not arrest the wrong one.

Once the ING forces were gathered, I and Lieutenant Colonel Waleed carefully explained the nature of the mission. Once the forces were briefed, the engagement criteria explained, and a final check of the TOC conducted, we proceeded under the guidance of our informants to the residences of the suspects. One by one, we conducted cordon-and-knocks on each house, carefully ensuring that we were not necessarily violent in their execution, so as to not irritate the innocent. But not at the expense of safety; we were poised to execute a "dynamic" entry if necessary. But complete surprise ensued, and not once were we forced to breach or fire our weapons. We carefully isolated each objective, knocked on the door, cleared the residence, and located the suspect, searched the residence, conducted tactical questioning, exploited the site, collected evidence, and moved on to the next residence. Seven times that night, and twenty-one suspects later, we were complete, just as the sun started to come up.

We were able to conduct initial processing and further tactical questioning back at Patrol Base Animal. After a call to our Task Force S-2, we moved them back to our task force TOC [and] turned them over to the S-2 for handover. The mission was a complete success. What became of the suspects is unknown, but we did not receive indirect fire on Patrol Base Animal for quite some time following that operation. Several months later, in another mission where we came under direct automatic weapons fire from that same vicinity, we located the mortar firing positions they had used to fire on us that day. Actually, the credit goes to Master Sergeant Russ, who noticed them. We excavated the area and found several mortar tubes, machine-gun ammunition, and a large amount of mortar rounds. This validated our earlier captures and was sent forward as evidence against them, as well as a few other detainees captured that day that corroborated information gathered from earlier detainees and informants.

Overall, this attack on Patrol Base Animal and our ING forces had a great effect on our mission. Our numbers were smaller, our morale lower, and our level of trust and confidence in those we were leading and training less sure. The "night of the long knives" mission helped set the conditions in correcting these problems and securing relative safety in our sector, at least for a few weeks.

Staff Sgt. Robert R. McBride, U.S. Army

Despite having survived more than a year in Iraq, Staff Sergeant McBride was happy to participate in a raid aimed at putting an end to mortar fire that had been harassing the soldiers of the 2nd Armored Cavalry Regiment in Najaf. Having made it through near misses and being a mortarman himself, McBride took the attacks personally.

ON JUNE 2, 2004, I received the mission for the following day that would turn out to be my section's last one together in Iraq, the most violent one of my 444-day deployment, and convinced the chain of command to award me the Silver Star Medal, an award that still baffles me today. Please bear with me as I lead you up to that day.

Being a nontypical kind of conflict, my section fit right in, as we were a nontypical section. We were a nine-man towed 120mm mortar section assigned to Iron Troop, 3rd Squadron, 2nd Armored Cavalry Regiment. None of my section's Hummers had armor

295

until the very last month or so of the deployment, and my truck never had any, so we were not really "armored," and we had not served as such during all of our deployment. Upon our arrival in Baghdad, we were very quickly assigned to providing escort duty for the Coalition Provisional Authority all over the Baghdad area and beyond, logging thousands of miles on the roads and hundreds of escort missions without losing a man or a vehicle. The vehicles I had at the time were two M998 troop carriers. I had rigged up some very crude mounts for the two M240 machine guns I had scrounged up for them—crude meaning a board strapped above the tailgate across the top of both backrests of the troop seats—so the gunner in the back had someplace to hang the bipod of the machine gun over when he engaged to the rear. If he engaged over the side, he used the troop seat back rest, and if he engaged forward, he just used the cab of the Hummer. In addition to these two trucks, I had my M1025 weapons carrier with another M240—less than ideal equipment, but my soldiers made it work and were damn proud of what they could do with so little. We were extended in Iraq, left Baghdad, and eventually wound up in Najaf where we eventually gained a brand-new soldier and a brand-new M1114. Things were about to get interesting, to say the least.

From the moment we began operations in the Najaf and Kuffa area, we were plagued by a 120mm mortar the insurgents had emplaced in a schoolyard about three hundred meters northwest of the Kuffa Mosque, using these buildings to prevent coalition forces [from] using airpower or indirect fires from destroying this mortar system. Its fires were getting more effective as days went on, and our efforts to locate its observers were proving to be futile. On one mission to find its observer, I was nearly knocked to my knees by a very close impact of this weapon while standing outside my truck, and then later I was shelled repeatedly by it while on guard duty at the front gate. Then it became personal when, after we had just conducted a long night operation, it started shelling our dining facility and the damn thing ruined my breakfast. Therefore, when I learned of the Iron Troop tasking with a raid to capture or destroy the mortar system and my section was going to be the troop main effort, I was more than pleased.

The raid was to take place at dawn on June 3, 2004, so we were up early and left the forward operation base (FOB) when it was still dark. Our movement was slow and steady until we reached the street where we would halt and wait for the morning sun to peek over the horizon. I had decided to take only my M1025 and our new M1114 on the mission, so I could put more of my men on the objective when our part of the mission kicked off. The rest of the troop team consisted of twelve M1025 trucks and their cavalry scout crews, and a tank platoon.

We crossed the line of departure (LD) at 0530 hours and headed for our objective. Shortly after LD, the insurgents attacked the troop with a series of command-detonated improvised explosive devices (IEDs) that had been buried alongside and in the road leading up to the objective. The blasts sent large clouds of smoke and debris into the air, completely blocking the view of the road ahead. I heard over the radio that the way was clear, so we pushed on through. On the other side of the debris from the IEDs, we began to establish the attack position and the inner and outer cordons. I left my truck to get a quick face-to-face with my other truck and to look toward the objective, when I saw a truck from the outer cordon coming back up the road very quickly. As it turned the corner, I saw that enemy fire had damaged it, and it was bringing casualties back to the attack position, which was also being used as the casualty collection point. First Sergeant Russel Reimers met the truck with his vehicle and began the casualty evacuation (CASEVAC) operations. At that moment, the attack position fell under attack from small-arms, RPG, and mortar fire.

The troop commander, Capt. Brandon Payne, was on the radio maneuvering the troop reserve to fill the gap in the outer cordon and continuing to develop the inner cordon. The enemy fire seemed to me to be concentrating on the first sergeant and the CASEVAC, so I made the decision to reposition my trucks in between the enemy fire and the first sergeant and directed my soldiers to identify and kill any insurgent they could. Once my soldiers started to engage, the enemy attack shifted, as I had hoped, onto my section, and the CASEVAC operation was successful. As the gunfire dwindled and the enemy broke off their attack, Spc. Devin Rogers called to me and pointed out where there was a bullet hole in our brand-new M1114. We both chuckled at it, and as I returned to my truck, I shouted something about it in the direction from which most of the fire had come from and offered an obscene hand gesture. The gesture and shout were answered by the zip of bullets passing just a little too close to me. There is just something intoxicating about being shot at and missed, so I yelled and gestured again like the idiot I can be at times.

When I got back to my truck, the troop commander ordered me to begin my movement to the objective. I loaded up my men, and we began our movement toward the school. When we turned up the street to the school, enfilading fire met us from several tall buildings, and we could finally see the fight that the inner and outer cordon were still in. We continued down the street with my unarmored truck in the lead and the uparmored truck in trail, one of many mistakes on my part that day that could have . . . [gone badly], but thankfully did not. I had one of the tanks knock a hole in the six-foot masonry wall for our entry point into the schoolyard and parked my trucks near that tank.

I dismounted my men except for the two gunners in the trucks, Spc. Emmett Jarvis in my truck, and Pvt. Louis Abreu in the other. They were to use their machine guns in support of the inner cordon and to cover us when we started to bring out captured personnel or equipment. We stacked on the wall and entered the schoolyard, getting our first good look at the school itself. It was a three-story I-shaped building when viewed from above, the long axis being about seventy feet with the top and bottom of the "I" being about thirty feet. Immediately we saw the now-abandoned 120mm mortar, already conveniently disassembled for us. I suspect that the insurgents were attempting to relocate it when an Abrams tank knocked their wall down. We broke into two four-man groups and set to our task of capturing the weapon and clearing the school. My driver, Spc. Nick Pangelinan, who was now carrying our dismounted radio, informed me that the inner cordon reported they could not put fires on a six-man squad stacking on the opposite side of the building preparing to attack my soldiers. I ordered Spc. Conyers Lamb and his team to stack on our side of the building and wait on them to come around, and that is where my leadership ability failed me. I could not think how to move my team, or maybe reposition Lamb's team, to a more defensible spot; I could only think of how to maneuver me, so I turned to Sgt. Ryan Gilbert and told him that I was going in. There I went into the first open door, catching a glimpse of a man with a rifle running by the window. As I crossed the room, I prepared a fragmentation grenade and eased a window open, peeking out. There were men stacked along the wall, their backs to me. I stuck my hand out the window and somewhat lazily tossed the grenade toward them and ran back toward the door. Sergeant Gilbert had entered the room now, and I told him, "*Frag Out!*" He turned to leave the room as the grenade detonated, shattering all the windows in the room. We both turned around and ran to the window to find that six insurgents lay dead or dying outside.

We rejoined our soldiers outside and again set about starting to recover the captured equipment, when the inner and outer cordon fell under attack from two platoon-sized elopements. The inner cordon also reported that they were receiving small-arms fire from the roof of the school. We then focused on clearing the school. Sergeant Gilbert saw a man duck into a room that turned out to be a small latrine. Rather than engage with small arms, Sergeant Gilbert wanted to engage with a grenade, and I concurred. I tell you, a fragmentation grenade makes quite a mess of a one-hole latrine and its occupant. It also fills a stairwell with choking smoke, as Spc. Brent Harmon will tell you, but he stood his ground and kept the second floor secure as we moved to the third floor.

Once we were on the third-floor balcony, our next stop was the roof. I saw the ladder to the roof, and we began to make our way to it. There was quite a lot of small-arms fire coming from the roof. I looked to Spc. Devin Rogers and told him to go to the opposite end of the balcony from me, prepare a fragmentation grenade, and we would engage the roof simultaneously with our grenades. The roof of the school had a low wall all the way around it, about two to three feet high and about four inches wide, a perfect place for hiding behind for shooting, and damn hard to get a grenade over from the balcony on the floor below. I counted to three, and Rogers and I threw our grenades kind of like a basketball hook shot. I saw Rogers' grenade clear the roof and thought mine did, too. I tucked up next to the wall, and out of the corner of my eye, I saw my grenade fall in slow motion down the side of the building. I remember thinking "Shit, this is going to hurt," and then it passed to the floor below us and detonated, shattering the glass on that floor. A soldier on the inner cordon later told me that he saw me throw it, saw it land on the four-inch ledge of the wall and roll twice before it fell off. Sometimes close does not count in grenades or horseshoes. Fortunately Specialist Rogers' hand grenade had the desired effect, sort of. The two insurgents on the roof, upon seeing the grenade attack, decided to jump off the roof of the three-story school, and [they] died because of their fall. Specialist Nick Pangelinan and I climbed onto the roof to make sure there was no one left up there and were standing up there as though we were immortal, when we both looked at each other with the same thought in our heads: get the hell off this roof before we get killed. We still laugh about that moment.

With the enemy finally reduced inside the school and schoolyard, we set about yet again to remove the captured arms and ammunition. It took several trips to get it all out to the waiting trucks, and on each trip, we were met with heavy small-arms fire. On one trip, I was carrying two 82mm mortar bipods. Running out of room on my truck, I decided to leave the insurgents a present when they came see what had become of their weapons. I put one bipod under each of the tracks on the Abrams tank next to my truck and got the driver's attention by banging on his hatch with my M4 [carbine]; he popped his hatch open, and I asked him if he would pull up about three feet. Bullets started smacking into the tank turret above us, and he slammed his hatch closed. I started back to the relative safety of the schoolyard for another trip and heard the tank's engine rev up. I turned and watched with great satisfaction as that wonderful war machine crushed those two bipods as if they were made of cardboard. I hope that young man got as big a kick out of that as I did. The 120mm mortar system, all its ammunition, two 82mm mortar tubes, their base plates and ammunition, several AK-47s, two RPG launchers with several rounds, dozens of assorted hand grenades, and a U.S.-made LAW (light antitank weapon) were loaded on trucks when the order was given to break contact and return to the FOB for some well-earned breakfast.

Absolutely none of this would have been possible without the brave men it was my honor, privilege, and blessing to lead. I would be terribly out of line if I did not mention them all. Sergeant Ryan Gilbert, my young but ever-so-intuitive right-hand man and often my conscience. Specialist Nick Pangelinan, my driver and shadow, ever-alert on the road, who could get a Humvee through the eye of a needle if he needed to. Specialist Conyers Lamb, my master of rigging things up and making them work; something out of nothing was no challenge for him. Specialist Emmett Jarvis, my pit bull; with him on the machine gun, I never worried about being covered. On a raid he was truly an unstoppable force. Private First Class Brent Harmon, my rock, so very cool and calm in a fight, with limitless endurance. Private First Class Glenn Brewer, my most versatile soldier. When paired with any in the section, they became a deadly "one, two punch." He was often taken from me to be the commander's gunner on certain missions. Specialist Devin "Dirty Red" Rogers, extremely intelligent and hardworking, but accidentprone and a dirt magnet. Private First Class Louis Abreu, a good heart and such a happy-go-lucky persona, attributes not normally associated with a warrior. He could turn it off in an instant and make his machine gun sing. Private First Class Trevor Hawthorn, the last man to join our team. He came to us in what would turn out to be our last months in country, and we all had our doubts about him. All those doubts went away on June 3, 2004, when he earned his combat infantryman badge (CIB). Last but not least, Private First Class Bradley Cuatt, "THE Cuatt," as he was known, accident prone and disorganized, but when the rubber met the road, he was there. When my section became "over strength" with personnel, he was moved to another platoon. He was severely wounded in the leg during a night ambush in Kuffa, Iraq. One of those things when the platoon did everything right but stuff still went wrong. I will always wonder what would have been if I had fought to keep him with me. It was an honor and a blessing to fight with these fine infantrymen. They were easy to lead, and they pushed me to be a better leader. I will be forever in their debt.

INDEX

Military Units

1st British Airborne, 68

1st Cavalry Division, 7th Cavalry Regiment, 2nd Battalion, 281, 286, 289, 292

1st Infantry Division, 7, 51, 203, 205
16th Infantry Regiment, 56, 61, 203–204, 213
5th Battalion, 203, 205, 207–208, 210, 212

1st Marine Regiment, 37, 121, 123
3rd Battalion, 121, 123

1st Raider Battalion, Edson's Raiders, 42

1st United Kingdom Division, 210

2nd Armored Cavalry Regiment, 203, 212, 295

2nd Infantry Division, 83

3rd Brigade (Grenada), 186, 188

5th Marine Regiment, 37, 123, 125

6th Regiment, 31

7th Army, 100

7th Infantry Division, 190, 200–201
Training Battalion, 80

7th Marine Regiment, 39, 45, 123, 125
1st Battalion, 39

8th Cavalry, 1st Battalion, Airborne, 141

9th Infantry, 20–21, 26

10th Mountain Division, 110, 238, 241–242, 245, 250
14th Infantry Regiment, 2nd Battalion, 242, 250
85th Regiment, 117
86th Regiment, 111, 117
87th Regiment, 110–112, 117, 241, 250
1st Battalion, 250
2nd Battalion, 111–112, 241

12th Parachute Regiment, 104

17th Cavalry, 1st Battalion, 281

22nd Infantry, 1st Battalion, 241–242

22nd Marine Amphibious Unit, 181, 185, 188, 201

23rd Infantry, 20–21

23rd Ranger Battalion, 166–167

24th Infantry Division, 3rd Brigade, 214

29th Marine Corps, 3

34th Armor Regiment,
1st Battalion, 213
2nd Battalion, 205, 211, 213

36th Division, 33

37th Armor, 4th Battalion, 213

40th Division, 224th Infantry Regiment, 131

44th Infantry Division, 99, 102

71st Infanty, 95–96

75th Infantry (Ranger) Regiment, 180, 189, 200–201, 223
1st Battalion, 180, 190
2nd Battalion, 180, 190–191, 197, 200
3rd Battalion, 189, 190–191, 197, 201, 223

82nd Airborne Division, 63, 65–66, 68, 71, 76, 177, 179–180, 184, 214, 281
504th Parachute Infantry Regiment, 2nd Battalion, 281
508th Parachute Infantry Regiment, 63, 68, 76–79
Long Range Surveillance Troop (LRST), 281

91st Infantry Division, 363rd Regimental Combat Team, 103

101st Air Assault Division, 214–215

101st Airborne, 68, 71

102nd Infantry, 9

106th Infantry Division, 80

114th Infantry, 95, 99
1st Battalion, 95

3rd Battalion, 95, 97
116th Infantry, 2nd Battalion, 51, 59
155th Aviation Company, 168, 171
160th Aviation Regiment, 1st Battalion, 223
197th Infantry Brigade, 18th Infantry,
    2nd Battalion, 214
325th Infantry,
    2nd Battalion (Airborne) (2-325),
        180, 184–186, 188
    DRF1 Battalion, 180
    DRF2 Battalion (3-325), 180, 184–185
407th Montagnard Scout Company
    (U.S. Army), 156–158, 167
422nd Regiment, 85, 90, 91
423rd Regiment, 80–81, 83, 86, 88–90
590th Field Artillery Regiment, 89
IV Army Corps, 23
    2nd Division, 23
VII Corps (Army), 203, 204
XVIII Airborne Corps, 179, 213, 281
    Long Range Surveillance
        Company, 281
Advisory Team 38 (U.S. Army), 154, 163
Allied forces, 7, 69, 76–77
ARVN (Army of the Republic of South
    Vietnam), 141–142, 152, 156, 158,
    160–162, 164–168, 171–173, 175
British forces, 7, 68, 124
Chinese forces, 123–126, 128–131,
    133, 137, 153
Coalition Provisional Authority, 296
Cuban forces, 178, 183–188
Devil Ranger Battalion, 204, 212
French forces, 7–9, 17–19, 22–23, 25–26,
    30, 32, 77, 156
German forces, 9, 11, 13, 17–18, 20–22,
    25, 27, 29, 32, 37, 50, 51, 54–56, 58–60,
    64, 69–76, 79, 81–83, 85–102, 104–109,
    112–119, 158
German Waffen-SS Panzer Division, 6,
    71–72, 95, 105
Iraqi forces, 203–206, 208, 210–211,
    213–215, 277, 281–286, 288–289,
291–293, 296–297
    Iraqi Civil Defense Corps
        (ICDC), 277
    Iraqi National Guard (ING),
        281–282, 285, 289, 292–295
Italian forces, 7, 114
Japanese forces, 35–47
Malaysian forces, 237–239, 243, 248,
    250–251, 253–255, 261–262
NVA (North Vietnamese Army), 153,
    168, 170
Oregon National Guard, 162 Infantry
Regiment, 2nd Battalion, 289
Pakistani forces, 238–239, 241, 243,
    249–251, 253, 261, 264–265
Panama Defense Force (PDF), 191,
    194–195, 201
People's Revolutionary Army (PRA)
    (Grenada), 178, 186–188
Russian Army, 94
Somali National Alliance (SNA), 224,
    226, 228
Task Force Ranger, 223–225, 227–228,
    240–244, 247–250, 252, 254–255,
    258–264
TM Dawg, 217–218, 221
U.S. Air Force (USAF), 51, 63, 158, 163,
    171, 178, 180–181, 190, 196, 201,
    213, 215
U.S. Army Air Corps, 6, 62
U.S. Army, 4, 7, 16, 23, 47–49, 63, 73,
    76, 79–80, 93–94, 99–100, 103, 111,
    115, 131, 142, 155–157, 163, 174, 178,
    182, 190–191, 203, 206, 213, 223,
    240–241, 267–268, 276, 280, 292, 295
U.S. Coast Guard, 44
U.S. Marine Corps, 3–4, 6, 20–21, 23, 32,
    35–37, 39, 41, 45, 121, 123–126,
    128–131, 181, 185–186, 188, 218
U.S. Navy, 6, 35, 44–45, 49–52, 58–59, 77,
    122, 174, 187, 190
U.S. Rangers, 166–172, 175, 180–181,
    183–184, 186, 188–193, 195–201, 204,

212, 223–229, 232, 239–245, 247–248, 250, 256, 258, 261–265, 271, 281
U.S. Special Forces, 223, 232
Viet Cong (VC), 142, 144, 146–154, 160, 162, 166, 168–170, 172–173, 175, 280
Wehrmacht, 102, 113, 116

People
Abreu, Louis, 299, 302
Adams, "Doc," 119
Addeo, Vincent, 114
Aideed, Mohamed Farah, 228, 240, 242–243, 247, 249
Alekno, Frank, 18
Amar, 1st Lt. ——, 293
Ato, Osman, 228, 241
Awale, Mohammed Hassan, 228, 231, 241
Baker, Sidney F. Jr., 207
Barnard, Larry, 198–200
Basilone, John "Johnnie," 48
Bellman, John, 234, 237
Benson, John, 112, 114
Bisco, Fred A., 51, 60, 61
Blackburn, Pvt. ——, 239
Blades, Sgt. ——, 55
Blue, Lt. ——, 56
Boucher, Charles Leo, 7
Bouma, Staff Sgt. ——, 195
Bowen, George, 52, 55
Bradley, Omar, 77–78
Brewer, Glenn, 302
Broughton, Levin B., 143
Brown, Jerry K., 141
Brown, Robert "Todd" Sloan, 267
Buck, Bruce S., 53
Burkett, Jack Clifton, 121
Carruth, Lt. ——, 9–10
Cascio, Brassie S., 74
Cavender, C. C., 91
Chiles, Cpl. ——, 42–43
Coleman, Spc. ——, 230–232, 234
Colson, Clarence, 55, 58

Colwell, Curtis, 53
Cooper, George, 13, 15
Croteau, Rene, 66
Crum, Robert Jr., 141, 144, 147, 153
Cuatt, Bradley, 303
Cullinane, Gerald B., 110
Dawson, Cpt. ——, 56, 60
Dennett, R. J., 64
Deponai, Cpt. ——, 270
Dewolf, Staff Sgt. ——, 277
Di Tomasso, Thomas, 223
DiGaetano, Vincent, 52, 60
Dolby, David, 149–150, 153
Downer, Andy, 72, 75
Draney, Tom, 104
Dunham, Pvt. ——, 199–200
East, Jared, 144, 147–150, 152
Edwards, Rembert A., 214
Eisenhower, Dwight, 61, 76–78
Eisminger, Cpt. ——, 220
Elliot, Jack, 72–74
Elmi, Osmar Salad, 228, 231, 241
Eversmann, Staff Sgt. ——, 230
Faulkner, Frank L., 16
Fernandez, Kenneth, 153
Ferry, Charles P., 241
Frick, Fred, 114
Gabine, Frank, 101
Gallagher, Richard J., 54, 57
Garrison, Maj. Gen. ——, 223, 228
Garwood, Bobby, 175
Gavin, James M., 62, 78
Geiger, Roy S., 46
Gilbert, Ryan, 299–300, 302
Glass, Pete, 286
Gould, Spc. ——, 233
Graney, Don, 154–155, 167, 172–173
Gray, Alfred M., 3
Gritzback, Dodi, 10, 12
Hamby, Giles, 174
Hamilton, Pvt. ——, 27–28
Haney, Robert, 287, 290–291
Hardy, James, 88

Hardy, Sgt. 1st Cl. ——, 223
Harley, Dennis M., 148
Harmon, Brent, 300, 302
Hawthorn, Trevor, 302
Henie, Sonja, 77
Henry, Hamilton, 156–157, 160, 162, 164, 173
Higgins, Patrick M., 177
Hitler, Adolf, 102
Hoi, Cpt. ——, 155, 167, 174
Hoover, Gerald, 147
Hosey, Don, 163
Hubbard, Art, 14
Hussein, Saddam, 203, 267
Hutch, Lt. ——, 59–61
Hutto, James C. "Buck," 62, 68
Jarvis, Emmett, 299, 302
Johnson, James L., 151–152
Joyce, Casey, 239
Karcher, Tim, 293
Kelly, Staff Sgt. ——, 192
Kennett, Cpt. ——, 114
Kernan, Col. ——, 192
Killgallen, Pvt. ——, 199–200
Kline, John, 79
Knuckus, Lt. ——, 60–61
Kovolenko, Harold, 148
Lai, Nguyen Tan, 156–157, 160–164, 173
Lamb, Conyers, 299, 302
Lamb, Spc. ——, 235–236
Lander, John, 119
Leslie, Mark, 280
Leszko, Stanley, 115, 118
Lindquist, Roy E., 62
Little, Staff Sgt. ——, 218–219
Lopez, Sgt. ——, 152
Lujan, Arsenio D., 151–152
Lycopolus, Staff Sgt. ——, 229–233
MacArthur, Douglas, 123
Martin, Robert, 99
Martin, Roy D., 141
Matthews, Tom, 223

McAuliffe, Anthony, 71
McBride, Robert R., 295
McCallum, David, 152
McCarron, William L., 144–147, 150–152
McGourty, James, 60
McKnight, Danny, 223
Mendez, Louis G., Jr., 62, 72
Mendillo, "Gwatsy," 12
Mertel, Kenneth D., 142–143
Metcalf, Adm. ——, 186
Mitchell, Francis, 97
Mitchell, Lt. ——, 68
Monooth, Bill, 105
Mozey, Cpt. ——, 145–148, 150–153
Mucelli, Joseph B., 154
Munro, Albert, 44
Nelson, Spc. ——, 230–232
Noriega, Manuel, 189–191, 201
Novellino, Joseph, 97–98
Olson, Lt. Col. ——, 216–221
Palassou, Robert, 103
Pangelinan, Nick, 299, 301–302
Parks, Milton, 145
Payne, Brandon, 298
Perino, Larry, 238
Pershing, John J., 9
Peterson, Kenneth, 57–58
Petro, James M., 203
Phillips, Sam, 174–175
Piasecki, Edwin, 52, 58
Pico, Sgt. "Doc," 285, 287, 289, 291–292
Poppendick, Ed, 35
Poynter, Ray "Top," 144, 146, 149–150, 152–153
Puller, Chesty, 39, 43–44, 46
Quinones, John, 287
Rainey, James, 281, 289–290, 292–293
Ramundo, Lewis J., 54, 61
Raysbrook, Robert D., 44
Reed, Gerald, 163
Reid, Col. ——, 216
Reimers, Russel, 298

Richards, Lt. ——, 42–43, 45–46
Richmond, Clarence L., 23
Ridgway, Matthew B., 62
Ritter, Allen, 151
Ritz, Mike, 185
Robinson, William, 149
Rodriguez, Angel, 153
Rogers, Devin "Dirty Red," 298, 300–302
Roper, William C., 53
Roth, Irvin, 95, 97
Russ, Master Sgt. ——, 295
Sampson, Jimmie, 148–149
San Miguel, Damien, 289
Sharp, Earl, 155
Smith, Arthur, 131
Smith, Gen. ——, 77–78
Spaulding, John, 49
Speakman, Robert E., 150
Stafford, Jeremy, 287, 291
Stalin, Joe, 77
Stangel, Staff Sgt. ——, 196
Steele, Mike, 223, 238
Stowers, Bucky, 42
Streczyk, Philip, 49, 52, 54, 57–58, 61
Strous, Spc. ——, 239
Struzik, Spc. ——, 230
Tai, Cpt. ——, 156–158
Tanksley, Clifton, 168, 170
Tetu, Sgt. 1st Cl. ——, 279
Thomas, Spc. ——, 231
Tilley, Virgil, 53, 55
Truman, Harry S., 77
Tugman, Jonathan E., 189
Tumlinson, 2nd Lt. ——, 279
Van Hoose, Paul, 155, 167, 172–173
Vandegrift, Alexander A., 39, 46
Vavrek, Lt. ——, 148, 150, 152–153
Vigil, Steven, 282
Villegas, Spc. ——, 276
Vinassa, Michael G., 148–149
Vote, Gary, 170
Waleed, Muhammed, 282–283, 291–294
Washington, Maj. ——, 59–61

Westby, Darryl, 158–160, 163, 165
White, Carroll B., 141, 150
Whitehead, Pvt. ——, 130
Wiegers, Cpt. ——, 88
Wilbanks, Hilliard "Willy," 171
Williams, Gene, 66
Williams, Jon, 152
Wood, Leonard, 115
Wooten, R. J., 166, 168, 172
Wozenski, Cpt. ——, 59–60
Yurek, Staff Sgt. ——, 229, 231–233, 235
Zahn, Brian, 207
Zufall, Robert, 286, 291

Places
Abdi House, Somalia, 242
Ardennes Forest, 72, 82
Australia, 48
Austria, 11, 102
Baghdad, Iraq, 281, 296
Bakara Market, Somalia, 229, 247–249
Bao Loc, Vietnam, 154, 166, 169, 171, 174
Barbados, 182, 185
Bastogne, France, 71
Belgium, 5, 71–73, 75, 82, 85
Berlin, Germany, 79, 94
Bleialf, Germany, 86, 88–93
Bobla, Vietnam, 155–157, 165–167, 175
Bois de Remieres, France, 11, 14
Camp Blanding, FL, 62
Camp Hale, 114, 116
Camp Myles Standish, MA, 79, 81
Camp Sissonne, France, 70
Camp Taji, Iraq, 281–282, 285–286, 292
Camp Wheeler, GA, 80
Cape Gloucester, New Britain, 49
Chaumont-en-Vexin, France, 9, 20
Chef du Pont, France, 65–66
China, 156
Chosin Reservoir, 123–124, 126–128, 131
Civil-Military Operations Center (CMOC), 273, 278

Colleville, France, 56–57, 59–61
Comte, Belgium, 73
Dilinh District, Vietnam, 154, 156,
    163–164, 167–168, 171, 173–174
East Hill, 125
England, 62, 67–68, 76, 81
Erria, Belgium, 72
Florio, Italy, 113, 115
Forbes Airfield, KS, 204, 214
Fort Benning, GA, 6, 62, 190, 226
Fort Bliss, TX, 223, 226
Fort Bragg, NC, 180, 224–226, 280
France, 63, 67–68, 70, 75–76, 79,
    81–82, 95
Frankfurt, Germany, 76, 79
Frequente, Grenada, 185, 187–188
Genicourt, France, 17
Germany, 5, 69, 76, 83, 93–94, 100, 102,
    144, 240
Glasgow, Scotland, 81
Görlitz, Germany, 94
Gothic Line, 104
Grand Anse Campus, Grenada, 184,
    186, 188
Grenada, 177–201
Guadalcanal, 35–39, 45, 48
Hagaru, Korea, 123–125, 128
Heartbreak Ridge, 132
Heidelberg, Germany, 100–101
Henderson Field, 47
Hill 955, 159, 165, 167–168, 170–171
Holland, 68–70, 72, 79
Howard Air Force Base, 201
Hunter Army Airfield (HAAF), 190
Ia Drang Valley, Vietnam, 142–143
Inchon, Korea, 121–122
Iraq, 203, 208, 212–214, 218, 267,
    295–296, 303
Italy, 103, 111, 115–116
Japan, 102, 122, 137
Koblenz, Germany, 93
Korea, 5, 121–122, 124, 126–127, 129,
    131, 133

Koto-ri, Korea, 123
Kuffa, Iraq, 296, 303
Kuwait, 203–204, 214, 218
Lam Dong Province, Vietnam, 154, 156,
    163, 170, 175
Lawson Army Airfield (LAAF), 191
Liege, Belgium, 71, 75
Lizzano, Italy, 119
Mandres, France, 10, 14
Matanikau River, 36, 39, 42, 45
Mogadishu, Somalia, 223–224, 226–227,
    229–230, 242–243, 247, 268
Monte Belvedere, Italy, 110,
    114–116, 119
Montharon, France, 17, 19
Mount Vaso, Italy, 103
Najaf, Iraq, 296
National Street, Mogadishu, Somalia,
    238–239, 251, 253–254, 256, 258,
    261, 263–265
New Port, Somalia, 248–249, 257
Nijmegen, Holland, 68–69
Normandy, France, 63–66, 68–69
North Korea, 122–123
Northern Ireland, 62
Olympic Hotel, Somalia, 229,
    253–255, 262
Pan American Highway, 190, 196
Panama, 177–201, 281
Paris, France, 20, 75–76
Patrol Base Animal, Iraq, 281, 283,
    293–295
Pearls Airport, Grenada, 181, 185
Peleliu, 49
Persian Gulf, 203
Point Salines Airstrip, Grenada,
    178–181, 183–184, 186–187
Poland, 55, 94
Pope Air Force Base, 180–181
Querciola, Italy, 111, 118–119
Republic of Korea (ROK), 122–123
Rio Hato Airfield, Panama, 189–191,
    196, 201

Riva Ridge, Italy, 112, 114
Rouen, France, 81–82
Safwan Airfield, 203, 213–214
Saint George's University, Grenada, 178–179, 185–188
Saint Laurent, France, 50, 56
Saint Vith, Belgium, 82, 86
Samarra, Iraq, 267–269, 271, 277–278
Sandbag Castle, 132, 135–136
Sarreguemines, France, 94–95
Saudi Arabia, 204, 208, 214
Schnee Eifel, 82–83, 85, 87
Schönberg, Germany, 82, 86–91
Seoul, Korea, 122
SHAEF (Supreme Headquarters Allied Expeditionary Force), 76–78
Siegfried Line, 82, 85
Soissons, France, 7–8, 22
Somalia, 223–266, 268
Somme-Py, France, 25–26
South Korea, 132
Southampton, England, 68, 76, 81
Soviet Union, 178, 208, 243, 249
TAA Roosevelt, 204–205
Tenaru River, 37, 48
Toul sector, France, 7–8, 15–16, 23
True Blue Campus, Grenada, 181, 184
Vidiciatico, Italy, 111
Vietnam, 156, 160, 174
Waal River, 68
Weinheim, Germany, 100
Wonsan, North Korea, 122–123
Yudam-ni, Korea, 124–125

General
A-7 fighter, 184–185, 187
A-10, 215
AC-130 Spectre gunship, 172, 191, 194
AH-6 Little Bird, 198, 231–232, 236
AH-64 Apache, 191, 194
AK-47, 151, 158, 232–233, 272, 276–277, 302
Army Commendation Medal, 292

B57 Canberra, 163
Battle of Norfolk, 203
Battle of the Black Sea, 228
Battle of the Bulge, 71–72, 74–75, 85, 95
bazooka, 52, 55, 57, 74, 87, 133, 191
Bouncing Betty mine, 132
Bradley fighting vehicle (Brad), 204, 207, 209, 211–213, 268–269, 271–274, 276–279
Bronze Star, 109, 115–116, 292
Browning automatic rifle (BAR), 5, 21, 53, 55, 114, 157, 161–162
BTR-60 armored personnel carrier, 178, 184
C-47, 63
C-130 cargo plane, 182, 185, 191, 194–195, 201
C-141, 181, 183–184
CH-47 Chinook, 141–142, 153, 179
Cobra gunship, 169, 250, 262
Colt pistol, 86
D-Day, 55, 61–63, 65, 80
Distinguished Service Cross, 17, 55, 61
Duke of Wellington, 81
F-4 aircraft, 161, 169
F-117 Stealth fighter, 191, 194
Fokker plane, 12, 13
Hellfire Valley, 124
Hill 95, 68
howitzer gun, 24, 179, 182
Huey gunship, 168
Humvee, 234, 237–239, 245–246, 248–250, 252, 254, 256–258, 261, 264, 273, 282–284, 295–296, 302
IED (improvised explosive device), 271, 274, 283, 285, 290, 297
James Parker, 62
Korean War, 99, 121–140
LCVP, 49, 51–52
Luger pistol, 14, 79
M1A1 Abrams, 206, 299, 301
M1 Garand rifle, 52, 104–105, 108, 115, 127, 137–138, 157, 213

M2 carbine, 52, 58, 61, 109, 127, 157

M4 carbine, 301

M9 earthmover, 207

M16 rifle, 147–149, 151–152, 157, 161–162, 166–167, 169, 257, 263, 265, 291

M60 machine gun, 147, 151, 167–168, 186, 230–231, 233, 254–255

M113 armored personnel carrier, 210, 264

M240 machine gun, 279, 296

M551 Sheridan, 179

M1025 weapons carrier, 296–297

M1114 truck, 296–298

M998 troop carrier, 296

Medal of Honor, 48, 99, 171

MG34, 112

MG42 machine gun, 107, 112, 116, 158

MH-60 Black Hawk, 231, 236

MK 19 grenade launcher, 220, 252, 255–257, 261

napalm, 161, 167, 172

NATO, 249

Navy Cross, 44

Nebelwerfer, 86, 96

O-1 aircraft, 158–159, 171

Operations,

Desert Storm, 203–222, 281

Drysdale, 124

Enduring Freedom, 281

Iraqi Freedom, 267–303

Just Cause, 189–190, 281

Market Garden, 68, 70

Urgent Fury, 177, 180, 182, 186, 188, 192

Organization of Eastern Caribbean States (OECS), 185

P-47, 117

President Adams, 48

RPD machine gun, 158, 164

RPG rockets, 197, 201, 213, 231–235, 242, 249, 252–253, 259–260, 262, 269–279, 298, 302

Silver Star medal, 98, 101, 116, 295

SKS rifle, 158, 161

Springfield rifle, 15

stalags (POW camps), 94

T-55 tank, 249–250, 264

Thompson submachine gun, 69, 74, 104–105, 107, 112, 157

UH-60 Black Hawk, 245, 258, 261, 288–289

United Nations, 122, 203, 205, 223, 226, 240–244, 249–250, 261

USS *Guam*, 185

USS *Independence*, 184

Vietnam War, 141–176, 240

World War I, 5, 7–33

World War II, 35–120, 132, 144

ZPU-4 antiaircraft guns, 191, 194, 201